Law for Professionals

The *Law for Professionals* book series contains publications in all fields of the law aimed at professionals and practitioners. The book series is dedicated to publish high quality books that provide in-depth insights into the workings and the practical functioning of the law, international organizations or regional legal frameworks. The authors contributing to the book series are experienced legal professionals and practitioners whose expertise combines theory and practice.

Benedikt Rohrßen

VBER 2022: EU Competition Law for Vertical Agreements

Digital, Dual, Exclusive and Selective Distribution plus Franchising

Springer

Benedikt Rohrßen
Taylor Wessing
Munich, Germany

ISSN 2662-141X ISSN 2662-1428 (electronic)
Law for Professionals
ISBN 978-3-031-35023-8 ISBN 978-3-031-35024-5 (eBook)
https://doi.org/10.1007/978-3-031-35024-5

This Springer imprint is published by the registered company Springer Nature Switzerland AG
The registered company address is: Gewerbestrasse 11, 6330 Cham, Switzerland

Preface

Who does not appreciate a **good shortcut?**

The Vertical Block Exemption Regulation ("VBER") is not just *a* shortcut—the **VBER** it is ***the*** **shortcut** to **legally certain distribution agreements**. This is because the VBER exempts all vertical agreements in principle from the prohibition of anti-competitive agreements, which would otherwise have to be assessed individually. It thus forms the **practical core of distribution and franchise law**, for all contractual structures that connect suppliers and buyers, importers, wholesalers, retailers, franchisees, or end users.

Vertical agreements are **ubiquitous** in the EU economy. Ubiquitous are also the restrictions of competition—out- and inside the vertical agreements, for whatever reason. For example, to protect the business/know-how, overcome hold-up issues, or maintain control over the distribution of one's products or services.

Restrictions of competition occur in a wide variety of forms—direct or indirect, by object or by effect. Often, a restriction does not arise from an isolated clause, but from the combination of several clauses or concerted practices. Whatever form they have: Where an agreement appreciably restricts competition, it is, in principle, void (and subject to fines).

Which **vertical agreements** are null and void—and **on which can companies rely?** The answer lies deep down in a **nested rule-exception mechanism of EU competition law**. As overarching principle, all anti-competitive agreements are prohibited and void. By exception, however, agreements may already fall outside the scope of competition law or may be exempt if their pro-competitive effects prevail. Whether they do or not requires an individual assessment of each agreement, with respective legal uncertainty.

The book shall be the **shortcut to understanding the VBER 2022** (i.e. the shortcut to the shortcut into the safe harbour) by providing concise, **practical guidance** on the VBER 2022—for private practitioners, in-house counsels (in- and outside the EU), as well as officers and judges. It includes contract clause examples for drafting distribution and franchise agreements, as well as tables and checklists for creating new and adapting existing agreements to the VBER. This **book has been written while accompanying the reform discussions** and the introduction of the VBER 2022 as an author, speaker, and private practitioner.

The law is **up to date** as of February 2023. Any **comments to further improve** the book are welcome, especially as this is the very first edition. If you have any questions, comments, or suggestions, please reach out to me (b.rohrssen@taylorwessing.com).

Thanks are due to my team, to Giorgia Carandente, Dr. Ulrich Spiegel, Maximilian Höving, Tobias Biller, Frank Wurm, David Sander and Luisa Feye. Thank you to everyone at Springer for their support and cooperation during writing and producing this book, especially Dr. Brigitte Reschke, Kay Stoll, and Sri Ranjani Ravi.

Last but not least, a **heartfelt thank you** to my beloved wife Daniela Trombetti and our sons Alessandro and Tommaso: grazie di cuore!

Munich, Germany
February 2023

Benedikt Rohrßen

Contents

About the Author

Benedikt Rohrßen is a German attorney-at-law and a partner at the international law firm Taylor Wessing. He leads the firm's Commercial Agreements & Distribution practice group. Benedikt specializes in the design and long-term strategic development of distribution and franchise systems, with a particular penchant for digital distribution and distribution-related competition law.

In addition, Benedikt serves on the editorial board of the Zeitschrift für Vertriebsrecht (Journal for Distribution Law), as a lecturer on commercial, distribution and competition law at the Munich Business School, as a lecturer on franchise law at the Deutsches Franchise Institut (Berlin) and is involved in various international organizations, including the T.R.A.D.E. Commission of the International Young Lawyers' Association (as whose President he served until September 2022), the International Distribution Institute, the International Bar Association, and the European Competition Lawyers' Association.

Numerous publications, lectures, and webinars attest to his proven expertise at the crossroads of distribution and competition law—including, beyond commenting on German commercial agency law, several dozens of contributions on franchising, selective distribution, and antitrust/competition law in various law journals such as ZVertriebsR, GRUR-Prax, IWRZ, BB, and IHR.

Abbreviations

BBl	"Bundesblatt," i.e. Federal Gazette publishing official texts of Swiss federal government (French: Feuille fédérale, FF; Italian: Foglio federale, FF; Romansh: Fegl uffizial federal, FF)
Christmas notice	Notice on exclusive dealing contracts with commercial agents, dated 24 December 1962
CMA	Competition and Markets Authority (UK)
ComCo	Competition Commission (Switzerland)
Commission Recommendation of 6 May 2003	Commission Recommendation of 6 May 2003 concerning the definition of micro, small, and medium-sized enterprises notified under document number C(2003) 1422 (Text with EEA relevance) (2003/361/EC)
Commission	European Commission
De Minimis Notice 1997	Commission Notice on agreements of minor importance which do not appreciably restrict competition under Article 81(1) of the Treaty establishing the European Community (de minimis)
De Minimis Notice	Communication from the Commission—Notice on agreements of minor importance which do not appreciably restrict competition under Article 101(1) of the Treaty on the Functioning of the European Union 2014/C 291/01
DRAFT VBER	Draft Vertical Block Exemption Regulation = Commission Regulation (EU) . . ./. . .of XXX on the application of Article 101(3) of the Treaty on the Functioning of the European Union to categories of vertical agreements and concerted practices, draft of 9 July 2021, C(2021) 5026 final
Draft VGL	Draft Vertical Guidelines = Annex to the Communication from the Commission, Approval of the content of a draft for a Communication

	from the Commission, Commission Notice, Guidelines on vertical restraints of 9 July 2021 C (2021)5038 final
ECLI	European Case Law Identifier. The identifier consists of five parts, in the following order, separated by a colon: ECLI: Country code: Court code: Year of decision: Unique identifying number. The courts mostly referred to are ECLI: EU:C—Decision by the Court of Justice of the European Union and ECLI:EU:T—Decision by the General Court of the European Union
Effect on Trade Guidelines	Commission Notice—Guidelines on the effect on trade concept contained in Articles 81 and 82 of the Treaty (2004/C 101/07)
Empowerment Regulation of 1965	Regulation No 19/65/EEC on the application of Article 81(3) of the Treaty to certain categories of agreements and concerted practices
ICC	International Chamber of Commerce
IPR	Intellectual property rights
MAP	Minimum Advertising Price
Market Definition Notice	Commission Notice on the definition of relevant market for the purposes of Community competition law (97/C 372/03)
Metro Criteria	Criteria for selective distribution falling outside Article 101(1) TFEU, developed by the ECJ in the Metro case
NAAT-rule	Non-appreciable affectation of trade rule
NCA	National Competition Authority
OIS	Online Intermediation Services
para.	paragraph
RPM	Resale Price Maintenance
RRP	Recommended Retail Price
SDS	Selective Distribution System
SME Recommendation	Commission Recommendation of 6 May 2003 concerning the definition of micro, small, and medium-sized enterprises.
Subcontracting Notice	Commission notice of 18 December 1978 concerning its assessment of certain subcontracting agreements in relation to Article 85(1) of the EEC Treaty
TT Guidelines	Technology Transfer Guidelines
TTBER	Technology Transfer Block Exemption Regulation

VABEO	Competition Act 1998 (Vertical Agreements Block Exemption) Order 2022
VBER 1999	Council Regulation (EC) No 1215/1999 of 10 June 1999 amending Regulation No 19/65/EEC on the application of Article 81(3) of the Treaty to certain categories of agreements and concerted practices
VBER 2010	Commission Regulation (EU) No 330/2010 of 20 April 2010 on the application of Article 101(3) of the Treaty on the Functioning of the European Union to categories of vertical agreements and concerted practices
VBER or VBER 2022	Commission Regulation (EU) 2022/720 of 10 May 2022 on the application of Article 101(3) of the Treaty on the Functioning of the European Union to categories of vertical agreements and concerted practices
VertBek	Swiss Vertical Notice ("Vertikalbekanntmachung") of 12 December 2022
VertBek-Erläuterungen	Explanations to the Swiss VertBek of 12 December 2022
Vertical Guidelines	Guidelines on vertical restraints, 2022/C 248/01
VGL	See "Vertical Guidelines"
WEKO	Wettbewerbskommission, see ComCo

List of Figures

List of Tables

EU Competition Law at a Glance

1

Abstract EU competition law is based on the overarching principle laid down in Article 101(1) TFEU: Agreements which restrict competition are prohibited and void. This hard principle, however, is softened by a nested rule-exception mechanism: agreements may already fall out of the scope of Article 101 TFEU—especially in case of so-called ancillary restraints—or are exempt, either because they fall into a group of agreements which is exempt or because the pro-competitive effects outweigh the anti-competitive effects in the individual case.

EU competition law—or EU antitrust law[1]—works with a quite nested rule-exception mechanism. The **overarching principle** is: Anti-competitive agreements are prohibited (Article 101(1) TFEU) and automatically void (Article 101(2) TFEU). **Exceptionally**, agreements may already fall outside the scope of Article 101(1) or are exempt (Article 101(3) TFEU). They may be exempt either because they belong to a category of agreements which usually is exempt (and no exception applies), or because the individual assessment shows efficiency gains which let the pro-competitive effects prevail.

This nested rule-exception mechanism is owed to the different interests and principles at stake: Prohibiting anti-competitive agreements contrasts with freedom of contract. Which is why further correctives have been put into place: Only agreements which appreciably affect competition require further review. As a **rule of thumb**: The higher the undertakings' market share, the more caution is required when implementing any practices which appreciably restrict competition.

Whether the positive effects outweigh the negative ones is not decided on the basis of a "rule of reason". The "rule of reason"-concept, developed under US

[1] Both terms are used synonymously here—as does the Commission as the competent competition authority for the VBER, cf. European Commission (2013).

B. Rohrßen, *VBER 2022: EU Competition Law for Vertical Agreements*, Law for Professionals, https://doi.org/10.1007/978-3-031-35024-5_1

competition law, serves as a corrective to the comprehensive "per se rule"[2] of the Sherman Act,[3] which applies without considering the specific circumstances (and can therefore also be called a "flat rule").

In contrast, EU competition law provides for a differentiated test program consisting of written and unwritten (pre-)exceptions from the overarching principle: **Article 101(1) and (3) TFEU** lay out the test for vertical agreements, while **case law** qualifies certain agreements to fall already out of the scope of Article 101 TFEU. While the cornerstones of European competition law, Articles 101 and 102 TFEU, remain the same for more than 50 years, they require regulations which further concretize and modernize them,[4] including the Vertical Block Exemption Regulation.

Agreements which fall **outside the scope of Article 101 TFEU** may for instance be (1) agreements within the same undertaking (agreements with the same group of companies; agency agreements), (2) **ancillary agreements** (e.g. restrictions which are necessary for protecting the know-how in franchise agreements as in the Pronuptia case[5]), (3) selective distribution agreements (restrictions necessary to maintain quality and ensure proper use, as in the Metro case [6]); or subcontracting agreements.[7]

Agreements fall outside the scope of Article 101 TFEU, because EU competition law follows an **effects-based approach** (as opposed to a purely form-based approach): EU competition law protects competition not for its own sake,[8] but for the sake of consumers—it is "a means for an end".[9]

Vertical agreements may or may not be exempt under the block exemption established by the Vertical Block Exemption Regulation, but may nevertheless benefit from the individual assessment under Article 101(3) TFEU. E.g., one party's market share may exceed 30%. In such case, one has to individually start checking whether the agreements fulfil Article 101(1) TFEU—and, only if so, if it nevertheless can be exempt individually under the conditions of Article 101(3) TFEU.[10]

The Vertical Block Exemption Regulation covers and exempts vertical agreements in general because the regulation presumes that vertical agreements

[2]Cf. Wolf (2020), para. 1010.

[3]The Sherman Antitrust Act of 1890 in principle prohibits, as a federal statute, any restraint of interstate or foreign trade activities; Wolf (2020), para. 1010.

[4]Bunte and Stancke (2022), § 1, paras. 97 et seq.

[5]ECLI:EU:C:1986:41; cf. Bechtold et al. (2023), AEUV Art. 101, para. 121.

[6]ECLI:EU:C:1977:167.

[7]Subcontracting Notice.

[8]For the general notion of "perfect competition" Jones et al. (2019), p. 7, for competition law Gerber (2020), pp. 11 et seq. and 16 et seq. On differences between US and EU law. Jones et al. (2019), pp. 38 et seq.

[9]Albers (2006), p. 11. Approaches that advocate a stronger integration of economic theories and methods into EU competition law are summarized as "more economic approach", cf. Mestmäcker and Schweitzer (2014), § 3, paras. 43 et seq.

[10]Cf. VBER, Recital No. 9.

generally have **efficiency-enhancing effects** which outweigh, i.e. compensate their anti-competitive effects.[11] As the Vertical Block Exemption Regulation provides a shortcut to legal certainty, practitioners often apply the VBER directly without assessing whether there is a restriction of competition at all.[12] At the same time, it is important to realise that the Vertical Guidelines are no regulation in terms of Article 288 TFEU, but "**soft law**".[13] They do not bind the courts or the national competition authorities;[14] Nevertheless, they provide helpful guidance as they are issued by the European competition authority, the European Commission.

What Has Changed from the VBER 2010 to the VBER 2022? In general, the VBER offers **more leeway** and **more exemptions** for suppliers. In addition, the VBER now explicitly covers the **online economy.**[15] The three conditions required for exemption and thus the basic test/its systematic approach remain unchanged: Exempted from the prohibition of anti-competitive agreements under Article 101 TFEU are (1) vertical agreements between undertakings (2) with market shares up to a maximum of 30%, which (3) do not contain any hardcore restrictions (see Fig. 2.1 in Sect. 2.1).

Nevertheless, there are quite a few changes, in particular, there are some new definitions (Article 1), specific limits for exempting dual distribution, rules for hardcore restrictions have been differentiated according to the different distribution systems (Article 4) and there are a few new rules for parity obligations.

The most obvious changes concern the hardcore restrictions (also called "**black clauses**"), which have been **restructured**. In general, the Vertical Block Exemption Regulation grants **more leeway** to suppliers. For example, exclusive distribution allows for shared exclusivity, i.e. the allocation of a territory to up to five exclusive distributors. In addition, suppliers can protect their exclusive or selective distribution system more and further reduce grey imports by passing on the territory/customer restriction downstream. By contrast, agreements with hybrid platforms are not covered by the VBER. In advance: The **safe harbour** of the VBER has become broader, but also narrower in some parts, and much more differentiated than before. Details are each shown in the appropriate place, and all changes summarized in Sect. 10.2.

---

[11] Cf. VBER, Recital No. 7 and 8.

[12] Cf. VGL, para. 7.

[13] Cf. Wijckmans and Tuytschaever (2018), para. 194. Cf. the VBER's heading "(Information)" respectively "Communication from the Commission".

[14] Which, by the way, the Commission itself confirms on other occasions, e.g. in the Effect on Trade Guidelines, para. 3: "Although not binding on them, these guidelines also intend to give guidance to the courts and authorities . . . .".

[15] Cf. Rohrßen (2021), p. 293.

1.1 Why EU Competition Law Matters

EU competition law matters for several reasons. In a nutshell, competition law shall foster a public good: **effective markets.**[16] But what do effective markets entail?

When it comes to vertical agreements and distribution of goods and services, the answer is given by the cornerstone of EU competition law, by Article 101(1) TFEU (which only changed numbers, while its content has always been the same: from Article 85[17] over Article 81[18] to Article 101):

Article 101(1) TFEU

1. The following shall be prohibited as incompatible with the internal market: all agreements between undertakings, decisions by associations of undertakings and concerted practices which may affect trade between Member States and which have as their object or effect the prevention, restriction or distortion of competition within the internal market, and in particular those which:
   (a) directly or indirectly fix purchase or selling prices or any other trading conditions;
   (b) limit or control production, markets, technical development, or investment;
   (c) share markets or sources of supply;
   (d) apply dissimilar conditions to equivalent transactions with other trading parties, thereby placing them at a competitive disadvantage;
   (e) make the conclusion of contracts subject to acceptance by the other parties of supplementary obligations which, by their nature or according to commercial usage, have no connection with the subject of such contracts.

Accordingly, **competition promotes efficiency and innovation** as it "contributes to improving the production or distribution of goods or to promoting technical or economic progress, while allowing consumers a fair share of the resulting benefit".[19] While the consumers "fair share" can clearly be associated with lower prices, competition law aims to protect more.

According to the European Court of Justice, "the ultimate purpose of the rules that seek to ensure that competition is not distorted in the internal market is to increase the well-being of consumers".[20] It shall serve "not only the immediate

[16] Gerber (2020), p. 13.

[17] Treaty on establishing the European Economic Community (also "Treaty of Rome"), signed 25 March 1957, in force since 1 January 1958.

[18] Treaty on establishing the European Economic Community, as modified by the Amsterdam Treaty 1997, signed 2 October 1997 and in force since 1 May 1999.

[19] Article 101(3) TFEU.

[20] ECLI:EU:T:2006:151 (Österreichische Postsparkasse), para. 115; ECLI:EU:C:1973:22 (Euroemballage), para. 25; ECLI:EU:C:2021:935 (Visma), para. 58. Further references in VGL, footnote 8.

interests of individual competitors or consumers but also protect the structure of the market and thus competition as such".[21] In other words: The direct objective of Article 101 TFEU is to maintain competition for the benefit of consumers, its indirect (or as the new Vertical Guidelines ("VGL") put it: the "wider") objective is to achieve "an integrated internal market, which enhances competition in the Union".[22] This is most important to understand, especially for non-Europeans: there shall principally be no partitioning of the internal market, despite the fact that the EU consists of 27 Member States, its market is a single one.

The legal reasons to comply—besides "compliance" as a value in itself[23]—can also be directly derived from EU competition law:

Article 101(2) TFEU

Any agreements or decisions prohibited pursuant to this Article[24] shall be automatically void.

And, if having an entire distribution system collapse would not already be disastrous, anti-competitive agreements are also subject to **fines.**[25] Fines are set by the European Commission according to Regulation 1/2003. They are determined by considering the gravity and the duration of the infringement (Article 23(3) of Regulation 1/2003). The overall limit of fines is **10% of the undertaking's total turnover**, generated in the business year preceding the decision, including the turnover generated by the entire group of companies, if the parent company had strongly influenced the subsidiary's operations during the infringement period (Article 23(2) of Regulation 1/2003).

Why comply with competition law? The fines awarded in the recent past, especially by the European Commission, may add a further layer of motivation to comply, as shown in Fig. 1.1.[26]

Accordingly, undertakings prefer not to receive letters from the European Commission or the national competition authorities inquiring about a particular agreement or practice, especially since non-compliance with competition law can also

[21] ECJ, Case C-8/08 (T-Mobile Netherlands BV v Raad van bestuur van den Nederlandse), para. 38.

[22] VGL, para. 5.

[23] Often referred to as "corporate compliance" as all strategies for ensuring lawful conduct (defined positively) or preventing breaches of law (defined negatively) of a company. It shall minimize liability risks (compensation payments, fines, loss of reputation) and strengthen the confidence of business partners and the market in the company. Pursuing compliance may even be a legal obligation in itself, namely for the management board, cf. Hölters and Weber (2022), § 93, para. 91.

[24] I.e.: Article 101 TFEU, which generally prohibits anti-competitive agreements.

[25] Cf. Commission (2013), p. 2.

[26] For more statistics see Commission (2021).

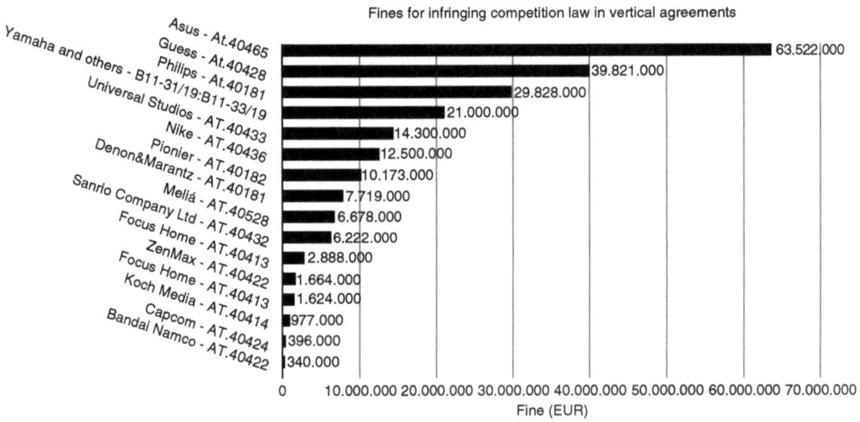

Fig. 1.1 Fines for unlawful vertical restraints

have **personal consequences** for employees. Such personal consequences may also consist of liability towards one's own company and termination of contract.[27]

Competition Law's Objective As the European Commission puts it very concisely: "Competition encourages companies to offer consumers goods and services on the most favourable terms".[28]

1.2 Where EU Competition Law Matters

EU competition law matters—**worldwide**. It applies directly in 30 countries—and beyond, as it also applies extraterritorially.

First, EU competition law applies **in all 27 Member States of the EU**. Second, it also applies in **three of four EFTA countries** (Iceland, Liechtenstein and Norway, excluding Switzerland), which together with the EU form the EEA. Thirdly, it applies beyond that—because EU competition law is already applicable when an agreement between two companies will have an effect in the EEA, regardless of their place of business.

This so-called **effects doctrine** was first developed by the United States Court of Appeals.[29] The European Court of Justice has not explicitly adopted the effects doctrine. It still adheres to the territoriality principle. In effect, however, the

[27] Cf. Hartmann-Rüppel and Nagel (2022), p. 234.

[28] European Commission (2023a).

[29] United States v. Aluminium Co of America, 148 F.2d 416 (2d Cir. 1945); cf. Wagner-von Papp and Wurmnest (2020), part 1, para. 1337; Ezrachi (2021), p. 702.

European Commission, the European General Court and, with some delay,[30] the European Court of Justice apply EU competition law with quite similar consequences as the effects doctrine:[31] "in order to justify the Commission's jurisdiction under public international law, it was (is) sufficient to establish either the qualified effects of the practice in the European Union or that it was implemented in the European Union".[32] In either case, EU competition law is applicable.

1.2.1 European Union

EU competition law applies in **all EU Member States** ("EU27"[33]), to state the obvious. Its territorial scope is precisely defined in Article 52 Treaty on European Union and Article 355 TFEU. To be precise, EU competition law applies in all 27[34] Member States of the EU (Article 52(1) TFEU), i.e.:

1. Kingdom of Belgium,
2. the Republic of Bulgaria,
3. the Czech Republic,
4. the Kingdom of Denmark,
5. the Republic of Croatia,
6. the Federal Republic of Germany,
7. the Republic of Estonia,
8. Ireland,
9. the Hellenic Republic,
10. the Kingdom of Spain,
11. the French Republic,
12. the Italian Republic,
13. the Republic of Cyprus,
14. the Republic of Latvia,
15. the Republic of Lithuania,
16. the Grand Duchy of Luxembourg,
17. the Republic of Hungary,
18. the Republic of Malta,

[30] Due to quite sharp criticism of the effects doctrine, especially from the United Kingdom in the 1970s and 1980s, cf. Wagner-von Papp and Wurmnest (2020), para. 1378.

[31] ECLI:EU:C:1972:70 (Imperial Chemical Industries), paras. 125 et seq.; ECLI:EU:T:2014:547 (Intel), paras. 233 et seq.

[32] ECLI:EU:T:2022:19 (RENV), para. 48. Which is why this approach has also been called Implementation Doctrine, cf. Ezrachi (2021), p. 703.

[33] EU27 refers to the entirety of all EU Member States, which are 27 now, after UK voted to leave.

[34] Following the "Brexit withdrawal agreement" (Agreement on the withdrawal of the United Kingdom of Great Britain and Northern Ireland from the European Union and the European Atomic Energy Community), the United Kingdom is, since 1 February 2020 no longer an EU Member State.

19. the Kingdom of the Netherlands,
20. the Republic of Austria,
21. the Republic of Poland,
22. the Portuguese Republic,
23. Romania,
24. the Republic of Slovenia,
25. the Slovak Republic,
26. the Republic of Finland, and
27. the Kingdom of Sweden;

including some and excluding other specific territories, especially outermost regions and overseas countries and territories, specified in the TFEU (Article 355 and Annex II).

1.2.2 European Economic Area

The principle of Article 101 and its block exemption VBER plus the VGL also apply—in a vastly identical wording—in **Iceland, Liechtenstein, and Norway** as they form part of the European Economic Area ("EEA").[35] The EEA Agreement has practically extended the territorial scope of the EU competition law to Iceland, Liechtenstein, and Norway:

The prohibition of anti-competitive agreements in Article 101 TFEU vastly corresponds to Article 53 of the EEA Agreement.[36] The VBER 2010 again has been incorporated into the EEA Agreement[37] (just slightly amended as regards the non-application of the VBER to parallel networks of similar vertical restraints[38]), and the same goes e.g. for the VGL,[39] the De Minimis Notice,[40] and the Subcontracting Notice.[41] The competent authority for monitoring compliance with competition rules in Iceland, Liechtenstein and Norway is the EFTA Surveillance Authority (ESA).

The VBER 2022 will presumably be incorporated into the EEA competition laws as its predecessor, the VBER 2010, by amending Annex XIV to the EEA

[35] Articles 53 and 54 of the Agreement on the EEA Treaty "copy and paste" the Articles 101 and 102 of the TFEU in order to apply to Iceland, Liechtenstein and Norway, too.

[36] Instead of "incompatible with the internal market" it refers to "incompatible with the functioning of this agreement", instead of "Member States", it refers to "Contracting Parties" and instead of "internal market" to "territory covered by this agreement".

[37] Decision of the EEA Joint Committee No. 77/2010 of 11 June 2010, OJ 2010 L 244, 35.

[38] Article 6 VBER 2010.

[39] EFTA Surveillance Authority, Notice of 15 December 2010, Guidelines on Vertical Restraints, published in the Official Journal of the European Union under 2012/C 362/01.

[40] EFTA De Minimis Notice.

[41] EFTA Subcontracting Notice.

Agreement, which contains the EEA competition rules. [42] This Annex will have to be amended by agreement by the EEA Joint Committee.[43] Considering the EEA's purpose, the VBER 2022 will presumably be transposed into EEA law without any or only minor changes since the EEA Agreement aims to create "a homogeneous European Economic Area"[44] and the EEA Joint Committee shall "take a decision concerning an amendment of an Annex to this Agreement as closely as possible to the adoption by the Community of the corresponding new Community legislation with a view to permitting a simultaneous application of the latter as well as of the amendments of the Annexes to the Agreement"[45]—with the objective of "guaranteeing the legal security and the homogeneity of the EEA".[46] To facilitate the acceptance of the VBER in the three EFTA States Iceland, Liechtenstein and Norway, the Commission has informally sought advice from experts of these states in order to involve them early and share their experience.[47]

1.2.3 Parallel Application of EU and National Competition Laws

In principle, EU Competition Law and the Member States' national competition laws may apply in parallel[48] where the conditions for applying the national law (s) are given (usually: that such Member State's market is affected).[49] The parallel application is confirmed by Article 3(1) of Regulation 1/2003.[50]

In case of conflict, the **EU Competition Law prevails**. Such prevalence has been established by the European Court early on, basing the precedence quite solemnly on the EEC Treaty, which has introduced its own legal system and created "a Community of unlimited duration, having its own institutions, its own personality, its own legal capacity and capacity of representation on the international plane and, more particularly, real powers stemming from a limitation of sovereignty or a transfer of powers from the States to the Community, the Member States have limited their sovereign rights, albeit within limited fields, and have thus created a body of law which binds both their nationals and themselves. The integration into the laws of each Member State of provisions which derive from the Community, and more generally the terms and the spirit of the Treaty, make it impossible for the States, as a corollary, to accord precedence to a unilateral and subsequent measure . . ." In short:

[42] Current version of Annex XIV: https://www.efta.int/legal-texts/eea/annexes-to-the-agreement.

[43] Article 98 et seq., Article102(1) EEA.

[44] Article 1(1) EEA Agreement.

[45] Article 102(1) EEA Agreement.

[46] Article 102(1) EEA Agreement.

[47] Commission Staff Working Document Evaluation of the VBER SWD/2020/0172 final, para. 1.2.

[48] Schultze et al. (2019), para. 95.

[49] In such case, NCAs may also act under EU competition law, cf. VGL, para. 265: NCAs may withdraw the benefit of the VBER in parallel.

[50] Clause 1 refers to vertical agreements, clause 2 to abuse of market power.

Table 1.1 Parallel application of EU and national competition laws

Situation	Consequence
An agreement or practice is prohibited by Article 101(1) TFEU, while allowed under national law	The agreement or practice remains prohibited [a]
An agreement or practice is permitted by Article 101(1) TFEU (e.g. a non-appreciable restriction) or exempt by Article 101 (3) TFEU (e.g. due to the VBER), while prohibited under national law	The agreement or practice remains permitted [b]

[a] ECLI:EU:T:2003:250 (Michelin II), para. 166 with further references

[b] ECLI:EU:C:1969:4 (Walt Willhelm), paras. 4 and 5; cf. Schultze et al. (2019), para. 96 with further references of ECJ case law. German law states this prevalence explicitly in § 22 GWB

> The precedence of Community law is confirmed by Article 189, whereby a regulation 'shall be binding' and 'directly applicable in all Member States'. This provision, which is subject to no reservation, would be quite meaningless if a State could unilaterally nullify its effects by means of a legislative measure which could prevail over Community law.[51]

This precedence goes for Competition Law as well as any other type of law:[52] Conflicts between EU antitrust law and national antitrust law must therefore be resolved in accordance with the principle of the precedence of Community law over national law.[53] Thus, applying national law may not lead to a result that contradicts European law. In practice, Table 1.1 shows what applies in which situation.

This prevalence of EU law has subsequently also been laid down in Article 3(2) (1) of Regulation 1/2003.

NCAs will therefore only apply EU law if it is stricter and/or provides further reaching measures.

To avoid that too many cooks in the kitchen cook different meals, the uniform application of EU law, even where applied by NCAs, is ensured by **the European Competition Network** ("ECN"). The ECN provides a forum for the competition authorities (both of the EU Member States and of the EU) to exchange information and assist each other.[54] Where NCAs apply EU Competition Law, its uniform application is assured by Regulation 1/2003,[55] especially through prescribing communication of draft decisions by NCAs and judgments of national courts (Article 11 (4), Article 11(6) and Article 15(2)) and establishing a clear precedence of Commission decisions over NCA decisions (Article 16).[56]

---

[51] ECJ, Judgment of 15 July 1964, Case No. 6/64 (Costa v Enel).

[52] Bechtold and Bosch (2021), Einleitung, para. 73.

[53] ECLI:EU:C:1969:4 (Walt Wilhelm), para. 6.

[54] Commission Notice on cooperation within the Network of Competition Authorities.

[55] Cf. Wijckmans and Tuytschaever (2018), para. 144.

[56] Thereby codifying ECLI:EU:C:2000:689 (Masterfoods), para. 60: "... where a national court is ruling on an agreement or practice the compatibility of which with Articles 85(1) and 86 of the Treaty is already the subject of a Commission decision, it cannot take a decision running counter to that of the Commission, even if the latter's decision conflicts with a decision given by a national court of first instance".

1.2.4 Switzerland

The Swiss competition law puts it—exemplarily—very clearly in Article 2(2) of its Federal Act on Cartels and other Restraints of Competition: "This Act applies to practices that have an effect in Switzerland, even if they originate in another country."[57] The Swiss Federal Court has been interpreting this provision broadly, including already practices which only potentially impact the market, by ruling "that foreign matters which have or may have an effect in Switzerland are also covered".[58]

Examples from contractual practice which therefore better shall not be followed have been stipulated in distributorship agreements by GABA, BMW and Nikon—and fined by the Swiss ComCo:

Example

"The distributor [Gebro] shall not make any active endeavours to solicit orders for the products [Gaba-Produkte] outside the territory [Österreich] and shall not establish any centre for the distribution of the products outside the territory. [The] distributor shall inform [the] principal [Gaba] of any request of supply of products coming from outside the territory. The principal or its affiliates shall not make any active endeavours to sell products in the territory."[59] ◀

Similar, but shorter, is the example of BMW, which has used the following "export clause" in its distribution agreements for selling its cars branded BMW and MINI throughout the EEA since 1 October 2003:

Example

"1.5 Export: The Dealer is not permitted to supply, directly or through third parties, new BMW vehicles and Original BMW Parts to customers in countries outside the EEA, nor to convert vehicles for such purposes."[60] ◀

Different wording in different distributor agreements concerning different levels of trade (especially wholesale and retail) by Nikon:[61]

---

[57] Taken from the, non-official, English translation of the Swiss publication platform for federal law: https://www.fedlex.admin.ch/eli/cc/1996/546_546_546/de.

[58] BGE 143 II 297, p. 307.

[59] Original English wording, cf. Swiss Federal Tribunal, Case No. 2C_180/2014 (BGE 143 II 297, 299).

[60] Swiss Federal Tribunal, Case No. 2C_63/2016, decision of 24 October 2017.

[61] Swiss Federal Administrative Tribunal, decision of 16 September 2016, Case No. B-581-2012; cf. also Meyer (2022), pp. 186 et seq.

Example

"Furthermore, the wholesaler or the authorized dealer undertakes not to sell the Nikon[-]products outside the EEA."[62]

(Selective distribution agreements between the Nikon subsidiaries in Germany [2004 to 2009], Austria [from 2006], Slovenia [from 2007] and Hungary and various wholesalers and retailers in the respective countries) ◀

Example

"In no event shall customer [dealer] directly or indirectly, transmit, send, or export any product outside the territory [USA]."

("Retail Dealer Sales Agreements" and "Internet Dealer Sales Agreements" between Nikon Inc., USA, and various US retailers). ◀

Example

"The distributor shall sell throughout the United Kingdom the products mentioned in the attached schedule [. . .]."

(Distribution agreement between Nikon UK limited, Great Britain, and various British retailers and wholesalers) ◀

Example

"However, the [D]istrib[u]tor may sell the products direc[tl]y or indirectly within any country of the European Community (EC), and[,] after its entry into force[,] [of] the European Economic Area (EEA), but the Distributor shall refrain, outside the territory and in [the] relation to the Products, from seeking customers, from establishing any branch and from maintaining any distribution depot."

(Distribution agreement between Nikon Europe B.V., Netherlands, and the Greek general importer) ◀

Example

"The Purchaser shall therefore acquire the right to purchase Products from Nikon for the purpose of further resale on the Territory [Poland]".

(Distribution agreements between Nikon Polska Sp. Z O.O, Poland, and various wholesalers and retailers in Poland) ◀

According to Article 5 of the Cartel Act, in particular "agreements that significantly impair competition on a market for certain goods or services and cannot be justified on grounds of economic efficiency" are inadmissible. Again, according to

[62] Swiss Federal Administrative Tribunal, decision of 16 September 2016, Case No. B-581-2012; cf. also Meyer (2022), pp. 186 et seq.

Article 6 Cartel Act, the Competition Commission may specify these conditions for efficiency exceptions by ordinance or general notice. The Competition Commission has already done this several times, most recently in the new vertical notice.

Compliance with the VBER provides a good indication for compliance with Swiss competition law, as the Swiss ComCo's Vertical Notice[63] closely follows the VBER 2010. It aims at applying vastly the same rules in Switzerland and the EU to avoid an isolation of the Swiss market.[64] There are only a few exceptions where a light "**Swiss finish**" is added, resulting in **a few stricter rules**.

The same now applies with the VBER 2022. The Swiss Competition Commission has published its draft of a "vertical notice" on 5 July 2022, together with the draft of explanations.[65] While the draft adopts many of the changes adopted by VBER 2022, the ComCo foregoes especially the explicit and more lenient rules for non-competes and the detailed rules on information exchange in dual distribution; it also stipulates a narrower definition of qualitative selective distribution (as selection of distributors shall be made "exclusively according to objective qualitative criteria based on the requirements of the product in question", while the EU VBER does not solely rely on the product, but may include services and even other goals as sustainability[66]). Actually, the exemption of qualitative selective distribution in Article 17 precisely lists the three "Metro" criteria. In the end, Swiss and EU competition law may also be very close here, provided that the term "product" is construed widely to include also aspects beyond the product itself—similar to the interpretation of "product" within the "Metro" criteria, which also encompasses the "aura of luxury", hence goes beyond the product itself.

After the EU (VBER) and the UK (VABEO[67]) on 1 June 2022, also Switzerland has now followed suit: The Competition Commission (ComCo) has finalised its counterpart to the Vertical Block Exemption Regulation on 12 December 2022: the Swiss Vertical Notice ("Vertikalbekanntmachung", short: "VertBek") including explanations ("Erläuterungen", short: "VertBek-Erläuterungen"), the latter are, however, significantly shorter than the EU Vertical Guidelines.[68] The VertBek came into

[63] VertBek 2022, paras. 10 et seq.

[64] Waser and Ondelli (2022), pp. 5 et seq., whereby they refer for the tight treatment of vertical restraints in the GABA case.

[65] WEKO (2022).

[66] Studienvereinigung Kartellrecht (2022), para. 35.

[67] Competition Act 1998 (Vertical Agreements Block Exemption) Order 2022, in short: VABEO, in force since 1 June 2022, thereby repealing the EU VBER 2010; for more details, see below.

[68] According to Article 5 of the Cartel Act, "agreements that significantly restrict competition on a market for certain goods or services and cannot be justified on grounds of economic efficiency" are unlawful. Again, according to Article 6 Cartel Act, the ComCo may specify these conditions for efficiency exceptions by ordinance or general notice. The ComCo has done so repeatedly, most recently in the VertBek 2022. The VertBek 2022 adapts Swiss vertical competition law to developments in the EU as well as to case practice in Switzerland (in particular to the Federal Supreme Court's leading decision on RRP). Accordingly, the ComCo's explanations focus on (i) vertical price agreements (paras. 4–9), on territory protection (paras. 10–14), selective distribution (paras. 15–22) and online sales (paras. 23–35).

force on 1 January 2023. With the Vertical Notice, the Competition Commission expressly intends to ensure that "in principle the same rules are applied in the EU and Switzerland".[69] The explanations are also explicitly based on the EU Vertical Guidelines, which "take into account the legal and economic conditions prevailing in Switzerland and also apply to Switzerland by analogy".[70]

Though the Swiss Vertical Notice is intended to avoid isolating Switzerland, there is "**no rule without exception**".[71] One of the differences that comes up clearly: While EU law now allows non-competes to "evergreen" and simply extend beyond a period of 5 years (provided there is the reasonable chance to terminate), Swiss law—as regards undertakings with market shares beyond 15%—limits non-competes to a 5-year-term.

The new Vertical Notice adapts Swiss distribution related competition law to developments in the EU as well as to case practice in Switzerland (in particular the leading decision of the Federal Supreme Court on price recommendations). Accordingly, the explanations of the ComCo focus on (1) vertical price agreements (paras. 4–9),[72] furthermore on **territorial protection** (paras. 10–14), selective distribution systems (paras. 15–22) and online sales (paras. 23–35). Especially the first two issues—vertical price agreements and territorial protection—may in practice result in differences and require review of agreements under Swiss law. For an overview, see Table 1.2.

Explicitly, the ComCo's explanations only refer to two rules which are "based on Swiss practice" (both concerning territory protection[73]), while they remain silent in regard of the other rules of the new VertBek. On the one hand, this might be interpreted as "eloquent" or "qualified" silence that in the other cases, the VertBek follows the same rules as the VBER. On the other hand, such "qualified silence" shall not be presumed too easily—which again would keep the door open to other deviations.

Aside from these differences in the details, time will tell whether the EU and Swiss competition rules will continue to vastly mirror each other[74]—as indicated by the ComCo. [75]**To be on the safe side**, agreements or practices which have or may have an effect in Switzerland require review under compliance with the Swiss competition laws, be it for a "**Swiss finish**" of the VertBek itself or be it for

---

[69] WEKO (2022).

[70] WEKO, VertBek-Erläuterungen 2022, para. 2.

[71] Cf. Bucher and Rohrßen (2023).

[72] A vertical price fixation occurs according to the Swiss Federal Court where the supplier transmits updated prices daily into the buyer's electronic cash register systems of the points of sale; in contrast, there is no agreement where price recommendations are laid down in catalogues, cf. Stäuber (2022), p. 391.

[73] VertBek-Erläuterungen (Swiss Explanatory Notes), Footnotes 39 and 40.

[74] Schmassmann (2022), pp. 144–146; Studienvereinigung Kartellrecht (2022), paras. 11 et seq., 35 et seq. and 39 et seq.

[75] VertBek, Recital VII: "In this sense, the European [EU] rules ... also apply analogously to Switzerland."

Table 1.2 Major differences of VBER (EU) and VertBek (Switzerland)

	VBER	Comparison [a]	VertBek
In force until	31 May 2034, transition period for existing agreements until 31 May 2023, Articles 10 and 11	<	No end date, transition period for existing agreements until 31 December 2023, Articles 21 and 22
Territorial scope	27 EU Member States	>	Switzerland
SME/limited market effect	Vertical agreements between small and medium sized enterprises are irrelevant (except for restrictions by object)	>	Vertical agreements between small enterprises are irrelevant (except for minimum/fixed prices or absolute territorial protection)
Market share threshold	30%, Article 3(1) VBER ≈ Article 18(2) VertBek		
Binding effect	VBER block-exempts and binds European authorities and courts	> [b]	Mere reflection of practice; no binding effect for the courts
Agency agreements	Not explicitly addressed in VertBek or its explanations. ComCo recognizes the agency privilege in principle, provided the agent does not bear significant risks, as under the VBER [c]		
Information exchange in dual distribution	Principles are the same [d]; however, the possibly different treatment in detail as a horizontal agreement under VertBek (Article 10(5)) and VBER (Article 2(6)) may lead to differences		
Price recommendations	Exempt as long as they not have the effect of fixed or minimum sales prices as a result of pressure or incentives	>	Price recommendations may qualify as a sanctionable RPM, absence of pressure or incentives does not constitute a "safe harbor"; considerable legal uncertainty [e]
Shared exclusivity	"maximum of five . . . exclusive distributors", Article 4(b)(i) VBER ≈ Article 4 VertBek		
Combining exclusive and selective distribution	Not exempt, to be assessed individually, VGL, para. 236 ≈ VertBek-Erläuterungen, para. 19		
Parity clauses	Wide retail parity obligations [f] required by OIS (e.g. hotel booking platforms) are excluded from the VBER (Article 5 (1)(d)), i.e. require an individual assessment. Other forms are exempt.	>	Wide parity obligations are not exempt as they are hardcore restrictions, Article 15(j) VertBek (specifically for retail parity obligations). Narrow ones can be exempt [g].

(continued)

Table 1.2 (continued)

	VBER	Comparison [a]	VertBek
Non-competes	Exempt if definite and ≤5 years, Article 5(1)(a) VBER ≈ Article 15(g) VertBek Tacitly renewable non-competes are exempt if buyer can reasonably withdraw from (terminate/renegotiate) at the end of the 5 years, VGL, para. 248 ≈ VertBek-Erläuterungen, para. 36		

[a] “>” stands for more, “<” for less leeway in the EU
[b] Due to the binding effect, the VBER provides greater legal certainty (“safe harbor”), subject to withdrawal
[c] Bucher (2020), pp. 233 et seq.; Bucher and Rohrßen (2023), Section II
[d] Article 10, paras. 2–5 correspond to Article 2, paras. 4–6 VBER
[e] VertBek-Erläuterungen, paras. 8 et seq.; Bucher and Rohrßen (2023), Section I
[f] Under EU law also called across-platform parity obligations, for details see Sect. 5.4
[g] VertBek-Erläuterungen, para. 36. Narrow parity obligations are unlawful in dealings with accommodation business Article 8a Swiss Unfair Competition Act

Switzerland’s own case law. This goes specifically for (1) exclusive purchasing obligations in contracts with Swiss-based distributors and general importers (as they may qualify as unlawful prohibition of passive sales) and (2) price recommendations (as they may qualify as price fixing even in the absence of any pressure or incentives, especially where there is a high degree of compliance by the buyers).[76]

While the ComCo’s guidance is not so elaborate as the Vertical Guidelines, the **test scheme** published by the ComCo itself, in Annex 1 to the VertBek is **helpful**, see the translation (with slight clarifications added) in Fig. 1.2.

1.2.5 UK

Moreover, undertakings distributing their goods or services in the EU and UK have to consider both sets of rules. This is one of the many effects of the Brexit. While EU competition law continued to apply during the transition period after the “Exit Day” of 31 January 2020 until 31 December 2020, UK has subsequently been setting up its own set of rules.[77] UK has now also put into place, with effect from 1 June 2022, the Competition Act 1998 (Vertical Agreements Block Exemption) Order, in short: VABEO.

Furthermore, on 12 July 2022 the Competition and Markets Authority published its guidance accompanying the UK’s block exemption for vertical agreements. **VABEO** and the **CMA Guidance** are, however, no copy and paste of the VBER. They are similar, but different. Like Switzerland, UK has its new VBER with an own touch, an “**English finish**”, as shown in Table 1.3.

[76] For details: Bucher and Rohrßen (2023).
[77] Cf. CMA (2020), p. 2.

Table 1.3 Major differences of VBER (EU) and VABEO (UK) [a]

	VBER	Comparison [b]	VABEO
In force until	31 May 2034, transition for existing agreements until 31 May 2023, Articles 10 and 11	>	1 June 2028, transition period for existing agreements until 1 June 2023, Articles 15 and 16
Territorial scope	27 EU Member States	>	4 UK countries (England, Wales, Scotland, Northern Ireland)
Market share threshold	30%, Article 3(1) VBER, or Article 6(1) VABEO		
Market share threshold exceeded	Exemption continues to apply for following 2 years, Article 8(d)	=	If ≤ 35%, the exemption continues to apply for following 2 years, Article 7 (2)
		>	If > 35%, the exemption continues to apply for one further year, Article 7(3)
Information exchange in Dual Distribution	Exempt if (1) directly related to vertical agreement and (2) necessary to improve product/distribution, Article 2(5)	<	Exempt if "genuinely vertical" [c], i.e. required to implement the vertical agreement and thus no restriction by object [d]
Shared Exclusivity	"maximum of five ... exclusive distributors", Article 4(b)(i)	>	"a limited number of buyers", Article 8(b), in proportion to the area/ customer group to preserve the distributors' interest to invest [e]
Combining exclusive and selective distribution	In same territory not exempt, VGL, para. 236	<	In same territory exempt if established at different levels of the distribution chain, VABEO Guidance, para. 8.71
Parity clauses	Wide retail parity obligations [f] required by OIS (e.g. hotel booking platforms) are excluded from the VBER (Article 5 (1)(d)), i.e. require an individual assessment. All other forms of parity obligations are exempt.	>	All wide retail parity obligations are not exempt as they are hardcore restrictions, Article 8(2)(f), regardless of online or offline.

(continued)

Table 1.3 (continued)

	VBER	Comparison [b]	VABEO
Non-competes	Exempt if definite and ≤5 years, Article 5(1)(a) VBER, or Article 10(2)(a) VABEO		
	Tacitly renewable non-competes are exempt if buyer can reasonably withdraw from (terminate/renegotiate) at the end of the 5 years, VGL, para. 248.	>	Tacitly renewable non-competes are not covered and require individual assessment, VABEO Guidance, para. 9.5.

[a] Thanks also to information provided by Paolo Palmigiano, Head of Competition, Trade and Foreign investment at Taylor Wessing LLP, London

[b] ">" stands for more, "<" for less leeway in the EU, while "=" or "~" stand for rules that are identical or essentially the same

[c] VABEO Guidance, para. 6.24 in relation to Article 3(5) VABEO

[d] Cf. VABEO Guidance, paras. 6.26 and 6.22

[e] VABEO Guidance, para. 10.59, thus close to the Draft VGL, para. 102, cf. Rohrßen (2021), p. 298 at footnote 92

[f] Under EU law also called across-platform parity obligations, for details see Sect. 5.4

Pan-European Distribution Systems

As EU, UK, and Swiss competition laws on distribution agreements have been developing differently—with the EU going forward and UK and Switzerland adding their specific finish, companies need to consider differences when designing their European distribution systems while aiming at a uniform agreement. Hence, one size may not fit all, but the amendments to be made are generally rather small. The devil, nevertheless, is in the details.

1.2.6 Rest of the World

EU competition law may also affect agreements concluded between undertakings based outside the EU—because of the **effects doctrine** (respectively the in effect same results reached by the European institutions' broad interpretation of the territoriality principle (see above)): Wherever an agreement or practice either has qualified effects in or was implemented in the European Union, **EU competition law applies**.

EU competition law can, however, be disregarded where vertical agreements only concern trade outside the EU, simply because Article 101 TFEU only concerns restraints of competition within the Union, explicitly: "agreements between undertakings . . . and concerted practices which may affect trade between Member States".[78]

Competition Compliance Checks
Check compliance with the competition law(s) of all market(s) concerned. Export restrictions can come costly.

1.3 The Principle: Prohibition of Anti-competitive Agreements

EU competition law follows quite a **nested rule-exception mechanism**, consisting of a very broad principle (anti-competitive agreements are prohibited), contrasted by exceptions (in particular agreements whose pro-competitive effects outweigh the anti-competitive effects are exempt).[79] The practically very relevant exceptions exist in form of block exemptions.

Article 101 TFEU prohibits anti-competitive agreements. It reads:

Article 101 TFEU

1. The following shall be prohibited as incompatible with the internal market: all agreements between undertakings, decisions by associations of undertakings and concerted practices which may affect trade between Member States and which have as their object or effect the prevention, restriction or distortion of competition within the internal market, and in particular those which:
   (a) directly or indirectly fix purchase or selling prices or any other trading conditions;
   (b) limit or control production, markets, technical development, or investment;
   (c) share markets or sources of supply;
   (d) apply dissimilar conditions to equivalent transactions with other trading parties, thereby placing them at a competitive disadvantage;
   (e) make the conclusion of contracts subject to acceptance by the other parties of supplementary obligations which, by their nature or according to commercial usage, have no connection with the subject of such contracts.

[78] Cf. VGL, paras. 178; ECLI:EU:C:1998:173 (Javico), para. 20: "... an agreement in which the reseller gives to the producer an undertaking that he will sell the contractual products on a market outside the Community cannot be regarded as having the object of appreciably restricting competition within the common market or as being capable of affecting, as such, trade between Member States."

[79] Cf. VGL, para. 6.

2. Any agreements or decisions prohibited pursuant to this Article shall be automatically void.
3. The provisions of paragraph 1 may, however, be declared inapplicable in the case of:
   - any agreement or category of agreements between undertakings,
   - any decision or category of decisions by associations of undertakings,
   - any concerted practice or category of concerted practices,

which contributes to improving the production or distribution of goods or to promoting technical or economic progress, while allowing consumers a fair share of the resulting benefit, and which does not:

(a) impose on the undertakings concerned restrictions which are not indispensable to the attainment of these objectives;
(b) afford such undertakings the possibility of eliminating competition in respect of a substantial part of the products in question.

This prohibition of anti-competitive agreements is the basis for the competition compliance test. As written above, this prohibition embeds quite a nested rule-exception mechanism, which is owed to the different interests and principles at stake: While in principle all agreements restricting competition are prohibited (Article 101(1) TFEU) and automatically void (Article 101(2) TFEU), individual agreements may already fall outside the scope of Article 101, be exempt through block exemption regulations or by the individual efficiency test in Article 101 (3) TFEU.

Article 101 TFEU thus works as a catch all, covering every agreement or practice which may affect competition ("all agreements between undertakings, decisions by associations of undertakings and concerted practices"). To ensure compliance with EU competition law, there is "no mandatory sequence for the assessment of vertical agreements".[80] In general, there are two ways: Either one follows the legal structure of the TFEU and the VBER[81] and applies the two-step-test by first examining whether Article 101(1) TFEU is fulfilled and, only in the affirmative, examining if the agreement or practice is exempt.[82]

Or, one takes the pragmatic shortcut offered by the VBER, examining directly whether an agreement is exempt under the VBER. As a last resort, if the vertical restraint agreed or requested to agree on fails the above test, is to review the agreement or practice individually under Article 101(3) TFEU.

---

[80] VGL, para. 7.

[81] Or other relevant block exemptions, see below, Sect. 1.6.

[82] Emmerich and Lange (2021), § 3, para. 4.

1.4 Agreements Outside Article 101 TFEU

No "rule of reason" applies under EU competition law, as the ECJ repeatedly notes:

> Those judgments cannot, however, be interpreted as establishing the existence of a rule of reason in Community competition law. They are, rather, part of a broader trend in the case-law according to which it is not necessary to hold, wholly abstractly and without drawing any distinction, that any agreement restricting the freedom of action of one or more of the parties is necessarily caught by the prohibition laid down in Article 85(1) of the Treaty. In assessing the applicability of Article 85(1) to an agreement, account should be taken of the actual conditions in which it functions, in particular the economic context in which the undertakings operate, the goods or services covered by the agreement and the actual structure of the market concerned ....[83]

Nevertheless: The prohibition of anti-competitive agreements only comes into play where the agreement "**may affect trade between Member States**", as required by Article 101(1) TFEU. Also, as unwritten requirement drawn from the provision's objective, **agreements of minor importance fall outside Article 101 TFEU**. As a test for both requirements, the actual situation of competition is to be compared with the one which would exist without the agreement in question.[84]

Agreements which either lack an effect on inter-Member States' trade or are of minor importance fall outside Article 101 TFEU and therefore do not require considerations under Article 101(3) TFEU and thus also not under the VBER. Insofar, there is a twofold threshold of appreciability: Article 101 only sets the relevant requirements for competition compliance if the agreement is capable of (1) **appreciably affecting trade within the EU** and (2) **appreciably affect competition**. As **exceptions** to the principle of Article 101(1) TFEU, they are **interpreted rather narrowly.**[85] This rule of interpreting exemptions rather narrowly is also applied by the European Court of Justice to the block exemption regulations, providing an exception to Article 101(1) TFEU:[86]

> It must be noted at the outset that, having regard to the general principle prohibiting anticompetitive agreements laid down in Article 85(1) of the Treaty, provisions in a block exemption which derogate from that principle cannot be interpreted widely and cannot be construed in such a way as to extend the effects of the regulation beyond what is necessary to protect the interests which they are intended to safeguard.[87]

This approach of narrow interpretation governs the practice of interpreting the exceptions to Article 101(1) TFEU.[88] Nevertheless, there is actually no general rule

---

[83] EU:T:2001:215 (Métropole Télévision), para. 76, with further references, e.g. to ECLI:EU:C:1991:91 (Delimitis), para. 31.

[84] ECJ, Case 22/71, para. 17 ECLI:EU:C:1971:113.

[85] VGL, para. 30, specifically for agency agreements.

[86] ECLI:EU:C:1994:257 (Peugeot), para. 8; Bunte and Stancke (2022), § 3, para. 126.

[87] ECLI:EU:C:1994:334 (BMW), para. 28 (ruling that the former Motor Vehicle Block Exemption Regulation No. 123/85 does not explicitly govern leasing).

[88] Cf. VGL, paras. 30 and 95.

that exceptions must be interpreted narrowly; the interpretation depends on the specific exception.[89] In fact, the very Commission confirms this **individual approach to interpretation** by applying the VBER "by analogy" to licensing of software rights.[90]

1.4.1 Agreements Between SME

In theory, **99% of the companies** operating in the EU[91] **would not have to worry about EU[92] competition rules** at all, because the Commission considers vertical agreements between **small and medium-sized enterprises**[93] (SMEs) out of the game, **unless** they apply **hardcore restrictions**[94] or **other restrictions by object.**[95] Restrictions by object are restrictions which "have as their object" to restrict the buyer, compared to restrictions by effect.[96] The exclusion is stipulated in the Effects Notice.[97] The reason for excluding agreements between SMEs is that they "are normally not capable of affecting trade between Member States".[98] The conditions under which companies qualify as SME are summarized in Table 1.4:

These thresholds (or: "ceilings" as the Commission puts it) shall not be exceeded together with so-called "linked enterprises",[99] to be measured on the basis of the "latest approved accounting period and calculated on an annual basis".[100] Here again, a "protection period" of 2 years applies, i.e. exceeding the numbers for a maximum of two consecutive years will not lead to lose the SME status.[101] Details of calculating staff numbers and financial amounts are laid down in Article 3 of the Annex to the Commission Recommendation of 6 May 2003 concerning the definition of micro, small and medium-sized enterprises.

[89] Rosenkranz (2015), pp. 783 et seq.

[90] VGL, para. 82.

[91] European Commission (2023b).

[92] For e.g. German national competition law, see Bundeskartellamt (2007).

[93] VGL, para. 28 refers to "small and medium-sized undertakings", which consistently should be abbreviated "SMU", while the Commission uses "SME" as well, as in other acts, e.g. in: Annex A to Commission Recommendation of 6 May 2003 concerning the definition of micro, small and medium-sized enterprises.

[94] Cf. Article 4 VBER.

[95] VGL, para. 28.

[96] Cf. the wording of Article 101(1) TFEU; for further details on restrictions by effect see the Commission's Guidance on restrictions of competition "by object" of 25 June 2014 (SWD(2014) 198 final).

[97] Effect on Trade Guidelines, para. 50.

[98] The Effect on Trade Guidelines, para. 50 refers to the relation between agreements without effects on trade and agreements between SME; De Minimis Notice, footnote 5.

[99] As defined in Article 3(3) of the Annex of the SME Recommendation.

[100] Article 4(1) of the Annex of SME Recommendation.

[101] Article 4(3) of the Annex of the SME Recommendation.

Table 1.4 What are SMEs?

SMEs are enterprises that fulfil two conditions:	
1	They employ less maximum 249 persons, and
2	their annual turnover does not exceed EUR 50 million or their balance sheet total does not exceed EUR 43 million [a]

[a] Article 2(1) of the Annex of the SME Recommendation

Where these thresholds are exceeded or the agreements contain restrictions by object, competition law compliance has to be reviewed more in detail. Within the thresholds and without restrictions by object, however, the Commission gives the comfort that it will "generally refrain from opening proceedings, due to a lack of sufficient interest for the Union, unless the undertakings individually or collectively hold a dominant position in a substantial part of the market."[102]

Competition Compliance for SMEs
While vertical agreements between SMEs are basically non-appreciable and thus fall outside Article 101 TFEU, being an SME is no carte blanche. Qualitative criteria (the agreement itself, kind and quantity of products, economic and legal context etc.) can outweigh quantitative criteria (the threshold of appreciability of 10% respectively 15% for agreements between competitors respectively non-competitors). In other words: The more serious the restriction of competition, the more likely it is to be appreciable. Especially, SMEs must not stipulate restrictions by object. SMEs may outgrow their status. Better be safe than sorry, therefore, **SMEs are recommended to comply with EU Competition Law**, too.[103]

1.4.2 Agreements of Only Local Effect

Agreements without effect on trade are not subject to EU competition law. Developed as case law by the EU courts,[104] the Commission has set out the Effect on Trade Guidelines[105] to give guidance on the effect on trade concept. These guidelines, applicable both to Article 101 (prohibition of anti-competitive agreements) and Article 102 TFEU (abuse of a dominant position),[106] establish the NAAT-rule, or

[102] VGL, para. 28.

[103] ICC (2015).

[104] Cf. Effect on Trade Guidelines, para. 18.

[105] Commission Notice—Guidelines on the effect on trade concept contained in Articles 81 and 82 of the Treaty (2004/C 101/07), "Effect on Trade Guidelines".

[106] Effect on Trade Guidelines, para. 2.

Table 1.5 The effect on trade guideline's negative rebuttable presumption

Vertical agreements are presumed to lack any appreciable effect on trade between the Member States if two requirements are given:	
1	The parties' aggregate market share on any relevant market amounts to maximum 5%, and
2	The supplier's aggregate annual turnover with the products [a] concerned by the agreement in the EU amounts to maximum EUR 40 million.

[a] Products covers both "goods" and "services", at least in the Effect on Trade Guidelines, cf. its footnote 10

non-appreciable affectation of trade rule.[107] This NAAT-rule works in both directions: it provides a "negative rebuttable presumption"[108] and a "rebuttable positive presumption".[109]

The Effect on Trade Guidelines provide a "**negative rebuttable presumption**"[110] for agreements which do not appreciably affect trade between the Member States—regardless of their restrictions, as shown in Table 1.5. According to the reasoning behind such agreements, they will be of a local, regional or national nature only. The Effect on Trade Guidelines thus also pave—theoretically—the road for agreeing on hardcore restrictions;[111] only theoretically, however, because this is where the respective **Member State's national competition law** comes into play.

In case of temporary (up to two successive calendar years) and minor (2% points of market share = maximum 7% and 10% of turnover = maximum EUR 44 million) excess of these two thresholds, the presumption continues to apply. Notably, the presumption shall not apply to emerging markets, where, instead, the parties' position on the market or strength in the technology concerned needs to be assessed.[112] As these two terms are rather abstract and thus open to interpretation, companies that intend to expand, thereby exceed the above thresholds and are risk-averse, are well **advised to comply with Article 101 TFEU** right away.

If an agreement is by its nature capable of affecting inter-state trade (e.g. a supply agreement concerns import or export or a distributorship agreement covers more than one Member State), appreciability is to be presumed if the turnover in the goods covered by the agreement exceeds EUR 40 million. The same shall "often be presumed"[113] if the market share threshold of 5% is exceeded—unless the agreement only covers part of a Member State.

---

[107] Effect on Trade Guidelines, para. 3.

[108] VGL, para. 25; Effect on Trade Guidelines, para. 50.

[109] Effect on Trade Guidelines, para. 53.

[110] Effect on Trade Guidelines, para. 50; VGL, para. 25.

[111] Effect on Trade Guidelines, para. 50: "...negative rebuttable presumption applying to all agreements ... irrespective of the nature of the restrictions contained ..., including ... hardcore restrictions .... In cases where this presumption applies the Commission will normally not institute proceedings either upon application or on its own initiative."; VGL, para. 25.

[112] Effect on Trade Guidelines, para. 52.

[113] Effect on Trade Guidelines, para. 53.

Table 1.6 Im- and exports and their effect on trade

	Effect on trade?
Imports into the EU	Possible. May be confined to one Member State and thus have no effect on Member State trade.
Exports out of the EU	In itself unlikely, but not impossible [a].
Re-imports into the EU	Possible, to be measured case-by-case [b]. Criteria: – prices appreciably different in- vs. outside EU – price difference not eroded by customs duties and transport costs – product volumes not insignificant compared to total market in EU (assessing the individual agreement, but considering also cumulative effects of similar agreements)

[a] ECLI:EU:C:1986:60 (Bulk Oil), para. 44
[b] ECLI:EU:C:1998:173 (Javico), paras. 18 et seq.; Effect on Trade Guidelines, para. 109; VGL, para. 178

After all, this **presumption is rebuttable**—and such rebuttal is likely to occur, especially where one of the parties to such agreement holds a dominant position in a substantial part of the EU market.[114]

> **Practical Tip**
> In order to minimise risk, companies that want to rely on the negative presumption do good in documenting to have passed the test. By such documentation, they can show the Commission their good faith. If companies acted in good faith that their agreements are covered by the negative presumption, the Commission will refrain from imposing fines.[115]

Three constellations of third-country business are typically covered,[116] as shown in Table 1.6.

1.4.3 Agreements of Minor Importance

The **De Minimis Notice**[117]—currently version 2.0[118]—sets out the quantitative thresholds under which agreements fall outside the scope of Article 101(1) TFEU.

[114] This goes specifically for agreements between SMEs with non-appreciable effects on the internal market, VGL, para. 28, but should apply here on this first step all the more.

[115] Effect on Trade Guidelines, para. 50.

[116] Wijckmans and Tuytschaever (2018), para. 3.139.

[117] Notice on agreements of minor importance which do not appreciably restrict competition under Article 101(1) of the Treaty on the Functioning of the European Union (De Minimis Notice), 2014/C 291/01.

[118] The Commission issued its first De Minimis Notice in 1997 Commission Notice No. 97/C 372/03, together with the Commission Notice on the definition of the relevant market No. 97/C 372/03. A new Draft Revised Market Definition Notice has been published on 13 January 2023.

Its development shows the Commission's **tendency to become more lenient** vis-á-vis vertical agreements: While in its 1997 version, vertical agreements were only considered as non-appreciably restricting competition where the parties' market shares reached maximum 10%,[119] its 2014 version sets the bar at 15%:

De Minimis Notice, para. 8:

The Commission holds the view that agreements between undertakings which may affect trade between Member States and **which may have as their effect [NOT: object] the prevention, restriction or distortion of competition** within the internal market, do not appreciably restrict competition within the meaning of Article 101(1) of the Treaty:

(a) if the aggregate market share held by the parties to the agreement does not exceed 10% on any of the relevant markets affected by the agreement, where the agreement is made between undertakings which are actual or potential competitors on any of those markets (agreements between competitors); or
(b) if the market share held by each of the parties to the agreement does not exceed 15% on any of the relevant markets affected by the agreement, where the agreement is made between undertakings which are not actual or potential competitors on any of those markets (agreements between non-competitors).

1.4.3.1 De Minimis Notice: Thresholds

Where the parties'—**non-competitors'—market shares amount to maximum 15%**, the respective vertical agreement is considered as not affecting (not "appreciably restricting") competition. Hence, there are **three negative preconditions**:

- First, the parties must not be competitors (**otherwise**, the **10%-threshold** applies—which in case of doubt the Commission will take as the relevant threshold[120]).
- Second, the **agreement must not contain restrictions by object**. Agreements containing restrictions by object are to be reviewed more closely,[121] as already confirmed by the European Court of Justice' decision in the Expedia case.[122] In practice, De Minimis is therefore—among the clauses explicitly listed in the VBER—relevant for the grey clauses listed in Article 5 VBER, but not for the black clauses listed in Article 4, as they all "have as their object" to restrict the buyer.[123]
- Third, the parties' **market shares must not exceed 15%** (10% with competitors).

[119] De Minimis Notice 1997, para. 9(b).

[120] De Minimis Notice, para. 9.

[121] De Minimis Notice, paras. 8 and 13.

[122] ECLI:EU:C:2012:795 (Expedia), para. 37.

[123] Similar Schultze et al. (2019), para. 164, who, however, do leave clauses beyond the black and grey clauses disregarded.

Table 1.7 How to calculate the market shares?

	Relevant product market	Relevant geographic market
Definition	All products/services that are substitutable by the consumer	Area where conditions of competition are sufficiently homogenous
Empirical evidence	Step 1: characteristics, intended use Step 2: prices	Prices and price differences
Details	Market Definition Notice, paras. 36 et seq.	Market Definition Notice, paras. 44 et seq.
Specifics for vertical agreements	In sectors where suppliers generally sell a portfolio of goods/services, the entire portfolio may be the relevant product market [a]. For multi-party agreements, Article 3(2) VBER applies. For franchisors that franchise a business method, also suppliers of substitutable goods/services who do not apply franchising are to be included [b]. Further details: Article 3 and 8 VBER; VGL, paras. 170–176; see Chap. 3	

[a] VGL, para. 172
[b] VGL, para. 173

Instead of 15%, a **5% threshold** applies if competition in a relevant market is restricted by the **cumulative effect of parallel networks**[124]—which again is more likely to exist if more than 30% of the market is covered with similar networks with similar effects.[125] In case of temporary (up to two successive calendar years) and minor (2% points of market share = maximum 7%, 12% and 15%) excess of this threshold, the presumption continues to apply.[126] How to calculate the relevant market shares is shown in Table 1.7.

As time horizon for drafting contracts, both the conclusion of contract and the time thereafter is relevant as agreements may "outgrow" or otherwise fall outside the thresholds and thus require adapting to the then applicable competition rules.[127]

1.4.3.2 The Market Definition Notice

The Market Definition Notice helps illustrating the Commission's approach how to define markets. As it dates back to 1997, the Notice is under revision, too.[128] According to the Commission's evaluation of the Notice, it **requires updating to the latest best practice**, especially as regards tools and techniques used for the market analysis. There is especially room for considering the impact of digitalization on the markets.[129]

The update of the Market Definition Notice shall:

[124] De Minimis Notice, para. 10.

[125] For Details, see VGL, paras. 257–261.

[126] De Minimis Notice, para. 11.

[127] The relevant time horizon depends on the competition issues at stake: in merger control, the time horizon is based on an analysis of past behaviour, cf. Market Definition Notice, para. 12.

[128] Commission (2022).

[129] Bundeskartellamt (2020, pp. 2–4).

- include guidance on using the small significant non-transitory increase in price test (SSNIP-test) for defining relevant markets;
- recognise additional parameters in digital markets, especially where products or services are marketed at zero monetary price;
- assess geographic markets under the impact of globalisation and import competition;
- include quantitative techniques, e.g. as regards exogenous shocks, price tests, critical loss analysis;
- include guidance on how to calculate the market shares in the online platform economy, updated to visits, click rates downloads, and other parameters of active use; and
- cover non-price competition (including innovation).[130]

The review has, as with the VBER update, resulted in a working document, which sums up the evaluation results.[131] The draft revised Market Definition Notice has been published on 8 November 2022.[132] It provides more extensive advice: While the 1997 version (when Amazon went public) contains 58 paragraphs, the **2023 version will contain about twice as many paragraphs** (113 paragraphs). The public consultation finished on 13. January 2023. The final version is expected to appear in 2023. It will shed light on how to delimit the relevant market in online platform economy (which was still in its infancy years when the Market Definition Notice had lastly been published), including on how to analyse the substitutability on the supply and the demand side as well as the geographic market.[133]

1.4.4 Agreements Based on State Action

Article 101 TFEU does—in lack of any competitive activity—not apply if an undertaking does not act on its own initiative but on the basis of state regulation—this is the "**State Action Defence**". This is also—indirectly—reflected in the VBER as its Article 4 only blacklists as hardcore restrictions the specific vertical restraints which are "**under the control of the parties**".

State Action Defence "Articles 85 and 86 of the Treaty apply only to anti-competitive conduct engaged in by undertakings on their own initiative (see to

[130] Commission Staff Working Document, Evaluation of the Commission Notice on the definition of relevant market for the purposes of Community competition law of 9 December 1997, SWD (2021) 199 final, pp. 66 et seq. and 68.

[131] Commission Staff Working Document, Evaluation of the Commission Notice on the definition of relevant market for the purposes of Community competition law of 9 December 1997, SWD (2021) 199 final: https://competition-policy.ec.europa.eu/system/files/2021-07/evaluation_market-definition-notice_en.pdf.

[132] https://competition-policy.ec.europa.eu/public-consultations/2022-market-definition-notice_en.

[133] Tinguely (2023), p. 25.

that effect, as regards Article 86 of the Treaty, Case 41/83 *Italy* v *Commission* [1985] ECR 873, paragraphs 18 to 20; Case C-202/88 *France* v *Commission* the so-called 'telecommunications terminals judgment [1991] ECR I-1223, paragraph 55; and Case C-18/88 *GB-Inno-BM* [1991] ECR I-5941, paragraph 20'). If anti-competitive conduct is required of undertakings by national legislation or if the latter creates a legal framework which itself eliminates any possibility of competitive activity on their part, Articles 85 and 86 do not apply. In such a situation, the restriction of competition is not attributable, as those provisions implicitly require, to the autonomous conduct of the undertakings (see also Joined Cases 40/73 to 48/73, 50/73, 54/73 to 56/73,111/73, 113/73 and 114/73 *Suiker Unie and Others* v *Commission* [1975] ECR 1663, paragraphs 36 to 72, and more particularly paragraphs 65, 66, 71 and 72).

Articles 85 and 86 may apply, however, if it is found that the national legislation does not preclude undertakings from engaging in autonomous conduct which prevents, restricts or distorts competition (Joined Cases 209/78 to 215/78 and 218/78 *Van Landewyck and Others* v *Commission* [1980] ECR 3125; Joined Cases 240/82 to 242/82, 261/82, 262/82, 268/82 and 269/82 *Stichting Sigarettenindustrie and Others* v *Commission* [1985] ECR 32831; and Case C-219/95 P *Ferriere Nord* v *Commission* [1997] ECR I-0000)."[134]

Examples for legislation or other state action which creates a framework which eliminates competitive activity usually involve collective price fixing or governmental price approvals, e.g. a law that prohibits dental care providers from advertising[135] or a decision taken by the government commissioner, laying down minimum prices for sales of cognac, both in cask and in bottle.[136,137]

Putting the above exception from Article 101 TFEU in a positive way, an agreement or practice only exists where the undertaking acts at its own initiative:

Anti-competitive Conduct at Own Initiative "As regards, first, the interpretation of the Articles of the Treaty, it must be recalled that Articles 81 and 82 EC apply only to anti-competitive conduct engaged in by undertakings on their own initiative. If anti-competitive conduct is required of undertakings by national legislation or if the latter creates a legal framework which itself eliminates any possibility of competitive activity on their part, Articles 81 and 82 EC do not apply. In such a situation the restriction of competition is not attributable, as those provisions implicitly require, to the autonomous conduct of the undertakings (Joined Cases C-359/95 P and C-379/

[134] ECLI:EU:C:1997:531 (Ladbroke Racing Ltd.), paras. 33 et seq.

[135] ECLI:EU:C:2008:157 (Ioannis Doulamis), para. 21.

[136] Commission Decision of 15 December 1982, Official Journal No. L 379/1, para. 48.

[137] Further examples can also arise from healthcare laws, cf. only Nolte (2022), Nach 101 AEUV, para. 544 with regard to the hardcore restriction on component suppliers, the former Article 4(b) (iv) VBER 2010.

95 P *Commission and France* v *Ladbroke Racing* [1997] ECR I-6265, paragraph 33).“[138]

1.4.5 Agency Agreements

Markets are ideally populated by many different players. And yet, EU competition law recognizes but a few. First of all, only the “**undertakings**” are bound by competition law. Second, competition law squeezes the players into a **dual scheme**: Either, they are suppliers or they are buyers.[139] This dualism may not always fit into the digital world, where platforms play a role, too, often multiple roles at once, both as buyers (of goods) and suppliers (of intermediation services)—and, in the case of dual distribution, even competitors (where we enter the crossroads to horizontal restraints).

In the world of competition law, only agreements between undertakings that are independent from each other matter. Because Article 101(1) TFEU stipulates that prohibited are only “all agreements between undertakings, decisions by associations of undertakings and concerted practices which . . . have as their object or effect . . . the restriction .... of competition”. If undertakings do not act as independent economic operators, their agreements fall out of Article 101(1) TFEU.

Not different undertakings, but the same—from a competition law perspective and thus exempt from competition law constraints—are especially **agreements between a principal and its agent** (provided the agreement meets the competition law specific notion). The same frequently applies to **agreements between businesses that are within the same group of companies**.

Excluding agency agreements is—historically—based on the early European soft law on competition: The Notice on exclusive dealing contracts with commercial agents, dated 24 December 1962 (and therefore called Christmas notice). According to that Christmas notice, “contracts made with commercial agents (. . .) do not fall under the prohibition in Article 85(1) of the Treaty”. A commercial agent, for to be distinguished from an independent trader, “must not by the nature of his functions assume any (financial) risk resulting from the transaction”, except for the del credere guarantee.[140] Even under the new VBER 2022/720, agency agreements continue to fall outside the scope of Article 101 TFEU—because and if they act as an “extended arm” of the supplier’s undertaking. The Vertical Guidelines of 2022 insofar are very similar to those of 2010;[141] additionally, they provide new guidance on (1) agents which have a dual role, i.e. act as agents and independent distributors for the same supplier[142] and on (2) agents in the online platform economy[143]

[138] ECLI:EU:C:2003:451 (Altair Chimica SpA), para. 30.

[139] VGL, para. 67.

[140] Notice on exclusive dealing contracts with commercial agents of 24 December 1962, para. I.

[141] VGL, paras. 29–46.

[142] VGL, paras. 36–40 and 45.

[143] VGL, paras. 46 and 63.

What is an agency agreement under EU competition law? An agency agreement is only deemed to exist where

▶ **Definition** the agent does not bear any significant financial or commercial risks regarding the contracts intermediated by the agent (concluded in its own name or on behalf of the principal/supplier[144]).

That means that **two requirements** need to be fulfilled in order to qualify as an agent (instead of an independent distributor):[145]

First, it must be an agreement where one person (the "principal") entrusts another (the "agent") to negotiate or conclude contracts for the purchase or sale of goods or services (no matter if in the agent's own name or on behalf of the principal)—it may therefore also encompass relationships which do not qualify as agency agreements under the national commercial/distribution laws.

Second, the agent must not bear any significant financial or commercial risks as regards the contracts intermediated. The significance test relates to the agent's remuneration. Irrelevant for assessing such risk are:

- that the agent's remuneration depends—as usual where no fixed commission is agreed—on its success in intermediating transactions;
- general investments, e.g. for premises or personnel that may be used for any type of activity.[146]

The Commission continues to distinguish three kinds of relevant risks:

- Contract-related risks, e.g. financing of stocks
- Market-related risks, e.g. equipment, premises, specific software
- Other risks on the same product market, e.g. delivery of products.

As an exception to the principle of Article 101 TFEU, it should be interpreted narrowly.[147] The following—non-exhaustive—checklist in Table 1.8 shall help identifying risks and amending agreements and contractual practice[148] correspondingly.

[144] Cf. Article 1(1) k) VBER 2022 according to which the term "buyer" includes undertakings which sell on behalf of another, thereby confirming that agents may fall under the VBER (cf. Higher Regional Court of Düsseldorf, ECLI:DE:OLGD:2017:1204.VI.U.KART5.17.00 (Expedia), para. 31, provided they fall into the scope of Article 101(1) TFEU, cf. Schultze et al. (2019), para. 294. (re Article 1(1)(h) VBER 2010).

[145] The Commission now differs between agents and independent distributors, cf. VGL 34, while in the past it was between "genuine" and "non-genuine" agents, which has been developed in light of the idea that agents may not be an "independent undertaking", but simply be "regarded as an auxiliary organ forming an integral part of his principal's undertaking" (ECLI:EU:C:1975:174 (Suiker Unie) para. 480), cf. Emde (2020), pp. 949 et seq.

[146] VGL, para. 32.

[147] Cf. VGL, para. 30.

[148] As it is that what matters in case contracts and practice diverge, cf. VGL, para. 34.

Table 1.8 Risks to avoid with agency agreements

#	Risk	Examples of which an agent must not incur any costs or risks for [a]
1	Contract-specific (i.e. directly related to the contracts intermediated)	– sales promotion (different from general advertising of the agent's activities), – stock maintenance, – transport, – transfer of property, – loss or damage, except where because of agent's fault, – customer's non-performance, except where because of agent's fault, hence must not assume a del credere liability [b]
2	Market-specific (i.e. to enter and operate in the specific market)	– equipment (e.g. petrol storage tank in petrol retailing, specific software), market-specific furniture (e.g. mannequins in the fashion industry), – premises, – training, – advertising
3	Role related risks—only relevant for dual role agents (i.e. distribution intermediaries which act for the same supplier as agent and distributor for different products on the same product market) [c]	– all significant risks above. Accordingly, the activities, obligations and rights of independent distributor versus agent must be delineated.

[a] Here listed in chronological order within the agent's activity, while the Commission starts with the risks related to the acquisition of property, cf. VGL, para. 33

[b] Cf. already the Christmas Notice, para. 1. Such del credere clause is allowed in most European countries, partly not regulated and thus subject only to general rules, partly regulated, often required to be in writing, limited to specific customers and in a few countries also only against special remuneration, especially Bulgaria (Article 35 Commercial Code), Croatia (Article 816 Croatian Code of Obligations), Finland (Article 17 Agency Act), Germany (§ 86b German Commercial Code), Italy (Article 1745 Civil Code), Slovenia (Article 819(3) Code of Obligations), Switzerland (Article 418c(3) Code of Obligations)

[c] Cf. VGL, para. 45; prior to the VGL 2022, the Commission had already dealt with dual role agents in its working paper from 2018: https://ec.europa.eu/competition/consultations/2018_vber/working_paper_on_dual_role_agents.pdf

A way out is that the principal covers such risks and costs. In general, **costs must** (1) **be covered** and (2) **be distinguishable**. Principals are free to decide how to cover the risks and costs. Two main methods exist:

- Reimburse the precise costs
- Reimburse via a lump sum scheme and reimburse any exceeding costs.[149]

[149] VGL, para. 35.

Contract Drafting Advice

To fall outside Article 101 TFEU, the distribution intermediary must only bear insignificant risks/costs related to the contracts concluded or intermediated on behalf of the principal. Risk otherwise: All clauses typical for agency agreements—vertical price maintenance, resale and sourcing restrictions—would qualify as restrictions by object and, in case of hardcore restrictions, make the entire agreement lose the benefit of the VBER. Except in case of efficiencies under Article 101(3) TFEU, the **agreement will be void** (Article 101 (2) TFEU) and may result in **fines** with EU and national competition authorities and **liability for damages** under civil law. While there is no case law, it is best practice to provide for (1) a catch-all clause to prevent costs being borne by the agent and (2) set up further control mechanisms to minimize risk.

Example Clause for New Agency Agreements:

The Parties acknowledge and agree that this agreement and the underlying relationship qualifies as agency—not as independent distributor—according to the European Commission's Guidelines on Vertical Restraints, paragraphs 29–46. Accordingly, the Agent will bear no or only insignificant, contract- or market-specific costs and risks in relation to the sale and promotion of the products. The Agent and its Affiliates shall during the Term of this Agreement not sell for its/their own account and risk Products. The Agent declares that it does not work

- for other principals than the Supplier/
- for principals other than those listed in Annex [•]

in the same relevant product market and must therefore not be considered as an independent economic operator. If the Agent intends to change, e.g. sell Products on its own account and/or work for others, the Agent must inform the Supplier. Any additional distribution requires the Supplier's approval.

The Agent warrants not to take any actions that would result in incurring any of the costs referred to in this Section without the prior consent of the Supplier.

Introducing the agency model with existing distributors may work in two ways: Either starting off fresh, with the agency agreements coming into effect only when the distributor agreements have expired or terminated. Or providing for a transition phase. In either case, a supplier who changes from independent distributors to agents, must—according to the Commission[150]—reimburse for investments made by the distributor which have not depreciated at expiry/termination as otherwise the agent would—in effect—arguably bear such costs. Reimbursing these costs shall, according to the Commission, only be dispensable if the costs relate exclusively to

[150] VGL, para. 39; Commission's Working paper from February 2021: Distributors that also act as agents for certain products for the same supplier, para. 20.

the sale of differentiated products not sold under the agency agreement, provided the agent can operate on the market without these products, as the costs related would otherwise again qualify as market-related costs.[151]

Example

If and as far as contract- or market-specific investments have not been depreciated upon expiry or termination of the Distributor Agreement, the Supplier will reimburse the Agent for such investments. ◀

The question is, whether online intermediation services (e.g. online marketplaces, app stores, price comparison tools, social media[152]) fit into this picture, i.e. whether they qualify as agents, and any sales requirements therefore lie outside the scope of Article 101 TFEU.

1.4.6 Intercompany Agreements

Agreements Concluded Between Companies Forming Part of the Same Group of Companies Can Fall Outside the Scope of Article 101 TFEU This exclusion, again, derives from a liberal construction[153] of Article 101 TFEU itself, based on the provision's purposes. While Article 101 TFEU's purpose is to protect competition for the sake of consumer welfare, it does not need to apply where there is **functionally no competition** due to organizational and legal ties between formally separate legal entities:

> The Court has also stated that the concept of an undertaking, in the same context, must be understood as designating an economic unit even if in law that economic unit consists of several persons, natural or legal (Case C-217/05 Confederación Española de Empresarios de Estaciones de Servicio [2006] ECR I-11987, paragraph 40).[154]

Actually, the ECJ early on showed a way to design distribution systems outside the limits of Article 101 TFEU (then: Article 85 of the EEC Treaty):

> The wording of Article 85 causes the prohibition to apply, provided that the other conditions are met, to an agreement between several undertakings. Thus, it does not apply where a sole undertaking integrates its own distribution network into its business organization.[155]

In such case, however, Article 102 TFEU may apply.

---

[151] VGL, para. 39.

[152] VGL, para. 64.

[153] In contrast to a "strict construction"; German lawyers tend to call it a "teleological interpretation" of the law, or, "teleological reduction" where the law's wording is reduced to a narrower content.

[154] ECLI:EU:C:2009:536 (Akzo Nobel), para. 55. This doctrine has been used to justify jurisdiction over companies outside the EU, cf. Ezrachi (2021), p. 704.

[155] ECLI:EU:C:1966:41 (Consten, Grundig), p. 340.

When does an economic unit exist? An economic unit exists according to the European Court's case law if a company (1) can and (2) does exercise significant influence over another.[156] Despite being separate legal entities, the conduct (market share, turnover)[157] of an affiliate can be attributed to a parent company if the affiliate does not determine its market conduct autonomously but essentially follows the parent company's instructions, primarily because of the economic, organizational and legal ties between these two legal entities. It is not necessary for the existence of an economic unit that formal decisions are made by the statutory organs. Rather, such an economic unit **may also be established informally**, especially based on **personnel ties** between the legal entities forming the economic unit. Existing as one economic unit is rebuttably presumed if the parent company holds 100% or nearly 100% of the shares in the subsidiary.

In plain words: Vertical agreements are only those between **different, independent undertakings**. Whether undertakings are independent is assessed on a functional test of whether a person performs an economic activity.[158] Connected undertakings, especially parents and their "children", are principally one undertaking.[159] This goes especially for the relationship between suppliers and their vertically integrated distributors.[160]

The clear consequence for designing distribution systems, as summed up by the ECJ:

> The Court of Justice has also held that 'in competition law, the term 'undertaking' must be understood as designating an economic unit for the purpose of the subject-matter of the agreement in question even if in law that economic unit consists of several persons, natural or legal' (judgment in Case 170/83 Hydrotherm v Compact [1984] ECR 2999, paragraph 11). . . .
>
> It follows that, where there is no agreement between **economically independent entities**, relations within an economic unit cannot amount to an agreement or concerted practice between undertakings which restricts competition within the meaning of Article 85(1) of the Treaty. Where, as in this case, the subsidiary, although having a separate legal personality, does not freely determine its conduct on the market but carries out the instructions given to it directly or indirectly by the parent company by which it is wholly controlled, Article 85 (1) does not apply to the relationship between the subsidiary and the parent company with which it forms an economic unit.
>
> While, admittedly, it cannot be excluded that the distribution policy applied by Parker, which consists of prohibiting its subsidiaries from supplying Parker products to customers

---

[156] ECLI:EU:C:1989:140 (Ahmed Saeed, Silver Line), para. 35 with further references; ECLI:EU:C:2019:499 (Italmobiliare), para. 88; ECLI:EU:C:1988:225 (Bodson), paras. 19 et seq.; ECLI:EU:C:1974:114 (Centrafram), para. 41.

[157] This economic unit-test is mostly used to attribute anti-competitive acts or market shares of the dependent companies to the parent company (and, finally, the turnover for calculating any fines).

[158] Wijckmans and Tuytschaever (2018), para. 3.07 on the VBER 2010; Ezrachi (2021), pp. 1 et seq.

[159] Article 1(2) VBER 2010; now Article 1(2) VBER 2022.

[160] VGL, para. 115.

established in Member States other than that of the subsidiary, may contribute to preserving and partitioning the various national markets and, in so doing, thwart one of the fundamental objectives to be achieved by the common market, it nevertheless follows from the abovementioned case-law that such a policy, followed by an economic unit such as the Parker group within which the subsidiaries do not enjoy any freedom to determine their conduct in the market, does not fall within the scope of Article 85(1) of the Treaty.

The Court therefore concludes that the Commission was correct in deciding that 'the subsidiaries' conduct is therefore to be imputed to the parent company' and that 'the integrated distribution system which ensures the sale of Parker products in Spain, France, Germany, Belgium and the Netherlands via the wholly-owned subsidiaries located there fulfils the conditions established by the European Court of Justice with regard to the non-applicability of Article 85.[161]

Single Economic Unit

A single economic unit in terms of competition law exists (and agreements between them thus fall outside of Article 101 TFEU) especially between:

- a parent company and wholly owned subsidiaries,
- parent company and majority owned subsidiaries,
- wholly owned subsidiaries.[162]

1.4.7 Agreements with Ancillary Restraints

Ancillary restraints fall **outside the scope of Article 101 TFEU**, too.[163] Ancillary restraints are those which are (1) necessary to restrict a commercial autonomy for implementing a main operation and (2) proportionate to the objectives underlying said main operation.[164] Thus, they are either neutral to competition or effect it positively. In the ECJ's words, the test is to "inquire whether that operation would be impossible to carry out in the absence of the restriction in question".[165] Whereby impossible does not mean "more difficult" or "less profitable", but "strictly indispensable". The test is to "inquire whether that operation would be impossible to carry out in the absence of the restriction".[166] This may even go for hardcore restrictions.[167]

[161] ECLI:EU:C:1996:405 (Viho), paras. 50–53.

[162] Wijckmans and Tuytschaever (2018), para. 3.30 on VBER 2010.

[163] Commission Guidelines on the application of Article 81(3), paras. 28 et seq.

[164] ECJ ECLI:EU:C:2014:2201 (MasterCard), paras. 91 and 107; ECLI:EU:C:2018:25 (F. Hoffmann-La Roche), para. 69; Commission Guidelines on the application of Article 81(3), para. 31.

[165] ECLI:EU:C:2014:2201 (MasterCard), para. 91.

[166] ECLI:EU:C:2014:2201 (MasterCard), para. 91

[167] VGL, para. 180.

Examples of ancillary restraints in case law include **licensing agreements** which restrict the conduct of third parties promoting the use of another product for the treatment of the same diseases:

> In view of the foregoing, the answer to the first part of the first question is that Article 101 (1) TFEU must be interpreted as meaning that an arrangement put in place between the parties to a licensing agreement regarding the exploitation of a medicinal product which, in order to reduce competitive pressure on the use of that product for the treatment of given diseases, is designed to restrict the conduct of third parties promoting the use of another medicinal product for the treatment of those diseases, does not fall outside the application of that provision on the ground that the arrangement is ancillary to that agreement.[168]

Another example of ancillary restraints are **franchise agreements** which stipulate restrictions necessary for the proper functioning of the agreement, especially to protect the franchise system's uniformity and reputation:

> Provisions which are strictly necessary in order to ensure that the know-how and assistance provided by the franchisor do not benefit competitors do not constitute restrictions of competition... Provisions which establish the control strictly necessary for maintaining the identity and reputation of the network identified by the common name or symbol do not constitute restrictions of competition....Provisions which share markets between the franchisor and the franchisees or between franchisees constitute restrictions of competition ...[169]

Though not made clear within the VGL, the Commission apparently considers **genuine testing** as a further example for agreements with ancillary restraints. Genuine testing occurs where suppliers test new products on the market by launching them in a limited territory/vis-à-vis a limited customer group. During such a launch period, they may prohibit active sales outside the test territory or beyond others than the test customer group, restricted, however to the necessary testing period.[170] Regularly, however, such genuine testing will be exempt under Article 4(b)(i) VBER, arguing that the other territories/customer groups have been reserved to the supplier, as the VGL stresses that reserving territories or customer groups does explicitly "not require the supplier to be commercially active in the territory or customer group"[171]—insofar, suppliers and their distributors who are within the VBER's 30% market share threshold benefit from this double safety net.

A further example of ancillary restraints are **joint venture agreements** which contains a non-compete to allow entering a new market together, up to the time to reach break-even:

[168] ECLI:EU:C:2018:25 (F. Hoffmann-La Roche), para. 75.

[169] ECLI:EU:C:1986:41 (Pronuptia), para. 27.

[170] VGL, para. 184.

[171] VGL, para. 123.

The non-competition clause can therefore be regarded as ancillary to the creation of TPS during the platform's crucial launch phase and can therefore be deemed pro-competitive in that it contributes to the creation of a new entrant on the French pay-TV market during that period. On the basis of the data supplied by TPS on the amount of the investments necessary for launching the platform, forecasts regarding accumulated losses, the time and the number of subscribers needed to reach break-even point and the rate of cancellation of subscriptions, and the company's performance over the first 18 months, the length of the launch phase can be estimated at three years. Consequently, the clause does not fall within the scope of Article 85(1) during the first three years of its application.[172]

1.4.8 Subcontracting Agreements

Subcontracting agreements **fall out of the prohibition of anti-competitive agreements**—as far as any of the following clauses are concerned, provided they are necessary:[173]

- Restriction of use: technology or equipment provided by the contractor may not be used except for the purposes of the subcontracting agreement,
- Confidentiality obligation: technology or equipment provided by the contractor may not be made available to third parties,
- Exclusive supply obligation: the goods, services or work resulting from the use of such technology or equipment may be supplied only to the contractor or performed on his behalf[174]

  "Subcontracting agreements" are legally defined by the Commission in its Subcontracting Notice as "agreements under which one firm, called 'the contractor', whether or not in consequence of a prior order from a third party, entrusts to another, called 'the subcontractor', the manufacture of goods, the supply of services or the performance of work under the contractor's instructions, to be provided to the contractor or performed on his behalf".[175] The typical scenario is that the buyer provides intellectual property rights to the supplier in order for the supplier to produces the goods to be sold to the buyer. The pro-competitive effect ideally arising out of this distribution of work is that companies, especially SMEs, can grow through the help of others.

  The reason for excluding subcontracting agreements from the scope of Article 101 TFEU is that **subcontractors**, in the cases defined in the Subcontracting Notice, **do not act as independent suppliers**. The subcontractor test therefore is

[172] Commission Decision of 3 March 1999 Case No IV/36.237 (TPS), para. 99 (with the clause quoted in para. 77).

[173] VGL, para. 47 appear to fall short by stating that subcontracting agreements "as a general rule" fall outside of Article 101(1) TFEU, but then clarify that restrictions beyond those necessary for subcontracting do fall under Article 101(1).

[174] Subcontracting Notice, para. 2.

[175] Subcontracting Notice, para. 1, sentence 3.

whether the subcontractor is by agreement limited to make "necessary use"[176] of specifications (in terms of industrial property rights, secret knowledge or manufacturing know-how, plans, dies, patterns or tools of the contractor which are contractor-specific in form, function or composition. The fine line is between specific information provided by the contractor on the one and general information reasonably obtainable on the other side as the subcontractor must not be deprived in developing its own business.[177]

Confidentiality obligations, contractual and post-contractual, are allowed. The same applies to the non-exclusive pass-on obligations of any foreground, or, as the Commission then put it, of any "technical improvements… made".[178] The same goes, of course at the crossroads with IP, for agreements where the contractor restricts the subcontractor in using the contractor's trademarks, trade name or get up.

1.4.9 Selective Distribution Systems Complying with "Metro"

Qualitative selective distribution systems **comply with Article 101(1) TFEU** if they fulfil **three conditions**:

1. The product, by virtue of its characteristics (in particular its high quality or technical development), requires qualitative selection in order to maintain quality and ensure proper use,
2. the selection criteria are objectively qualitative and applied in a non-discriminatory manner and
3. the selection criteria are necessary.[179]

These conditions must exist objectively, considering the interests of the consumer. Dogmatically, these "Metro" criteria are a teleological reduction of Article 101(1) TFEU, namely of the characteristic "prevention, restriction or distortion of competition". Though intra-brand competition—namely price competition—is presumably reduced in selective distribution (because the prices within a selective system typically diverge less than in the case of free competition of all possible resellers, including pure online players). At the same time, however, inter-brand competition with regard to customer services is promoted. The foundation for this was laid by the European Court of Justice in its Metro/SABA decision[180]—giving the criteria their name as "Metro" criteria.

[176] Subcontracting Notice, para. 2, sentence 3.

[177] Subcontracting Notice, para. 2, last sentences.

[178] Subcontracting Notice, para. 3, sentence 1.

[179] ECLI:EU:C:1977:167 (Metro), para. 21; ECLI:EU:C:2011:649 (Pierre Fabre), para. 41 with further references.

[180] ECLI:EU:C:1977:167.

1.5 Block Exemptions as Safe Harbour

While the EU's primary competition law, Articles 101 and 102 TFEU, has remained the same (the only change from the original Articles 85 and 86 in 1957 to the Articles 81 and 82 in 1999 was from "common" to "internal market"),[181] the Commission as competent European competition authority has been constantly developing the secondary competition law. With the most recent reform process, the Commission aims at making EU competition law fit for the challenges of the digital economy and maintaining legal clarity, thus reducing the administrative burden of the companies.

The Commission's tool kit consists of both **soft law** (binding the Commission itself) and **hard law** (binding generally, including the courts): notices, guidelines and—most of all—of block exemption regulations. These block exemption regulations shall enable market participants to easily self-assess if an agreement or practice falls inside or outside the allowed limits of EU competition laws.

The self-assessment is the rule since 2003—when EU competition law shifted from notification (undertakings had to notify the Commission about agreements and practices and the Commission decided about their exemption[182]) to self-assessment. This shift is laid down in the regulation on the implementation of the rules on competition,[183] whose Article 2 sentence 2 states: "*The undertaking or association of undertakings claiming the benefit of Article 81(3) of the Treaty shall bear the burden of proving that the conditions of that paragraph are fulfilled.*"

The block exemption regulations shall serve as a reliable shortcut to the exemption of Article 101(3) TFEU. Compared to a self-assessment based solely on Article 101(3), the block exemption regulations are far more concrete and offer a "safe harbour" as they apply as binding laws throughout the EU, unlike the Article 81 (3) Guidelines. Therefore, it is advisable to head for the safe harbour.[184]

The block exemption regulation's structure is basically the same: They describe the "blocks" of agreements which may be exempt (including the market shares) and stipulate lists of "black" (prohibited so-called "hardcore restrictions", agreement not exempt), "white" (allowed, agreement exempt) and "grey" (prohibited, agreement, however, exempt) clauses. The block exemption regulations are generally made for specified periods, as required by Article 2(1) of Regulation No. 19/5/EEC on application of Article 85(3) of the Treaty to certain categories of agreements and concerted practices. The practically most relevant block exemption regulations **for vertical restraints** are shown in Table 1.9.

---

[181] Slightly different: "common market" in 1957 instead of "internal market".

[182] EEC Council: Regulation No 17: First Regulation implementing Articles 85 and 86 of the Treaty. The Commission decided whether "*there are no grounds under Article 85(1) or Article 86 of the Treaty for action on its part in respect of an agreement, decision or practice*". With the increasing number of notifications, the Commission started providing comfort letters to deal efficiently with them.

[183] Council Regulation (EC) No 1/2003 of 16 December 2002.

[184] Bunte and Stancke (2022), § 3, para. 125.

Table 1.9 Overview of most relevant Vertical Block Exemption Regulations

#	Title	Scope	In force until
1	Regulation 2022/720 on vertical agreements and concerted practices	"Umbrella regulation" for all vertical agreements	31 May 2034
2	Regulation 461/2010 on vertical agreements and concerted practices in the motor vehicle sector	Motor vehicle aftermarket: Spare parts for motor vehicles and repair and maintenance services	31 May 2023
3	Regulation 316/2014 on technology transfer agreements	Technology rights licensing agreement or assignment of technology rights for production	30 April 2026

Contrary to vertical restraints, there is no "umbrella" **regulation for horizontal restraints**. The practically most relevant block exemption regulations for horizontal restraints are shown in Table 1.10.

While drafts for new horizontal competition rules have been published on 1 March 2022[185]—for specialisation agreements,[186] for R&D agreements[187] and accompanying Horizontal Guidelines[188]—and should have been implemented with effect of 1 January 2023, the feedback of the public consultations required further work on the drafts. To ensure legal certainty for businesses, the European Commission extended the validity of the existing regulations in the meantime. According to information provided by the Commission to the author,[189] the new horizontal competition rules shall enter into force before the expiry of the HBERs in June 2023.

Moreover, there are currently only two block exemption regulations governing **specific sectors**, as shown in Table 1.11.

To enhance interpreting the Block Exemptions, the Commission also publishes notices which explain the Commission's intentions behind the Block Exemptions. For distribution and supply agreements, especially the following are relevant:

[185] Cf. the analysis of the drafts by Giedke et al. (2023), pp. 67 et seq.

[186] Draft for a Commission Regulation on the application of Article 101(3) of the Treaty on the Functioning of the European Union to certain categories of specialisation agreements, OJ 2022/C 120/01, https://eur-lex.europa.eu/legal-content/EN/TXT/?uri=CELEX:52022XC0315(01).

[187] Draft for a Commission Regulation on the application of Article 101(3) of the Treaty on the Functioning of the European Union to certain categories of research and development agreements, OJ 2022/C 120/02, https://eur-lex.europa.eu/legal-content/EN/TXT/?uri=CELEX%3A52022XC0315%2802%29.

[188] Draft for a Communication from the Commission—Guidelines on the applicability of Article 101 of the Treaty on the Functioning of the European Union to horizontal co-operation agreements, OJ 2022/C 164/01, https://eur-lex.europa.eu/legal-content/EN/TXT/?uri=OJ%3AC%3A2022%3A164%3AFULL.

[189] Email of 6 February 2023.

Table 1.10 Horizontal Block Exemption Regulations ("HBERs")—overview

#	Title	Scope	In force until
1	Regulation 1218/2010 on specialisation agreements	Unilateral, reciprocal specialisation or joint production	30 June 2023 [a]
2	Regulation 1217/2010 on R&D agreements	R&D agreements	30 June 2023 [b]

[a] Originally until 31 December 2022, extended by Regulation (EU) 2022/2456 of 8 December 2022 amending Regulation (EU) No 1218/2010

[b] Originally until 31 December 2022, extended by Regulation (EU) 2022/2455 of 8 December 2022 amending Regulation (EU) No 1217/2010

Table 1.11 Sector-specific block exemption regulations

#	Title	Scope	In force until
1	Regulation 169/2009/EEC Application of the competition rules to transport by rail, road and inland waterways	Rail, road and inland waterways [a], only applicable to SMEs [b]	n/a [c]
2	Regulation 906/2009 on certain categories of agreements, decisions and concerted practices between liner shipping companies [d]	Liner shipping companies	24 April 2024

[a] For air transport, no block exemption regulation is in place. Regulation No. 3652/93 has expired and no new one has been made, even though the Commission is authorized to set one up according to Regulation No. 487/2009

[b] Cf. its Article 3 with the limits to the carrying capacity of each grouping

[c] Different from the other block exemptions, this one is not limited in time because it is not based on Regulation No. 19/5/EEC on the application of Article 85(3) of the Treaty to certain categories of agreements and concerted practices, whose Article 2(1) stipulates that a regulation made pursuant to Article 1 shall be adopted for a specified period

[d] Based on Council Regulation (EC) No 246/2009 of 26 February 2009 on the application of Article 81(3) of the Treaty to certain categories of agreements, decisions and concerted practices between liner shipping companies (consortia)

- Guidelines on Vertical Restraints, OJ C 130, 19.5.2010, pp. 1–46,
- Commission notice—Supplementary guidelines on vertical restraints in agreements for the sale and repair of motor vehicles and for the distribution of spare parts for motor vehicles OJ C 138, 28.5.2010, pp. 16–27,
- Guidelines on the applicability of Article 101 of the treaty on the Functioning of the European Union to horizontal co-operation agreements OJ C 11, 14.1.2011, pp. 1–72,
- Guidelines on the application of Article 101 of the Treaty on the Functioning of the European Union to technology transfer agreements OJ C 89, 28.3.2014, pp. 3–50.

1.6 Outside the VBER: The Article 101(3) TFEU Exception

How to handle agreements which appreciably restrict competition, but fall outside the VBER, either because their restrictions are materially not exempt or because one of the parties' market shares exceeds 30%? Even though they fall outside the safe harbour, they may be exempt in the individual case from the prohibition of Article 101(1) TFEU[190] if they fulfil the four conditions of Article 101(3) TFEU:

Article 101(3) TFEU

The provisions of paragraph 1 may, however, be declared inapplicable in the case of:

- any agreement or category of agreements between undertakings,
- any decision or category of decisions by associations of undertakings,
- any concerted practice or category of concerted practices,

which contributes to improving the production or distribution of goods or to promoting technical or economic progress, while allowing consumers a fair share of the resulting benefit, and which does not:

(a) impose on the undertakings concerned restrictions which are not indispensable to the attainment of these objectives;
(b) afford such undertakings the possibility of eliminating competition in respect of a substantial part of the products in question.

Article 101(3) TFEU sets up two positive and two negative requirements:

Positive:
- Contribution to improving production or distribution or to promoting technical or economic progress
- Allowing consumers a fair share of the resulting benefit

Negative:
- Restriction must not be not indispensable (i.e. must be necessary[191]) to attain the above objectives, and
- Restriction must not allow eliminating competition regarding a substantial part of the products.

---

[190] VGL, para. 48.

[191] Cf. Article 101(3) TFEU's triple negatory wording ("...which does not (a) impose ... restrictions which are not indispensable ...").

Assessing whether an agreement can rely on the benefit of Article 101(3) TFEU thus requires considering the positive and negative effects of vertical agreements. These effects vary between the various vertical restraints.

Potential positive effects especially include:

- lower prices;
- promotion of non-price competition;
- improvement in the quality of services;
- the addressing of vertical externality issues (i.e. indirect costs or benefit that is produced by another party's activity[192]);
- addressing the free rider problem;
- opening up or entering new markets;
- addressing the certification free rider issue;
- addressing the hold-up problem,[193] specifically in franchising;
- achieving economies of scale and distribution;
- ensuring uniformity and quality standardization;
- addressing capital market imperfections.[194]

Potential negative effects especially include:

- anti-competitive foreclosing of other suppliers or buyers, by raising barriers to entry or expansion;
- softening of competition and/or facilitating collusion between competing suppliers (especially: reducing inter-brand competition);
- softening of competition between the buyer and its competitors or the facilitation of explicit or tacit collusion between competing buyers, often referred to as the reduction of intra-brand competition, where it concerns distributors of the goods or services of the same supplier; and
- creating of obstacles to market integration, in other words: partitioning the internal market, thus limiting the consumer's choice to purchase goods or services.[195]

Both positive and negative effects of vertical restraints may reinforce each other where several suppliers and buyers organise distribution in the same way, resulting in cumulative effects.[196] When negative effects reinforce each other, this may lead to the withdrawal of the benefit of the Regulation.

---

[192] Cf. Niels et al. (2016).

[193] Hold-up problems are basically situations of underinvestment, where a party to a contract is refrained from investing because it is concerned not to get it returned, cf. the examples in the VGL, paras. 16(e) and (f), 313, 314, 316, 319, 327, 329, 330 and 378.

[194] VGL, para. 16.

[195] VGL, para. 18.

[196] VGL, para. 22.

What shall not occur: foreclosure of markets, softening of competition (both inter-brand and intra-brand[197]) or conclusion, where companies fail to offer products or services at the most favourable terms (prices or other)—and neither, EU-specifically, the creation of obstacles to market integration.[198] Where such effects occur, companies are on the road to dominance:

> The degree of market power required to establish a restriction of competition within the meaning of Article 101(1) of the Treaty is less than the degree of market power required for a finding of dominance under Article 102 of the Treaty.[199]

Insofar, certain behaviours may still be allowed under such elevated market shares, while they may be prohibited in case of a dominant market position. Again, the Commission provides guidance for self-assessing if an agreement benefits from Article 101(3) TFEU, namely through its "Guidelines on the application of Article 81 (3) of the Treaty",[200] in short: Article 81(3) Guidelines.

Examples of Agreements which are Exempt under Article 101(3) TFEU

- territory restrictions for the sake of genuine testing or staggered introduction of new products to the market;[201]
- selective distribution, prohibition of active sales between authorised distributors, if necessary for authorised wholesalers to invest in promotional activities in each of their territories;[202]
- exclusive agency provisions preventing the principal from appointing other agents regarding specific transactions, customers or territories; single branding provisions, post-term non-competes;[203]
- agreements preventing the parties from carrying out independent research and development;[204]
- rent and lease agreements;[205]
- agreements relating to the provision of online intermediation services (if they restrict competition at all and if they do not already enjoy the De Minimis Notice's exemption);[206]

[197] Where, however, reduced intra-brand competition (i.e. regarding goods/services of same supplier) unlikely impacts consumers negatively where inter-brand competition is strong, cf. ECJ, ECLI:EU:C:1977:167 (Metro), para. 22; ECJ, ECLI:EU:C:2021:935 (Visma), para. 78; VGL 21 and footnote 25.

[198] VGL, para. 18.

[199] VGL, para. 11.

[200] Article 81(3) Guidelines.

[201] VGL, para. 184.

[202] VGL 184, even though the Commission's point is questionable as to which it should not be practical to specify the promotional efforts in the agreement.

[203] VGL, para. 43.

[204] VGL, para. 61.

[205] VGL, para. 61.

[206] VGL, para. 107.

- exclusive distribution agreements: as pro-competitive effects, exclusivity may incentivise distributors to invest in developing the supplier's brand or in providing demand-enhancing services. Rule of thumb: The more exclusive distributors in a particular territory, the less likely they will be incentivised to invest in promoting the supplier's products and brand, as the other exclusive distributors that share the territory may free-ride on their investment efforts;[207]
- selective distribution combined with a location clause[208]
- quantitative selective distribution,[209]
- restriction of active cross-supplies between authorised distributors (to remain free under the VBER);[210]
- RPM for a limited period of time;[211]
- non-competes in return for transfer of substantial know-how,[212]
- franchising;[213]
- quantity forcing, e.g. minimum purchase requirements, stocking requirements or non-linear pricing (e.g. conditional rebate schemes or two-part tariffs, consisting of a fixed fee plus a price per unit), or English clauses (i.e. requiring the buyer to report better offers, allowing the buyer to accept them only if the supplier does not match the offer);[214]
- exclusive supply;[215] or
- restrictions on the use of marketplaces,[216] or

[207] VGL, paras. 125 et seq., especially para. 136, with further examples in para. 141 ("multiple exclusive dealerships") and para. 142 ("exclusive customer allocation").

[208] VGL, para. 162 (particularly if the combination is necessary to protect the distributor's substantial, relationship-specific investments).

[209] VGL, para. 163. While inter-brand competition is not directly affected, intra-brand competition is not foreclosed if the selected distributors are free to sell competing brands.

[210] VGL, para. 183, e.g. if necessary for authorised wholesalers to invest in promotional activities in the territory in which they distribute to support sales by authorised retailers (provided such promotional activities cannot be specified in the distribution agreement).

[211] VGL, para. 195, e.g. for introducing a new product to induce distributors to better consider promoting the product, provided there are no realistic and less restrictive alternative means of incentivising the distributors, or also in uniform distribution systems such as franchising to organise a coordinated short-term low-price campaign, usually of 2–6 weeks in most cases.

[212] VGL, para. 317.

[213] VGL, para. 169. As far as obligations are necessary to protect IPRs or to maintain the franchise network's uniformity (common identity and reputation), they already fall outside the scope of Article 101(1) TFEU. Other restrictions, especially on selling (e.g. selective distribution) provide an incentive to the franchisees to invest in the franchise concept and help maintaining the uniformity, thereby "offsetting" the loss of intra-brand competition. Non-competes aim to exclude free-riding (i.e. avoiding competing brands from benefiting from its trade name).

[214] VGL, para. 320.

[215] VGL, para. 331, with an example on an intermediate product market where the supplier makes considerable investment for producing a new component.

[216] VGL, para. 342, e.g. if restrictions aim at protecting the brand, provided they are necessary, i.e. the brand protection cannot be achieved through using an own brand shop within the marketplace. Restrictions are rather to fulfil Article 101(3) TFEU if the suppliers impose and control compliance throughout the system.

- less likely in practice: tying, i.e. "where customers that purchase one product (the tying product) are required also to purchase another distinct product (the tied product) from the same supplier or someone designated by the latter".[217,218]

Appendix: Test Scheme for Vertical Agreements Under Swiss Law[219]

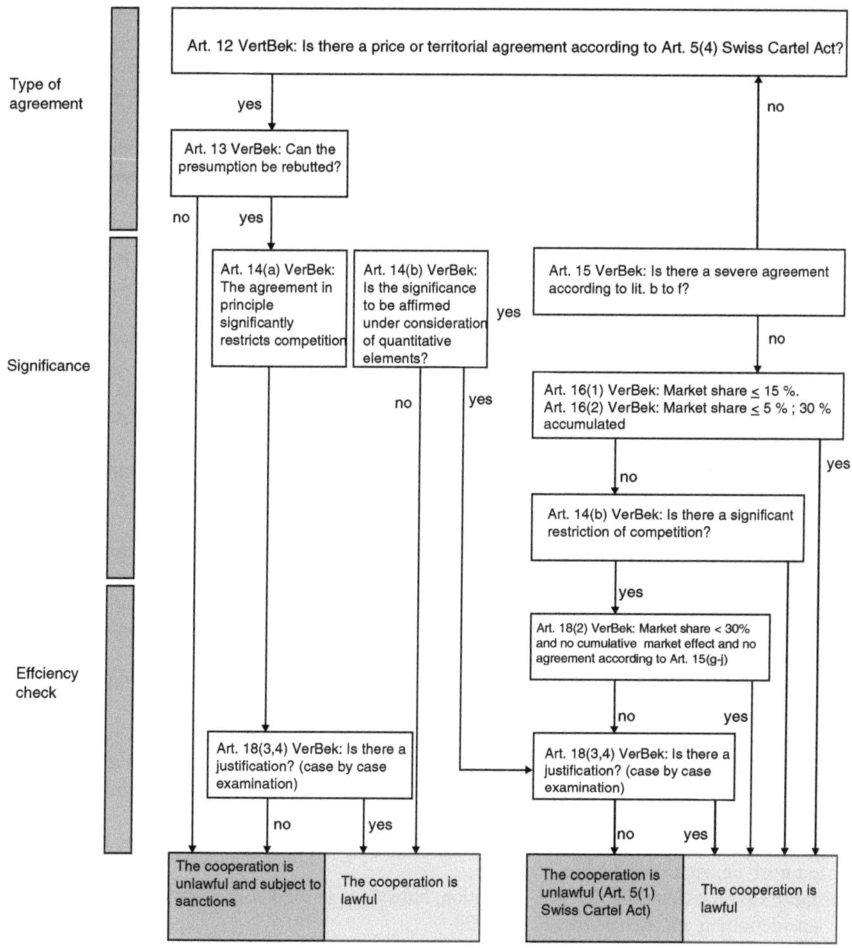

Fig. 1.2 Test scheme for vertical agreements under Swiss Law

[217] VGL, para. 389.

[218] VGL, para. 397: Tying may facilitate joint production or joint distribution. For Article 101 (3) TFEU, tying must allow consumers a fair share of the benefit, especially by partially passing on cost reductions to consumers.

[219] From Annex 1 of the VertBek 2022, translated by the author.

References

Albers M (2006) Der "more economic approach" bei Verdrängungsmissbräuchen: Zum Stand der Überlegungen der Europäischen Kommission. Nachträglich angefertigte, leicht veränderte und um Fußnoten ergänzte Fassung des Vortrages anlässlich des Hamburger Kartellrechtssymposiums 2006. In: Ahrens B, Behrens P, von Dietze P (eds) Marktmacht und Missbrauch. Nomos, Baden-Baden, pp 11–24

Bechtold R, Bosch W (2021) Gesetz gegen Wettbewerbsbeschränkungen (GWB), 10th edn. C.H. Beck, Munich

Bechtold R, Bosch W, Brinker I (2023) EU-Kartellrecht, 4th edn. C.H. Beck, Munich

Bucher R (2020) Dual distribution and agency agreements under the Swiss Cartel Act – AdBlue: decision of the Swiss Competition Commission of 2 December 2019, 22-0485. ZVertriebsR 2020:231–236

Bucher R, Rohrßen B (2023) Vertriebskartellrecht EU / Schweiz – Der "Reboot" im Vergleich. ZVertriebsR 2023:Issue 3

Bundeskartellamt (2020) Evaluation of the commission notice on the definition of the relevant 58 market for the purposes of Community competition law. https://www.bundeskartellamt. Accessed 9 Feb 2023

Bundeskartellamt (2007) Information leaflet of the Bundeskartellamt on the possibilities of cooperation for small and medium-sized enterprises. https://www.bundeskartellamt.de/SharedDocs/Publikation/EN/Merkblaetter/Leaflet%20-%20Cooperation%20for%20SMUs.pdf?__blob=publicationFile&v=3. Accessed 12 Feb 2023

Bunte H, Stancke F (2022) Kartellrecht mit Vergaberecht und Beihilferecht, 4th edn. C.H. Beck, Munich

CMA (2020) Guidance on the functions of the CMA after the end of the Transition Period 2020. https://www.gov.uk/government/publications/guidance-on-the-functions-of-the-cma-after-the-end-of-the-transition-period. Accessed 9 Feb 2023

Commission (2013) Competition: antitrust procedures in anticompetitive agreements. https://competition-policy.ec.europa.eu/system/files/2020-12/antitrust_procedures_101_en.pdf. Accessed 9 Feb 2023

Commission (2021) Statistics on Cartel cases. https://competition-policy.ec.europa.eu/cartels/statistics_en. Accessed 9 Feb 2023

Commission (2022) Competition: Commission seeks feedback on draft revised Market Definition Notice (Press release 8 November 2022 IP/22/6528). https://ec.europa.eu/commission/presscorner/detail/en/ip_22_6528. Accessed 9 Feb 2023

Emde R (2020) Das Handelsvertreter-Kartellrecht nach den Leitlinien zur GVO 2790/99 (VO 2790/99). BB 2020:949–955

Emmerich V, Lange K (2021) Kartellrecht, 15th edn. C.H. Beck, Munich

European Commission (2013) Competition: antitrust procedures in anticompetitive agreements. https://competition-policy.ec.europa.eu/system/files/2020-12/antitrust_procedures_101_en.pdf. Accessed 12 Feb 2023

European Commission (2023a) Antitrust overview. https://competition-policy.ec.europa.eu/antitrust_en. Accessed 13 Feb 2023

European Commission (2023b) SME definition. https://single-market-economy.ec.europa.eu/smes/sme-definition_en. Accessed 12 Feb 2023

Ezrachi A (2021) EU competition law. An analytic guide to the leading cases, 7th edn. Hart, London

Gerber D (2020) Competition law and antitrust. A global guide, 1st edn. Oxford University Press, Oxford

Giedke A, Stief M, Stachowitz S (2023) Die Reform der Gruppenfreistellungsverordnungen – FuE- und Spezialisierungs-GVO 2023. WuW 2023:67–73

Hartmann-Rüppel M, Nagel S (2022) Durchsuchungen des Bundeskartellamts. CB 2022:230–236

Hölters W, Weber M (2022) Aktiengesetz, 4th edn. C.H. Beck/Vahlen, Munich

ICC (2015) Why complying with competition law is good for your business, practical tools for smaller businesses to improve compliance. https://iccwbo.org/publication/icc-sme-toolkit-complying-competition-law-good-business/. Accessed 12 Feb 2023

Jones A, Sufrin B, Dunne N (2019) EU competition law. Text, cases and materials, 7th edn. Oxford University Press, Oxford

Mestmäcker E, Schweitzer H (2014) Europäisches Wettbewerbsrecht, 3rd edn. C.H. Beck, Munich

Meyer C (2022) Neue Regeln für den Vertrieb in der Schweiz. ZVertriebsR:184–188

Niels G, Jenkins H, Kavanagh J (2016) Economics for competition lawyers, 2nd edn. Oxford University Press, Oxford

Nolte S (2022) Nach Art. 101 AEUV. In: Langen E, Bunte H-J (eds) Kartellrecht, vol 2, 14th edn. Luchterhand, Munich

Rohrßen B (2021) Online-Vertrieb in der EU – Vertriebskartellrecht: Die neue Vertikal-GVO 2022. ZVertriebsR 2021:293–298

Rosenkranz F (2015) Die Auslegung von Ausnahmevorschriften. JA 2015:783–788

Schmassmann M (2022) Revision der Vertikalbekanntmachung. SZK/RSDC 2022:144–146

Schultze J-M, Pautke S, Wagener D-S (2019) Vertikal-GVO, Gruppenfreistellungsverordnung für vertikale Vereinbarungen, 4th edn. Deutscher Fachverlag, Frankfurt am Main

Stäuber R (2022) Preisbindung durch Preisempfehlung – Urteile des Schweizer Bundesgerichts zu Hors-Liste-Arzneimitteln NZKart:388–391

Studienvereinigung Kartellrecht (2022) 013-00007: Revision Vertikalbekanntmachung (VertBek) – Stellungnahme vom 02.09.2022 an die Wettbewerbskommission. https://www.studienvereinigung.de/publikationen/stellungnahmen. Accessed 9 Feb 2023

Tinguely B (2023) La distribution sur internet dans le nouveau droit européen – et futur droit suisse? – des accords verticaux. sic! 2023:11-26

Wagner-von Papp F, Wurmnest W (2020) 1. Teil Grundlagen. In: Säcker F-J, Karpenstein U, Ludwigs M (eds) Münchener Kommentar zum Wettbewerbsrecht, vol 1/2, 3rd edn. C.H. Beck, Munich

Waser A, Ondelli V (2022) Ein "Swiss Finish" im Vertriebskartellrecht. SZK/RSDC 2022:5–9

WEKO (2022) WEKO updates vertical agreement rules, 14 December 2022. https://www.newsd.admin.ch/newsd/message/attachments/74457.pdf. Accessed 12 Feb 2023

Wijckmans F, Tuytschaever F (2018) Vertical agreements in EU competition law, 3rd edn. Oxford University Press, Oxford

Wolf M (2020) I. Freistellung (Art. 101 Abs. 3 AEUV). In: Säcker F-J, Karpenstein U, Ludwigs M (eds) Münchener Kommentar zum Wettbewerbsrecht, vol 1/2 (Band 1, 2. Teil. Europäisches Wettbewerbsrecht), 3rd edn. C.H. Beck, Munich

VBER 2022: The Safe Harbour for Distribution Agreements

2

Abstract The Vertical Block Exemption Regulation ("VBER") is the heart of European competition law. It is of utmost practical relevance as it provides a safe harbour for distribution agreements, i.e. provides a safe harbour in the open sea of distribution related competition law. Under the broad prohibition of anti-competitive agreements, the Vertical Block Exemption Regulation aims at allowing a legally certain self-assessment of vertical agreements by abstractly exempting agreements ("blocks")[1] and thereby extending the rule-exception principle of Article 101 TFEU[2] by a further rule-exception principle.[3]

In practice, the Vertical Block Exemption Regulation—the first of which entered into force[4] on 1 May 1967—has acquired enormous importance[5]: It is the **"heart" of competition related distribution law**[6] and the VBER 2022 has been "an important policy project because vertical agreements, for example between suppliers of goods and services and their distributors, are ubiquitous in all sectors of the EU economy".[7] The Vertical Block Exemption Regulation, together with the guidelines published by

[1] The VBER refers to "certain categories of vertical agreements" (Recital 1), which it exempts block-wise (Recital 2).

[2] Cf. for example Hopt (2019, XII.3); Wolf (2020, para. 1020 et seq., also on the overall interpretation of the ECJ that Article 101(3) supplements the prohibition in para. 1.).

[3] See the prohibitions and derogations of Article 4 VBER.

[4] Regulation 67/67/EEC on exclusive distribution agreements, replaced in 1983 by Regulation 83/83 on exclusive distribution agreements and Regulation 84/83 on exclusive purchasing agreements, supplemented by Regulation 4987/88 for franchise agreements. From 2000 onwards, the first "Vertical Block Exemption Regulation" No. 2790/99 applied, replaced by Regulation No. 330/2010.

[5] Cf. Martinek et al. (2016, § 31 para. 23); Rohrßen (2019, p. 342 footnote 7 with further references).

[6] Rahlmeyer et al. (2020, Preface).

[7] European Commission (2021b, IP/21/3561).

B. Rohrßen, *VBER 2022: EU Competition Law for Vertical Agreements*, Law for Professionals, https://doi.org/10.1007/978-3-031-35024-5_2

the European Commission, have served well and have brought some simplification and legal certainty to supply and distribution agreements.

The VBER 2022 has **adapted this safe harbour to the technical development**—the **digitalisation of distribution**—and replaced the former Vertical Block Exemption Regulation 2010/330. The legal trigger has been that the Vertical Block Exemption Regulation expired on 31 May 2022.[8] The VBER 2022 updates the Vertical Block Exemption Regulation to take account of market developments, in particular "the growth of e-commerce"[9] and thus works as a "reboot" according to EU Commissioner Vestager:

> What we need is not so much a reset – it's more what, in Hollywood,[10] they **call a "reboot"**. When they reboot old movies and TV shows, they bring back the characters we know, but with the details refreshed and **updated for a new era**. And that's pretty much what competition policy needs. Not to change what our policy is about – but to make sure that the tools we have to achieve those goals are up to date." [11]

The basic test of exemption with its three requirements remains the same. Exempt from the prohibition of anti-competitive agreements under Article 101 TFEU are (i) vertical agreements between undertakings (ii) with market shares up to a maximum of 30%, which (iii) do not contain any hardcore restrictions—Articles 2–4 VBER. Contractual provisions on commercial agents will also remain exempt from antitrust law.

The Basic Test of Exemption Under the VBER

The three conditions for exemption and thus the basic test remain unchanged. Exempt from the prohibition of anti-competitive agreements under Article 101 TFEU continue to be

(i) vertical agreements
(ii) between undertakings with market shares up to a maximum of 30%, which
(iii) do not contain any hardcore restrictions (Articles 2–4 VBER).

Commercial agency agreements also remain exempt from antitrust law.[12]

---

[8] Article 10 VBER. The former VBER No. 2790/1999 was also limited in time, as was Regulation (EEC) No. 1983/83 with regard to exclusive distribution agreements and No. 1984/83 with regard to exclusive purchasing agreements.

[9] VBER, recital 2.

[10] Maybe even more in Silicon Valley.

[11] Vestager (2020).

[12] VGL, para. 29 et seq., following the Commission's "Working paper: Distributors that also act as agents for certain products for the same supplier" of February 2021. On platforms as commercial agents Rohrßen (2019, p. 159).

Nevertheless, the VBER has undergone some changes, in particular in Article 1 (definitions /examples),[13] Article 2 (the exemption on dual distribution), Article 4 (hardcore restrictions) and Article 5 (non-compete or parity obligations). The **most significant changes**, because changes in the entire structure, experience the **black clauses**[14] or **hardcore restrictions**. They are now much broader in scope,[15] as had been expected.[16] For example, suppliers may now protect their exclusive distribution system better and prevent grey imports to a greater extent by passing on the exclusive obligation to downstream trade levels. Furthermore, the **"grey clauses"**[17]**/ non-competition clauses** are supplemented by a provision on parity obligations of online platforms. In addition, the Vertical Guidelines contain numerous new interpretative notes from the European Commission.

In total, the **safe harbour** provided by the VBER will mostly be **broader**, **in some parts, however, narrower** and receive significantly **more differentiated regulations** than before. Whether such differentiated, extensive wording is necessary is debatable.

The VBER addresses dual distribution in particular detail, thus mirroring the factual development of suppliers acting on both levels. Dual distribution especially concerns intra-brand competition—and the new rules focus less on distribution as such than on information exchange, following the contributions that stakeholders made during the consultations period,[18] especially the additional public consultation on proposed guidance relating to information exchange in the context of dual distribution, intended to be added to the Vertical Guidelines.[19] While the draft set the threshold for the safe harbour very low, the VBER 2022 in its final version now requires passing a two-limb test for information exchange to be exempt from Article 101(1) TFEU.

The Commission has been pursuing three different objectives[20] with this new VBER:

[13]The new definitions include the following five terms: "supplier" (not so much a definition than an example/clarification), "exclusive distribution system", "active sales", "passive sales" Restriction of active or passive selling (Article 1(1)(n) Draft Vertical Block Exemption Regulation).

[14]On the term CG Competition, European Commission (2002, July 2022, p. 22 term continuously used, even though the Glossary has been archived as some definitions are no longer valid due to changes in legislation).

[15]Article 4 now consists of >800 words, previously only about 340.

[16]Cf. Rohrßen (2017, p. 281 at footnote 87).

[17]"Grey" because only the provision itself is *not* exempted, in contrast to "black" clauses/hardcore restrictions under Art. 4, cf. Bechtold et al. (2023, Vertikal-GVO, Art. 2 para. 2); Zöttl (2020, Vertikal-GVO, Art. 5 para. 2 footnote 5).

[18]European Commission (2021a).

[19]European Commission (2022a).

[20]European Commission (2020).

1. Eliminating false positive and reducing false negative[21] results: As "false positives" (i.e. exempting agreements though they fail to sufficiently certain satisfy Article 101(3)[22]), the Commission considered dual distribution and parity obligations under the VBER 2010. Whereas "false negative" results (i.e. not exempting agreements though satisfying the conditions of Article 101(3) TFEU),[23] the Commission considered active sales restrictions and specific online restrictions.
2. Updating the VBER to the market developments, especially the continued strong growth of e-commerce in general and especially of online platforms.
3. Reducing compliance costs by simplifying rules and streamlining the guidance.

The hardcore restrictions concerning **territory or customer restrictions** have been structured anew, namely according to the different types of distribution systems. Moreover, definitions of active and passive sales are now laid down in the VBER (not just, as before, the non-binding VGL), thus also bind national authorities and courts. The VBER provides for a new approach to active versus passive sales.

The VBER 2022 is also **more lenient on exclusive distribution**: The VBER 2022 allows to allocate an exclusive territory not only to one, but up to five exclusive distributors, [24] thus increasing intra-brand competition in such exclusive territory. Whereas under the VBER 2010, the 1:1 rule applied, i.e. one territory, one distributor, which stakeholders considered inflexible, not meeting the business requirements, making them either cut down territories into small parts or prefer selective distribution —which anyway has been on the rise during the VBER 2010, especially in order to control the increasing online business of distributors.[25]

Moreover, suppliers may now request their distributors to pass on the restriction of active sales into exclusive territories to the buyers' customer (so-called "direct customer", hence only one level down in the supply chain in order to avoid arbitrage arising out of parallel sales, thereby providing a further incentive to exclusive distributors to invest. Combining exclusive and selective distribution, however, is still not block exempted,[26] also not on different levels of a distribution network. This is in order to avoid that national markets become sealed off, while the internal market objective is to allow the free flow of goods and services throughout the EU. New is also the **exemption for protecting distribution** (exclusive or selective) in one

[21] Commission's wording seemingly influenced by pandemic.

[22] European Commission (2020, p. 16 before footnote 61).

[23] European Commission (2020, p. 17 behind footnote 63).

[24] Such a fixed number provides more legal certainty than the open wording of the Draft VBER which allowed for shared exclusivity of "a limited number of buyers", "determined in proportion to the allocated territory or customer group in such a way as to secure a certain volume of business that preserves their investment efforts" (Draft VGL, para. 102), cf. Rohrßen (2021, p. 298 at footnote 92).

[25] Rohrßen (2017, p. 279 et seq.).

[26] VGL, para. 236.

territory from sales from the outside, thus closing a loophole that undermined especially selective distribution in the past.

The VBER 2022 also **allows dual pricing**, based on the Commission's evaluation that online sales have become an established sales channel which no longer needs the special protection that the Commission has granted in the past. Instead, the Commission believes that the level playing field between offline and online sales needs to be re-balanced to incentivize brick and mortar shops. Accordingly, the Commission has basically abolished the equivalence principle.

In turn, a **new online-sales specific hardcore restriction** has been adopted and placed into Article 4(e) VBER. Article 4(e) VBER provides the general framework for assessing online sales restrictions. The limit for such online sales restrictions is the "**effective use**" test. According to the Commission, the VBER hereby just codifies the Coty ruling—which, however, has not answered all the questions explicitly the same way that Article 4(e) now does. In any case, Article 4 (e) VBER is based on the Coty case, in which the European Court of Justice ruled that marketplace bans do neither constitute protection of the goods' luxury image and para. 69 (marketplace bans do not constitute hardcore restrictions, neither a restriction of customers within Article 4(b) VBER 2010 nor a restriction of passive sales to end users within Article 4(c) VBER 2010 and may already fall out of the scope of Article 101(1) TFEU, at least in the concrete case which concerned a selective distribution system primarily designed to protect the goods' luxury image.[27] The court's ruling set an answer to this specific case and in the aftermath many suppliers, especially of luxury goods, relied on that ruling. Nevertheless, the ruling did not end the debate; Instead, a new debate started about whether and to what extent the ruling, limited, as the case was, to luxury goods, could be transferred to non-luxury goods.[28]

The new online-sales specific hardcore restriction also allows to restrict online advertising as long as supplier and buyer do not agree on closing down the entire online advertising channel. The reasoning behind it: Distributors (on whatever level of market) shall be able to set up and advertise their own online store.

[27] ECLI:EU:C:2017:941 (Coty) para. 36 (selective distribution system for luxury goods, designed to preserve the goods' luxury image, is outside of Article 101 TFEU if (i) resellers are chosen pursuant to objective-qualitative criteria, (ii) laid down uniformly and applied in non-discriminatory manner and (iii) stick to the necessary—i.e. in line with the Metro Criteria), para. 58 (supplier may prohibit its selective distributors of luxury goods to use discernible third-party platforms if necessary to protect the goods' luxury image) and para. 69 (marketplace bans do not constitute a restriction of customers within Article 4(b) VBER 2010 or a restriction of passive sales to end users within Article 4(c) VBER 2010.

[28] Cf. only the opposing views: "marketplace bans are block-exempted", European Commission (2018, page 4), versus Coty does not "allow conclusions on the decision's transferability to other branded goods", is "not necessary to generally prohibit the use of marketplaces", and raises the "question which conclusions should be drawn from the Coty case regarding hardcore restrictions under Article 4 VBER in cases where online marketplaces (...) are the dealer's primary distribution channel" (Bundeskartellamt (2018, p. 2 et seq.).

As regards Online Intermediation Services ("OIS"), the Commission considers them not easy to classify under the VBER's dualistic scheme of supplier or buyer, while actually they are regularly to be classified as suppliers of input services. The example par excellence for OIS are online platforms if and as far as they facilitate transactions. Mere resellers, on the contrary, are no OIS in terms of the VBER.

Hybrid platforms are in many cases, but not per se, carved out from the VBER: If a platform sells a product A and provides OIS to suppliers selling product B on the platform, these are two different markets.

No news on commercial agents: According to the VGL, [29] agency agreements continue to fall outside of the scope of Article 101(1) TFEU if they do not bear any significant financial or economic risks (insofar, the concept of agency under competition law may differ from commercial law/contract law). Where agents do not fit that role, they are buyers under VBER. New is, however, the guidance on dual role agents, a new market reality for quite some time now.

RPM is still a hardcore restriction, and the same goes for **MAP**.[30] RPM may, however, be efficiency enhancing.

Also, sustainability is now addressed in the VGL. It is rather a topic for horizontal agreements. In selective distribution, sustainability can be used as a selection criterion—nothing new insofar.

Finally, the VBER has become slightly more lenient as regards the **evergreening of non-competes**: The automatic renewal does not automatically take away the safe harbour, as long as the other party can terminate after five years. The further, more procedure-related provisions on e.g. withdrawal are less relevant for suppliers and their buyers than for enforcers.

All in all, the VBER, as the Commission promotes it, **aims at providing a shortcut on the road to exemption**, thus reducing compliance costs by concretizing and simplifying[31] the rule of Article 101 TFEU. **Attention**, however, needs to be paid as "shortcuts make long delays."[32] This goes because the shortcut is not always as clear to see or as safe as the standard route. While the VBER may vastly be clear (there is always room for improvement, e.g. further streamlining of terms), the Vertical Guidelines could, from the perspective of undertakings, be formulated still more concrete in some parts. This request concerns especially all the parts of the Vertical Guidelines where the Commission leaves backdoors open, e.g. by referring to "the particular circumstances", "subject to paragraph [•]", "generally unlikely", etc.[33] By doing so, the Commission, to some part understandable, leaves

[29] VGL, para. 30.

[30] MAP is indirect means to hardcore restrictions, just meant as important clarification, before not perhaps drafted super clearly.

[31] Cf. the European Commission (2022d).

[32] Tolkien (1954, Chapter 4).

[33] Cf. the "non-exhaustive" black and white lists, softened by the caveat that "the inclusion of a particular type of information . . . does not imply that the exchange of information will fulfil the two conditions . . . in all cases" (VGL, para. 99–101).

room for development and adaption of the VGL to a further changing business environment. Not being covered and thus not being exempt by the VBER does, however, not mean that the agreement is prohibited and void, but requires a very detailed self-assessment.

The Commission's Schedule for updating the EU Competition Law[34] provides for 2023 and 2024 to update the Motor Vehicle Block Exemption Regulation—which expires on 31 May 2023—and the Consortia Block Exemption Regulation—which expires on 25 April 2024. The MVBER will presumably stay exactly the same because the draft MVBER[35] foresees to prolong the validity of the existing MVBER for 5 years until 31 May 2028, with the Commission taking care of an evaluation before its expiry. Within that period, the Commission expects that "currently emerging trends, such as those resulting from vehicle digitalisation and new mobility patterns, will have been consolidated".[36] These trends especially include the data generates by the cars' sensors, which will likely influence repair and maintenance services.

2.1 Article 2 VBER: Exemption for Vertical Restraints

Article 2(1) VBER exempts vertical agreements from Article 101(1) TFEU provided the supplier's and buyer's market shares reach 30% as a maximum (Article 3) and the agreement is free from hardcore restrictions (Article 4), see Fig. 2.1.

Freedom from hardcore restrictions means that the agreement must be free from stipulations which have as their object resale price maintenance, territory or customer restrictions or restrictions on the sale spare parts, except for those shown in Table 2.1.

Though formally the Vertical Guidelines are merely a "Communication from the Commission"[37] and therefore bind, following a respective and ideally consistent practice, the European Commission as competition authority.[38,39] As guidelines of the Commission, they are not binding on the courts or national competition authorities. Nevertheless, they have developed into a "de facto standard"[40]: The national competition authorities and the courts revert to the guidelines for interpretation—even though with at times considerably different results, as the

[34] European Commission (2021c).

[35] European Commission, C (2022) 4324 final/of 30 June 2022.

[36] European Commission (2022b).

[37] Cf. its title, thus a legal instrument developed in practice, beyond the instruments listed in Article 288 and 290 TFEU.

[38] Cf. Rohrßen (2016, p. 278).

[39] Prior to the new VBER 2022, there have been proposals to make the Vertical Guidelines binding, cf. Rohrßen (2019, p. 347, footnote 92).

[40] Bernhard (2020, Vertikal-GVO, Einleitung para. 17).

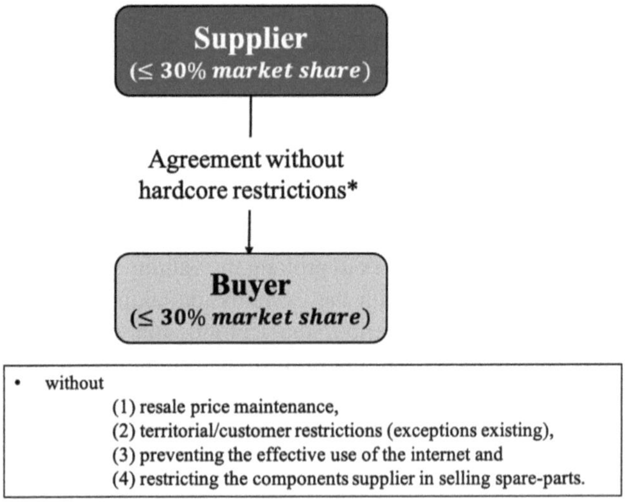

Fig. 2.1 Block Exemption under the VBER—The Road to Exemption

case law evolving around marketplace bans in Germany in the past decade illustrates.[41]

Further, Vertical Block Exemption Regulation and the Vertical Guidelines contain several caveats, scattered throughout both documents:

- "… defines a category of vertical agreements that the Commission regarded as normally satisfying the conditions laid down in Article 101(3) of the Treaty"[42];
- "… should not be applied mechanically, as each agreement must be evaluated in the light of its own facts"[43];
- "… these Guidelines are also without prejudice to the case-law of the General Court and the Court of Justice of the European Union"[44];
- "Although these Guidelines seek to give an overview of the various justifications for vertical restraints, they do not claim to be complete or exhaustive"[45];
- "… does not imply that the exchange of such information will fulfil the two conditions …"[46];
- "it is unlikely that the commission will prioritize enforcement action in respect of vertical agreements relating to the provision of online to mediation services where the provider has a hybrid function"[47]

[41] Especially under the VBER 2010, German courts have developed a rather differentiated view of restrictions of online sales, which created legal uncertainty for suppliers and distributors, cf. Rohrßen (2016, p. 278).

[42] VBER, Recital 1.

[43] VGL, para. 2.

[44] VGL, para. 2.

[45] VGL, para. 16.

[46] VGL, para. 101.

[47] VGL, para. 109.

Table 2.1 Exceptions from Hardcore Restrictions

Restricting …		Passing on?
The buyer's	Maximum sale price or recommendation of a sale price, as far as this does not restrict the buyer's ability to determine its sale price	No
	active sales into exclusive territories or to exclusive customer groups,	The buyer's direct customers
	Sales (active and passive) to unauthorized distributors in territories where a selective distribution system for these goods/ services is operated,	The buyer's customers, all down the distribution chain
	The buyer's place of establishment,[a]	No
	sales (active and passive) by wholesalers to end users,[b]	No
	Sales (active or passive) of components[c] deemed for incorporation, to the supplier's competitors,	No
	Online sales, including online advertising, as far as this does not prevent the effective use of the internet for selling nor have as object closing the entire online advertising.	No, explicitly prohibited ("effective use of the internet by the buyer or its customers"[d])
The supplier's	Sales of components as spare parts to end users or service providers not entrusted by the buyer.	No

[a]Referring only to "outlets where direct sales take place" (ECJ, EUCLI:C:2011:649 (Pierre Fabre), para 56), specifically only to "physical" and not to virtual outlets (cf. VGL, para. 231)
[b]Thereby keeping the wholesale and retail levels separate, cf. VGL, para. 225, following the practice of the Commission and the ECJ in the Metro case, cf. Schultze et al. (2019, para. 755)
[c]I.e. any intermediate goods (VGL, para. 226), i.e. any goods "for use as an input to produce other goods (…) [and that] are generally not recognisable in the final goods" (VGL, para. 287)
[d]VBER, Recital 15 and Article 4(e) VBER

On the one hand, these caveats are understandable, especially in the light of the twelve-year term of the VBER and the potential need or wish of the Commission to adapt to new developments. On the other hand, however, these caveats reduce the legal certainty which the VBER is aiming to provide, especially in the light of the undertakings' self-assessment.[48] Whether such self-assessment is possible without expert legal advice may become more doubtful, be it only for self-assurance or shifting liability risks.

[48]For which the Vertical Guidelines shall be of help, cf. VGL, para. 101.

2.2 Structure, Definitions, and Players of the VBER

The VBER's Objective Is to Enable the Undertakings' Self-Assessment It is structured as any other regulation, providing definitions for the sake of clarity upfront in Article 1. The most important terms—as they lay the ground for being exempt from Article 101 TFEU for distribution agreements—are two: (i) Vertical agreements (i.e. an agreement between undertakings operating at different supply chain levels) which contain (ii) vertical restraints (i.e. restrictions of competition).[49] The devil, however, is often in the details, as the VBER foresees detailed principles for and exceptions from hardcore restrictions. Accordingly, outside **counsels** may be needed /sought, at least in cases which play **in the grey area** – and thereof exist quite a few considering all the caveats the Commission has scattered throughout its Vertical Guidelines.

Besides the agreement itself, it is essential to categorise the players under the categories provided by the VBER. The distinction is easy, as there are basically only two categories—suppliers and buyers:

> The VBER categorises undertakings active in the supply and distribution chain as suppliers or buyers. Depending on whether an undertaking falls within one category or the other, the VBER may apply differently.[50]

Though in the end, all melts down to suppliers and buyers of the products or services concerned, there are many subcategories of players, characterizing their position/level on the market more specifically. The overview in Table 2.2 shows the diversity of business relationships in distribution and shall facilitate categorizing the players concerned under the new VBER and the Vertical Guidelines, here sorted from upstream to the downstream market level and within each group from general (undertaking) to special (connected undertaking) term.

Plus, of course, there are the competent authorities as the European Commission and the Competition authority of the Member States. Not specifically covered by the VBER, but by other laws, are the "gatekeepers"—whose activities the EU further regulates in its Digital Markets Act.[51]

For interpreting agreements and their effects on the market, it also helps understanding the different types of goods and services foreseen by the VBER, shown in Table 2.3:

[49] Article 2(1) and Article 1(1)(a) and (b) VBER.

[50] Draft Vertical Guidelines, para. 61.

[51] Regulation (EU) 2022/1925 of 14 September 2022. Cf. Rohrßen (2020, p. 79 on the draft Digital Markets Act).

Table 2.2 VBER—The Players[a]

#	Name	Definition/Role
1	Supplier	Not defined. Example given in Article 1(d) VBER: includes an undertaking that provides online intermediation services
2	Undertaking active in the platform economy	Not defined, used in Recital 10 VBER and VGL, paras. 46, 62–65, 68, 193: Such undertakings are often qualified as agents in contract or commercial law. The term apparently includes OIS (cf. VGL, para. 68) and, understood broadly, any other undertaking buying or selling online.
3	Agent	Defined in VGL, para. 29: Person entrusted with the power to negotiate and/or conclude contracts on behalf of another person ("the principal"), either for the purchase or for the sale of goods/services.
4	Dual-role Agent	Not defined. Explained in VGL, para. 45: An independent distributor that also acts as agent for different goods on the same product market for the same supplier.
5	Principal	Indirectly defined in VGL, para. 29: Person entrusting another person ("agent") with the power to negotiate and/or conclude contracts on its behalf, either for the purchase or for the sale of goods/ services.[b]
6	Category Captain	Not defined. Used in VGL, para 385: Supplier in category management agreements, i.e. agreements where the distributor entrusts the supplier with the marketing of a category of products
7	Buyer (= Final Consumer or Undertaking)	Not defined. Example given in Article 1(1) (k) VBER: includes an undertaking which, under an agreement falling within Article 101(1) of the Treaty, sells goods or services on behalf of another undertaking
8	Distributor (selective /authorised)	Not defined. Examples given in Article 1(1) (g) VBER. Authorised distributor
9	Premium Distributor	Defined in VGL, para. 16(d): Distributors who have a reputation for stocking only quality goods or providing quality services.
10	Authorised distributors/Members of the selective distribution system	Defined in VGL, para. 227 as "authorised distributors", hence the distributors in a selective distribution system. Used in VBER, Article 4(c)(i)-(iii) and VGL, para. 202.
11	Unauthorised distributor; also: non-authorised[c]	Not defined, used in Article 1(1)(g) and Article 4(b) (ii), (c)(i)(2) and (d)(ii) VBER, referring to the distributors that are not members, but outsiders to a selective distribution system.
12	Independent distributors	Not defined. Used in VBER, Recital 12 and VGL, para. 34, 36-40, 45, 94, 116. Relating to distributors which act as undertakings on their own, different from agents or vertically integrated distributors.

(continued)

Table 2.2 (continued)

#	Name	Definition/Role
13	Multiple dealership	Defined in VGL, para. 141: Same person (dealer) appointed as exclusive dealer by several suppliers
14	Customers	Not defined. Used in Recital (7) VBER and elsewhere. Relating to buyers of the buyer, e.g. within the definition of active and passive sales
15	Group of customers, customer group	Not defined. Used in Article 1(1)(h) to define an exclusive distribution system. Relating to buyers of the buyer, e.g. within the definition of active and passive sales
16	Direct customers	Not defined. Used in Article 4(b)(i), Article 4(c)(i)(1), Article 4(d)(i)—in contrast to customers, to the buyer's direct buyer in order to distinguish the exempted passed-on territorial/customer restriction in exclusive from selective and free distribution—even though the term "direct customers" appears unnatural or superfluous as customers usually refers to one's (direct) buyers, while those further down the supply chain are simply "Customers of the buyer "(as defined in the VBER 2010[d]) or "the buyer's customers" (as used in Recital 15 and Article 2(3) VBER).
17	Consumers	Defined in VGL, footnote 161: all direct or indirect users of the products covered by the agreement, including producers that use the product as an input, wholesalers, retailers and final consumers, i.e. natural persons who are acting for purposes which are outside their trade or profession
18	Final consumers	Defined in VGL, footnote 161: natural persons who are acting for purposes which are outside their trade or profession
19	End user	Defined in VGL, para. 3: undertakings and final consumers, namely natural persons who are acting for purposes which are outside their trade, business, craft, or profession.
20	OEM	Defined in VGL, para. 245: Original Equipment Manufacturer.
21	Single-home users	Users of OIS who use only one platform, in contrast to those who multi-home.[e]

[a]In the order of the supply chain, with general terms upfront
[b]Cf. VGL, para. 29
[c]Cf. VGL, para. 154 and 157; mainly used: "unauthorised distributors"
[d]Defined in Article 1(1)(h) VBER 2010 as "an undertaking not party to the agreement which purchases the contract goods or services from a buyer which is party to the agreement". Now, the term has simply been deleted, though it could have served here to make the regulation clearer
[e]VGL, para. 364

Table 2.3 VBER—Types of Goods and Services

#	Name	Definition/Role
1	Goods	Not defined. Final goods and intermediate goods, unless defined otherwise in the context, cf. VGL, para. 287
2	Components	Any intermediate goods, cf. VGL, para. 226
3	Tying products and tied products	Defined in VGL 389 Situations where customers that purchase one product (the tying product) are required also to purchase another distinct product (the tied product), e.g. in the case of the producer of 'powder-actuated fastening nail guns, nails, and cartridge strips Hilti supplying cartridge strips only when purchasing together with nails[a]
4	Experience products	VGL, para. 137 and 162 Products hard to judge before consumption
5	Credence products	VGL, para. 137 and 162 Products hard to judge even after consumption
6	Quality goods/quality services	Not defined. VGL, para. 16(d)
7	Complex products	VGL, para. 137, 140, 162, 197(d)
8	Intermediate (d) goods[b]/services	VGL, para. 3, 59, 67(e), 104-107, 140, 176, 226, 233, 244, 287, 307, 321, 328, 329, 331, 366, 370 products that are sold to various types of professional buyers (VGL, para. 140) = component (VGL, para. 331)
9	Final goods/services	VGL, para. 3, 59, 134, 287, 288, 331 Final goods or services are, directly or indirectly, sold to end users, which often rely more on brand and image (VGL, para. 287)
10	Must-stock item	Not defined. Used in VGL, para. 301 to describe goods that on which a buyer relies for its sales activities because many customers prefer it.

[a]ECLI:EU:T:1991:70 (Hilti) para. 16
[b]Sometimes also "intermediate products", cf. VGL, para. 307

2.3 Exemption of Vertical Restraints: Principal Scope

Vertical agreements exempt by the VBER include not only more or less complex distribution agreements, but also straightforward supply agreements where the buyer buys the products for its own use (not for resale or assembling and resale). By including supply agreements, the VBER differs from the past as the predecessors of Regulation 2790/99 only covered "certain categories of exclusive dealing agreements" (Regulation No. 67/67), "categories of exclusive distribution agreements" (Commission Regulation No. 1983/83), or "categories of exclusive purchasing agreements" (Commission Regulation (EEC) No 1984/83) respectively.

Basically, **vertical agreements can be exempt** by the VBER, **regardless of the type of goods or services concerned**. However, the VBER **excludes** vertical agreements which focus on the **assignment or use of intellectual property rights** by the buyer (Article 2(3) VBER), e.g. as simple ancillary IP clauses as:

Example

Buyer must not infringe the copyright of Supplier. Accordingly, Buyer must not make copies and resell or make copies and use the software in combination with other hardware.[52] ◀

Example

Buyer is only entitled to resell under the condition that its customers do not infringe the Supplier's copyright. ◀

Illustrated, the exemption rules as shown in Table 2.4 apply to different goods and services.

2.4 Exemption of Vertical Restraints: Re-Exceptions/Limits

2.4.1 Agreements with Associations, Article 2(2) and Article 9 VBER

While Article 2(2) VBER exempts vertical agreements between associations of undertakings,[53] vertical agreements between an association and its individual member or supplier are only **exempt** under the VBER if they fulfil **two** further **requirements**:

(i) The members of the association must be retailers of goods (not services[54]);
(ii) no individual member of the association (together with its connected undertakings) has a total annual turnover exceeding EUR 50 million,[55] or EUR 55 million for more than two consecutive financial years.[56] Said turnover is to be calculated according to Article 9(1) VBER, taking the turnover achieved during the previous financial year, including the party's connected undertakings,

[52] Cf. VGL, para. 81.

[53] To be precise: Article 2(2) sentence 2 VBER.

[54] Cf. recital 3 VBER, Article 2(2) sentence 2 VBER, confirmed by VGL, para. 69.

[55] Article 2(2) sentence 1 VBER.

[56] Article 9 sentence 1 VBER: The EUR 50 million threshold may be exceeded up to 10% maximum for two consecutive years, thereby adding some flexibility to the threshold.

Table 2.4 Block exemption rules per different goods and services

	Principle	Exception			
Products	All, including selling hard copies of software[a] or selling software for use by the customer[b]	Software licensing for mere reproduction and distribution of the software[c]	Selling automotive aftermarket goods	Renting and leasing,[d] although it could be qualified as a service,[e] a term which the Commission itself interprets broadly[f]	Producers of agricultural products may fall out of Article 101[g]
Block Exemption	Covered by VBER	Covered by TT-BER (by analogy[h])	Covered by MVBER which requires compliance with both VBER and MVBER[i]	(-)	(-)

[a]VGL, para. 83
[b]Because software sales focus on distributing a product, whether incorporated in a hard copy or not. This qualification, however, still needs to be clarified, cf. Beisel and Andreas (2017, § 18 para. 72 with further references)
[c]Because the main object of such software licensing is not the purchase or distribution
[d]VGL, para. 61: "because in that case there is no sale or purchase of goods". Accordingly, the Commission does not qualify leasing as service either
[e]The term "service" derives from the Franchise Block Exemption Regulation, cf. Article 1(3)(a) and (b), cf. Bernhard (2020, Art. 1 VBER para. 19)
[f]VGL, para. 3 and explicitly para. 59; Bernhard (2020, Art. 1 VBER para. 19)
[g]Cf. Article 210(a) Regulation (EU) No 1308/2013: "Article 101(1) TFEU shall not apply to agreements ... of producers of agricultural products that relate to ... agricultural products and that aim to apply a sustainability standard higher than mandated by Union or national law, provided ... only impose restrictions of competition that are indispensable ...".; cf. VGL, para. 8 footnote 16
[h]TT-BER Guidelines, para. 48; not covered directly by Technology Transfer Block Exemption Regulation either because licensing is no production in terms of TT-BER, cf. TT-BER Guidelines, para. 62
[i]Article 4(1) MVBER: "Pursuant to Article 101(3) of the Treaty and subject to the provisions of this Regulation Article 101(1) of the Treaty shall not apply to vertical agreements relating to the conditions under which the parties may purchase, sell or resell spare parts for motor vehicles or provide repair and maintenance services for motor vehicles, which fulfil the requirements for an exemption under Regulation (EU) No 330/2010 and do not contain any of the hardcore clauses listed in Article 5 of this Regulation."

excluding however any taxes and other duties and excluding the turnover created by dealings between the party and its connected undertakings.

The ratio behind these additional requirements is that exemption shall (only) help small and medium-sized[57] retailers in joint purchasing.

2.4.2 Agreements on Intellectual Property Rights, Article 2(3) VBER

Intellectual property rights (or: "IPR") under the VBER include especially industrial property rights (including trademarks[58]), know-how, copyright and neighbouring rights.[59] Agreements relating to the assignment or use of IPR are **exempt** under the VBER **under the following**—according to the Commission: five[60]—**conditions**:

(i) The agreement is a vertical agreement,[61] i.e. according to its very definition, an agreement on the purchase, sale, or resale of goods or services.[62] This is not the case, according to the Vertical Guidelines, e.g. for
- licensing agreements for using a certain recipe to produce a drink, including industrial franchise agreements[63];
- pure merchandising licences (of trademarks or signs),
- sponsorship contracts, or
- copyright licensing/broadcasting contracts.[64]

While, however, pure licensing agreements shall not be covered by the VBER according to the Commission; they may be exempt by analogy.[65] Accordingly, the Commission considers the Vertical Block Exemption Regulation and the

[57] Cf. the definition of SMEs above, limited also to the threshold of EUR 50 million turnover.

[58] Specifically mentioned in VGL, para. 79 as one of the three main intellectual property rights ("IPRs") for implementing vertical agreements.

[59] These are the examples given by Article 1(1)(i) VBER.

[60] Actually, conditions three and four set appear redundant, as vertical agreements are only those which cover the purchase, sale or resale of goods or services.

[61] The VBER by way of title, scope and definition in Article 2(1) only exempts vertical agreements, i.e. those on purchasing or (re)selling goods or services.

[62] Article 1(1)(a) VBER.

[63] VGL, para. 85.

[64] VGL, para. 74.

[65] Cf. VGL, para. 82. This analogy is corroborated by the Commission's exclusion of trademark licensing from the TT-BER because it "often occurs in the context of distribution and resale ... and is generally more akin to distribution agreements" (Technology Transfer Guidelines, para. 50); cf. Schultze (2019, para. 413 et seq.).

Technology Transfer Block Exemption Regulation for manufacturing and distribution licences concerning football or film merchandising products.[66]

(ii) The IPR is assigned or licensed for use by the buyer (and not by the supplier; in such case, the subcontracting notice may apply, see above[67]). Conversely, agreements on the transfer of know-how from the buyer to the supplier are not exempt, as they miss the above condition.[68]

(iii) The agreement's primary object shall neither consist in assigning nor licensing[69] the IPR to the buyer. This requirement appears redundant, considering that the Commission already excludes pure licensing agreements under the first condition, "vertical agreement".

(iv) The provisions on assignment or use of IPR are directly related to the use, sale or resale of goods or services by the buyer or its customers, i.e. not related to the manufacture of goods, but, to the marketing of goods or services.[70] Examples according to the Vertical Guidelines are franchising agreements where the franchisee resells goods from the franchisor under the franchisor's trademark,[71] or supply agreements where the supplier supplies a concentrated extract and licences the buyer to dilute and bottle the extract before selling it.[72]

(v) The provisions on assignment or use of IPR do not contain restrictions of competition which have the same object as vertical restraints not exempted under the VBER, i.e. the agreement must not have as the object of any of the hardcore restrictions of Articles 4 nor of any of the excluded restrictions of Article 5 VBER. E.g. an exclusive trademark licence must comply with the exclusive distribution rules of Article 4 VBER.[73]

---

[66] Cf. European Commission, Case AT.40436, C(2019) 2172 final (Nike) para. 130; Case AT.40432, C(2019) 5087 final ("Hello Kitty") para. 99.

[67] The VBER may also apply, as Article 2(3) does not generally cover all "vertical agreements containing provisions on intellectual property rights", but only reduces the exemption of Article 2(1) VBER in relation to "vertical agreements containing provisions which relate to the assignment to the buyer or use by the buyer of intellectual property rights".

[68] VGL, para. 75.

[69] The VBER speaks of "use by the buyer of IPR", Article 2(3) sentence 1 VBER, i.e., read together with the alternative "assignment to the buyer" as referring to licensing.

[70] VGL, para. 77.

[71] The VGL are insofar consistent with the TT Guidelines, para. 50: "Trademark licensing often occurs in the context of distribution and resale of goods and services and is generally more akin to distribution agreements than technology licensing. Where a trademark licence is directly related to the use, sale or resale of goods and services and does not constitute the primary object of the agreement, the licence agreement is covered by Commission Regulation (EU) No 330/2010."

[72] VGL, para. 77.

[73] VGL, para. 80.

The latter appears indeed "peculiar"[74] as Article 5 itself only excludes the exemption of Article 2 VBER for the respective obligation (e.g. a non-compete), while the remaining agreement is, if covered by the VBER, exempt. Whereas, a literal interpretation of Article 2(3) VBER would exclude the entire agreement from the safe harbour.

Exempt are therefore, e.g. franchising agreements where the franchisee buys goods or services from the franchisor or a third party and distributes them by using the franchisor's IPR.[75] They are covered by the VBER as also Article 5(3)(d) VBER confirms which exempts the post-contractual protection of know-how transferred by the supplier to the buyer (as is typical for franchise agreements).[76] Distribution agreements on software licensing may also be exempt as far as the licence is not the primary object of the agreement (see above).[77]

Not exempt under the VBER are therefore e.g. pure licensing agreements including production franchise agreements and merchandising agreements, sponsorship contracts, copyright licensing contracts.[78]

2.4.3 Dual Distribution: Agreements of Competitors, Article 2(3) VBER

Dual Distribution is defined by the VBER as

▶ **Definition** "the scenario where a supplier sells goods or services not only at the upstream level but also at the downstream level, thereby competing with its independent distributors."[79]

As a principle, agreements between competitors are **not exempt** under the VBER, Article 2(4) sentence 1 VBER. This very principle has been existing with the very wording also under the VBER 2010[80] and the VBER 1999.[81]

Compared to the Draft VBER 2021,[82] the final VBER 2022 has reworked the requirements for vertical agreements between competitors, making it **easier to enter into the VBER's safe harbour**. The draft provided for an additional market

[74] Wijckmans and Tuytschaever 2018, para. 4.28).

[75] VGL para. 72(d), 86 et seq.

[76] Bechtold et al. (2023, Art. 2 Vertikal-GVO para. 8).

[77] Bechtold et al. (2023, Art. 2 Vertikal-GVO para. 8), limiting the VBER, however, to software sold via physical carriers.

[78] VGL, para. 74.

[79] VBER, Recital 12.

[80] Article 2(4) sentence 1 is identical in VBER 2022 and VBER 2010.

[81] Article 2(4) sentence 1 VBER 1999 is almost identical; the first sentence has only been cut into two from the VBER 2010 onwards.

[82] Draft VBER of 9 July 2021, C (2021) 5026 final.

threshold of 10% for vertical agreements between competitors: From a combined market share of more than 10% at retail level, the exchange of information in a vertical relationship between competing undertakings should fail to be block exempt[83] because of the risk of collusion involved. Instead, the rules on horizontal agreements should apply, in particular the Horizontal Guidelines.[84],[85] Many details on how to design a competition law compliant information exchange remained unclear, also because the Horizontal Guidelines so far addressed the specificities of dual distribution only selectively.[86]

The **draft of new Horizontal Guidelines** has been **published**[87]; they are expected to come into effect in 2023. Apparently, the draft VBER was dominated by horizontal concerns on dual distribution, while the public consultation showed that it principally may positively affect intra-brand and inter-brand competition (with franchise systems as a typical example). The 10% threshold, set in square brackets, apparently was a test balloon set up by the European Commission.[88] According to the guidance provided by the draft Horizontal Guidelines, agreements between competitors, whether reciprocal or not, require a **two-step assessment, first under the Horizontal Guidelines**, then under the **VBER** and the **Vertical Guidelines**. The only **exception** are the dual distribution scenarios covered by Article 2(4) and (5) of the VBER: they are just covered by the VBER and its Guidelines.[89]

While the Draft VBER reduced the exemption for dual distribution by introducing a further market share threshold of maximum 10% hold in aggregate by supplier and buyer on the retail level,[90] the final version of the VBER 2022 goes without such additional conditions. Instead, the VBER 2022 elaborates and thus provides more legal certainty on information exchange and limits its concerns to hybrid platforms which it does not exempt (Article 2(6) VBER, see below).

Undertakings qualify as competitors if they are either **actual or potential competitors**. This definition in Article 1(1)(c) VBER is in line with the case law.[91] While actual competition may be easy to assess, potential competition is rather wide and means that an undertaking would, "on realistic grounds and not just as a mere theoretical possibility, be likely within a short period of time, to make the

---

[83] Article 2(4) and (5) Draft VBER.

[84] European Union (2011a).

[85] The reference to the Horizontal Guidelines can already be found in the Vertical Guidelines 2010, cf. para. 212.

[86] Therefore understandably critical Haberer and Fries (2021, footnote 25).

[87] Draft Horizontal Guidelines, 19 April 2022, Official Journal 2022/C 164/01.

[88] As also shown by the square brackets in which the percentage was set in the draft VBER.

[89] Draft Horizontal Guidelines of 19 April 2022, para. 357 (dual distribution); para. 48 (relationship between horizontal and vertical rules in general).

[90] Rohrßen (2021, p. 296).

[91] E.g. ECLI:EU:C:2020:52 (Generics (UK) and Others) para. 32: "The latter requirement *[i.e.: a negative and appreciable effect on competition]* means, with respect to horizontal cooperation agreements . . . that the coordination involves undertakings who are in competition with each other, if not in reality, then at least potentially".

necessary additional investments or incur other necessary costs to enter the relevant market. Compared to the VBER 2010, it has slightly changed, as the possibility of entering the market need not necessarily be triggered by "a small but permanent increase in relative prices".[92] The test, in short, boils down to whether the undertaking has "both real and concrete possibilities and the capacity to enter the market".[93] Criteria to be considered according to the Commission are

- time: "normally not longer than a year" according to the Vertical Guidelines (this is criterion goes very, if not too, far as it should be very easy for a supplier with a European distribution network to start direct (e.g. online) sales);
- structure of the market;
- economic and legal context; there must be no insurmountable entry barriers.[94]

By way of exception, vertical agreements between competitors can be exempt by the VBER under **two conditions**:

(i) the agreements are non-reciprocal and
(ii) the supplier and the buyer do not compete at the level of trade where the buyer buys the contract goods or services.[95]

What Article 2(4) exempts is dual distribution, i.e. vertical agreements between undertakings which compete at the downstream level,[96] while agreements between undertakings competing at the upstream level shall not be block-exempt. If not block-exempt, the agreements may still be exempt by Article 101(3) TFEU. Insofar, the new Horizontal Guidelines will ideally provide guidance; the Vertical Guidelines in any case refer to their respective future version.[97]

Non-reciprocal according to the Vertical Guidelines means "in particular"[98] that the buyer of the contract goods or services does not also supply competing goods or

[92] Article 1(1)(c) VBER 2010.

[93] EU:C:2021:243 (Lundbeck), para. 54.

[94] VGL, para. 90.

[95] For future versions, the wording could be further streamlined: Why use two different terms used in the same provision law for presumably the same thing: Article 2(4)(a) says "where it buys", Article 2(4)(b) VBER "where it purchases".

[96] VGL, para. 94 et seq.

[97] VGL, para. 9; Christodoulou and Holzwarth (2022, p. 542 et seq.).

[98] Apparently, this is a further backdoor left open by the Commission as the Vertical Guidelines remain silent on what other situations should be excluded (and the predecessor, the Vertical Guidelines of 2010, remained silent at all about when an agreement was "non-reciprocal").

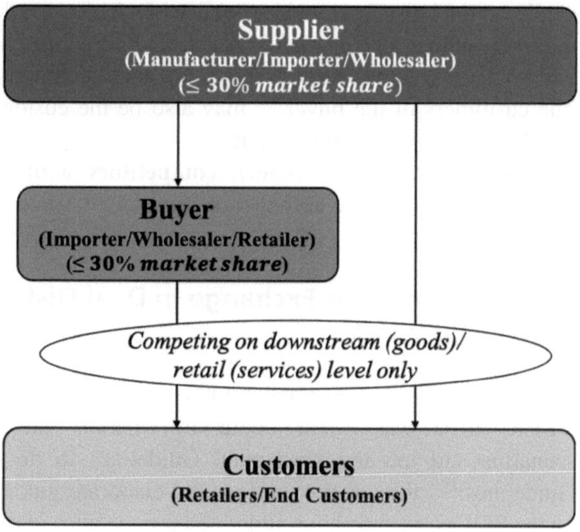

Fig. 2.2 Dual Distribution – The Scenario

services to the supplier.[99] The purpose of this condition is to exempt only those agreements which do not relate to the competitive relationship, but exclusively to the supply and distribution: If each party is supplier and buyer of the other for the contract goods or competing goods, these agreements are not exempt by the VBER.[100]

The changes in Article 2(4) from VBER 2010 to VBER 2022 in sentence 1 are of clarifying nature, while the changes in sentence 2 broaden the room for exemption, distinguishing between the supply of goods and the provision of services. The main feature is that competition may only occur on the downstream level where the Commission sees the potential anti-competitive effects outweighed[101]:

Vertical agreements between **competitors acting as suppliers of goods** are exempt if they compete only on the downstream level, irrespective of the upstream level at which the supplier operates, as summarized in Fig. 2.2. Whereas under the VBER 2010 the supplier needed, as a condition for the exemption, to be active as "a manufacturer and distributor", it now suffices if the supplier is active (clarified: "at the upstream level") as a manufacturer, importer, or wholesaler and (clarified: at a downstream level") as an importer, wholesaler, or retailer. The exemption therefore

[99] VGL, para. 93.

[100] Cf. – on Article 2(4) VBER 2010 – Bechtold et al. (2023, Art. 2 Vertikal-GVO para. 12 et seq.); Schultze (2019, para. 473).

[101] VGL, para. 95, very abstract comparison of the effects of dual distribution on competition, very similar to the wording of the predecessor (VGL 2010, para. 28), more concrete on positive effects of the information exchange in dual distribution for production and distribution the European Commission (2022e, p. 2. and 4).

applies to dual distribution, irrespective of whether the dual relationship occurs at the importer, wholesaler or retailer level, as long as the buyer acting as an importer, wholesaler, or retailer downstream is not also a competitor upstream. In other words: The customers of the buyer[102] may also be the customers of the supplier, but the supplier must not be among them.

Vertical agreements between **competitors acting as service providers** are exempt if they compete at the retail level only (Article 2(4)(b) VBER 2010).

2.5 Information Exchange in Dual Distribution, Article 2(5) VBER

Exchanging information may both have pro- and anti-competitive effects. So far, the VBER 2010 was silent about information exchange in dual distribution scenarios and left the Horizontal Guidelines to do the job.[103] The Horizontal Guidelines,[104] though providing quite elaborate guidance in para. 55–110, based on the ECJ's case law, have addressed the specifics of dual distribution so far only in a few points, leaving practically relevant details open, including what information a supplier may demand from its customers with whom it competes.[105] There has also been hardly any case law which could provide further guidance. One of only a few has been the Danish Hugo Boss decisions by the Danish NCA (confirmed by the Danish Competition Appeals Tribunal) on Hugo Boss disclosing information on its own planned promotional retail campaigns to its distributors.[106] This lack of any safe harbour has resulted in quite some, well-deserved, critical remarks[107]—well-deserved because dual distribution is on a rise as is the e-commerce, making direct sales very easy to handle—and thus making a safe harbour for information exchange practically very relevant. Notably, such information exchange can occur in any form, including the CEOs of undertakings exchanging their future pricing concepts at the bar on the occasion of an industry meeting.[108]

[102] Previously defined under Article 1(1)(i) VBER 2010 as "an undertaking not party to the agreement which purchases the contract goods or services from a buyer which is party to the agreement" as the term served to blacklist the passing on of the restriction of active sales into exclusive territories or to customer groups further down the distribution chain, cf. Article 4(b) (i) VBER 2010—while such passing on is exempt under the VBER 2022.

[103] VGL 2010, para. 211 footnote 1: "Direct information exchange between competitors is not covered by the Block Exemption Regulation, see Article 2(4) of that Regulation and paragraphs 27-28 of these Guidelines." However, on a literal interpretation, Article 2(4) VBER 2010 did not exclude the information exchange.

[104] European Union (2011b, The Horizontal Guidelines replaced the Notice of agreements, decisions and concerted practices concerning inter-company cooperation of 29 July 1968).

[105] Rohrßen (2021, 296 at footnote 58 et seq.).

[106] European Commission (2022f, p. 14).

[107] E.g. Auf'mkolk (2011, 710); Fritzsche (2011, p. 212 et seq. ("Only of limited use in practice"); Lübbig (2011, p. 7).

[108] Example taken from Bunte and Stancke (2022, § 8 para. 33).

Now, **information exchange is regulated more in detail**, both by Article 2(5) VBER and the Vertical Guidelines in para. 96-103. By way of principle provided by Article 2(4) VBER, all information exchange relating to implementing the vertical agreement is exempt if the **above two conditions** are fulfilled (i.e.: (i) the agreement is non-reciprocal and (ii) the supplier and the buyer do not compete at the level of trade where the buyer buys the contract goods or services). This goes, however, positively formulated, **only** for information (i) directly related to the implementation of the vertical agreement and (ii) necessary for improving the production or distribution of the contract goods or services as only those are deemed to be efficiency-enhancing. Actually, Article 2(5) VBER is formulated as a double negative: "The **exceptions** set out in paragraph 4, points (a) and (b) [i.e. exempting dual distribution] shall **not** apply [shall not be exempt] to the exchange of information between the supplier and the buyer that is either **not** directly related to the implementation of the vertical agreement or is **not** necessary to improve the production or distribution of the contract goods or services, or which fulfils **neither** of those two conditions". The last clause shows what matters: Both conditions must be fulfilled for information exchange between competitors to be block-exempt.[109]

For information exchange, **any information either way**—supplier to buyer or buyer to supplier—**suffices**. Though information exchange may in its literal interpretation of "exchange" be understood as a two-way-communication, the term is interpreted quite broadly by the Commission, encompassing also unilateral information, provided proactively by one party without any request from the other.[110]

The Vertical Guidelines provide—explicitly non-exhaustive—a white list and a black list of information, as summarized in Table 2.5. These information items are to be used for orientation, do however not save the self-assessment in the individual case—or, as the Vertical Guidelines put it: These examples "may, depending on the particular circumstances" (hence not definitely are, but need to be checked in the individual case) be exempt, respectively are "generally unlikely" (but not completely excluded) to do so. [111]

The Fig. 2.3 illustrates the underlying **rule of thumb**. In general, the more detailed and the more targeted the information, the less likely it will be exempt. Compliance with the information exchange rules requires that all information supplied or received be audited as to (i) what kind of information it is (see Fig. 2.3) and (ii) who has access and (iii) whether to set limits to the information exchange (setting up firewalls, separating distribution levels such as wholesale and retail, restricting accesss to e.g. CRM software, encrypting/aggregating data, sharing only aged data, cooling off-periods for staff changing from direct to indirect sales, etc.) and (iv) document such rules in compliance/distribution/information exchange policies or data exchange agreements. This applies all the more as far as information on prices is

[109] This is also confirmed in reverse by VGL, para. 98 where the Commission relates to whether an information exchange is directly related to the implementation of the vertical agreement *and* necessary to improve production or distribution.

[110] VGL, para. 97.

[111] VGL, para. 99 and 100.

Table 2.5 Information Exchange in Dual Distribution—White vs. Black List

White List of Information (likely block-exempt)	Black List of Information (unlikely block-exempt)
Technical information, registration, certification, handling, use, maintenance, repair upgrading or recycling	
Logistical information on production and distribution	
Customer purchases, preferences, and feedback (as far as not used for territory or customer restrictions)	Identified end users unless necessary for • satisfying such end users requirements (adapting goods, granting special conditions including customer loyalty schemes, providing pre- or after-sales services, including guarantee services), • implementing or monitoring compliance with a selective or exclusive distribution agreement which allocates particular end users to the supplier or buyer
Pricing information: • prices at which the supplier sells contract goods or services to the buyer[a]; • recommended or maximum resale prices (as far as not used for resale price maintenance)	Future prices at which supplier or buyer intend to resell[b]
Marketing of the contract goods or services, including promotional campaigns and on new goods	
Performance-related information, including aggregated information by the supplier to the buyer on marketing and sales activities of other buyers (as far as not enabling the buyer to identify activities of particular competing buyers	
	Information on buyer's private label products[c] exchanged between the buyer and a manufacturer of competing goods, unless the manufacturer also produces the buyer's goods

[a]Considering that the supplier will hardly sell the goods at secret prices to the buyer, the supplier needs at least to be allowed to communicate the current price in order to conclude and perform the sale. If the information on the sales price could be considered a restriction of competition at all, it should in any case fall outside the scope of competition law for being an ancillary agreement. Accordingly, listing the current price as an example which "may, depending on the particular circumstances" fulfil the two conditions for exemption appears rather odd

[b]Very logical in the light of Article 4(a) VBER and in line with the German Bundeskartellamt (2017, para. 95 et seq.)

[c]VGL, para. 100: "goods sold by a buyer under its own brand name"

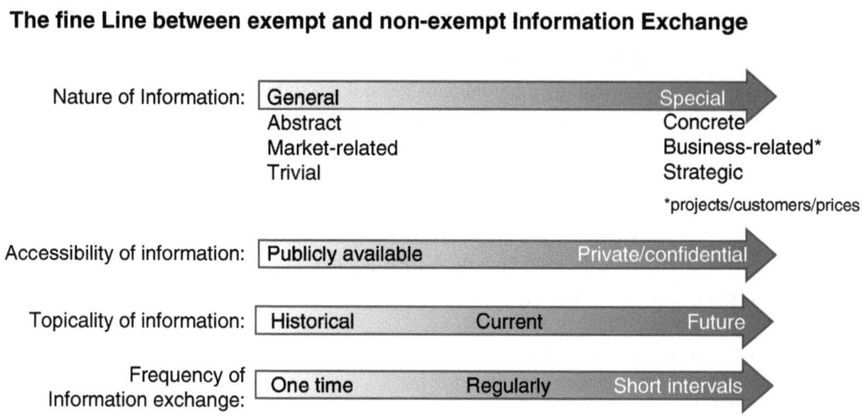

Fig. 2.3 Information Exchange—Exempt vs. Non-exempt Information

concerned—or, as the ECJ has put it: "Price coordination agreements are by their very nature among the worst kind of infringements of Article 101 TFEU and Article 53 of the EEA Agreement".[112]

There are, however, **ways out**, allowing to implement an agreement between competitors and exchange information which may be too sensitive to be exempt. Though these measures do not bring such information to the road of exemption, they allow to minimize competition concerns on the level of Article 101(3) TFEU. Such measures especially include to:

- reducing and aggregating the information subject to exchange,
- delaying the time between generation of the information and its exchange,
- implementing technical, organisational or other administrative measures, e.g. setting up "firewalls" respectively ringfencing measures (i.e. separating information streams), thereby restricting the access to said information between those responsible for the supplier's upstream activities from those responsible for the supplier's downstream direct sales activity,[113]
- implementing legal measures to separate information streams by having another legal entity carrying out the competing activity.

2.6 Hybrid Online Platforms, Article 2(6) VBER

No exemption under the VBER applies to "vertical agreements relating to the provision of online intermediation services where the provider . . . is a competing undertaking on the relevant market for the sale of the intermediated goods or

[112] ECLI:EU:T:2019:515 (Sony), para. 33.

[113] VGL, para. 103.

Table 2.6 Sector-Specific Block Exemption Regulations

BER	Subject of Agreement
Technology Transfer BER[a]	Licensing or assigning of technology rights for production (assigning only where risk of exploitation remains with the assignor)
R&D BER[b]	Joint R&D and/or joint exploitation of joint R&D results
Specialisation Agreements[c]	Unilateral or reciprocal specialisation or joint production
Motor Vehicle BER[d]	Motor vehicle aftermarket (NOT purchase, sale and resale of new motor vehicles for which the VBER applies[e])

[a]Commission Regulation (EU) No 316/2014
[b]Commission Regulation (EU) No 1217/2010
[c]Commission Regulation (EU) No 1218/2010
[d]Commission Regulation (EU) No 461/2010
[e]Article 3 MVBER

services"[114] (i.e. for hybrid online platforms). The rationale behind this non-exemption is that "such providers have an incentive to favour their own sales".[115] This motivation is not entirely convincing. While there may be a natural tendency of favouring oneself, the VBER only applies up to market shares of 30%.

The Commission appears to have recognised this and provides some **comfort to smaller and medium-sized platforms** by stating in the Vertical Guidelines that "appreciable anti-competitive effects are unlikely where the provider of the online intermediation service does not enjoy market power . . . for example because it has only recently entered such market (start-up phase)".[116]

Reading Article 2(6) VBER and the Vertical Guidelines together, it reads like the result of keeping all doors open for imposing or not imposing measures upon the online intermediation services, focusing perhaps slightly too far on the big platforms. Whether the VBER is the right place to tackle this issue, is questionable—for the time being, the question has been answered by the Commission in the affirmative. At least, the Commission acknowledges that the dual distribution agreements with OIS do not necessarily restrict competition, or may lack appreciability on the markets for (i) the provision of online intermediation services and (ii) for the sale of the intermediated goods or services.[117] Finally, the Commission provides some comfort by stating in the Vertical Guidelines "that it is unlikely that the Commission will prioritise enforcement action in respect of vertical agreements relating to the provision of online intermediation services where the provider has a hybrid function."[118]

Agreements on providing online intermediation services therefore require assessment under the Horizontal Guidelines. The Horizontal Guidelines have been under

[114]Article 2(6) VBER.
[115]VGL, para. 105.
[116]VGL, para. 107.
[117]VGL, para. 107.
[118]VGL, para. 109.

review, too. In March 2022, they were expected to come into effect on 1 January 2023.[119] The draft Horizontal Guidelines have been approved by the Commission on 19 April 2022 and the public consultation was closed on 26 April 2022. They are expected to come into effect in June 2023. The draft Horizontal Guidelines focus on "Commercialisation Agreements" in Chapter 5, while Chapter 6 is dedicated to "Information Exchange" in its various forms and contexts. For dual distribution scenarios, the draft refers to the Vertical Block Exemption Regulation, while all other agreements between (actual or potential) competitors will be dealt with in the future Horizontal Guidelines.[120] Hybrid platforms are, however, not explicitly covered by the chapter on commercialization, but in the chapter on information exchange.[121] Altogether, a possible restrictive effect on competition and efficiency gains of such information exchange is to be assessed on a case by case basis, considering especially[122] the nature of information (whether commercially sensitive or rather not, as in the case of public information, whether aggregated or individualised data), the age of the information and the characteristics of exchange.

2.7 Priority of other Block Exemption Regulations

The VBER is the "umbrella" BER, serving as a catch-all for vertical agreements when no other, specific BER covers the agreement concerned. That is what Article 2(7) VBER states—and thus nothing new.

This priority goes especially for horizontal agreements, i.e. agreements between competing undertakings (as also established by Article 2(4) VBER)). More specific are especially the block exemption regulations (or their future successors) shown in Table 2.6.

References

Auf'mkolk H (2011) Der reformierte Rechtsrahmen der EU-Kommission für Vereinbarungen über horizontale Zusammenarbeit. WuW 2011:699–712

Bechtold R, Bosch W, Brinker I (2023) EU-Kartellrecht, 4th edn. C.H. Beck, Munich

Beisel D, Andreas F-E (2017) Beck'sches Mandatshandbuch Due Diligence, 3rd edn. C.H. Beck, Munich

Bernhard J (2020) Vertikal-GVO, Einleitung, Art. 1-3, Art. 6-10. In: Säcker F-J, Karpenstein U, Ludwigs M (eds) Münchener Kommentar zum Wettbewerbsrecht, vol 1/2, 3rd edn. C.H. Beck, Munich

Bundeskartellamt (2017) NCA's Guidance note on the prohibition of vertical price fixing in the brick-and-mortar food retail sector, July 2017. https://www.bundeskartellamt.de/SharedDocs/

[119] European Commission (2022c); see already at footnote 356.

[120] Draft Horizontal Guidelines of 19 April 2022, para. 356 and 357.

[121] Draft Horizontal Guidelines, 19 April 2022, para. 435–461.

[122] The Draft Horizontal Guidelines explicitly state as "caveat" that the discussion of potential efficiency gains from information exchange is neither exclusive nor exhaustive, cf. footnote 259.

Publikation/EN/Others/Guidance_note_prohibition_vertical_price_fixing_LEH.pdf?__blob=publicationFile&v=2. Accessed 12 February 2023

Bundeskartellamt (2018) Competition restraints in online sales after Coty and Asics - what's next? https://www.bundeskartellamt.de/SharedDocs/Publikation/EN/Schriftenreihe_Digitales_IV.pdf?__blob=publicationFile&v=3. Accessed 12 February 2023

Bunte H-J, Stancke F (2022) Kartellrecht, 4th edn. C.H. Beck, Munich

Christodoulou K, Holzwarth J (2022) Die neue Vertikal-GVO: Das moderne Vertriebskartellrecht 3.0. NZKart 2022:540–547

European Commission (2002) Glossary of terms used in EU competition policy, July 2022, p. 7, 22 https://ec.europa.eu/translation/spanish/documents/glossary_competition_archived_en.pdf. Accessed 10 February 2023

European Commission (2020) Commission Staff Working Document Executive Summary of the Evaluation of the VBER {SWD(2020) (https://eur-lex.europa.eu/legal-content/EN/TXT/?uri=CELEX%3A52020SC0172). Accessed 10 February 2023

European Commission (2021a) Summary of the comments received in response to the public consultation on the draft revised rules for the review of the Vertical Block Exemption Regulation (EU) No 330/2010. https://competition-policy.ec.europa.eu/system/files/2021-11/contributions_summary_draft_revised_VBER_and_VGL.pdf. Accessed 10 February 2023

European Commission (2021b) Antitrust: Commission invites interested parties to provide comments on draft revised Vertical Block Exemption Regulation and Vertical Guidelines. IP/21/3561. 9 July 2021. https://ec.europa.eu/commission/presscorner/detail/en/ip_21_3561. Accessed 10 February 2023

European Commission (2021c) Mergers and Antitrust – Timetable. https://ec.europa.eu/competition/antitrust/legislation/timeline_table_M_AT_final.pdf. Accessed 12 February 2023

European Commission (2022a) Draft new section dealing with information exchange in dual distribution. https://competition-policy.ec.europa.eu/system/files/2022-02/guidance_information_exchange_VBER_dual_distribution_2022_0.pdf. Accessed 10 February 2023

European Commission (2022b) Antitrust: Commission invites comments on draft proposals for the future of the Motor Vehicle Block Exemption Regulation and Supplementary Guidelines. Press release of 6 July 2022, IP/22/4282, https://ec.europa.eu/commission/presscorner/detail/en/ip_22_4282. Accessed 10 February 2023

European Commission (2022c) 'Freeze and Seize Task Force': Almost €30 billion of assets of Russian and Belarussian oligarchs and entities frozen by the EU so far Freeze and Seize Task Force' with U.S. and Ukrainians (europa.eu)). Accessed 10 February 2023

European Commission (2022d) Explanatory note on the new VBER and Vertical Guidelines. explanatory_note_VBER_and_Guidelines_2022.pdf (europa.eu)). Accessed 10 February 2023

European Commission (2022e) Draft new section dealing with information exchange in dual distribution, 4 February 2022. https://competition-policy.ec.europa.eu/system/files/2022-02/guidance_information_exchange_VBER_dual_distribution_2022_0.pdf. Accessed 10 February 2023

European Commission (2022f) Expert Report on the review of the VBER, Information Exchange in dual distribution, Final Report. kd0122032enn_VBER_dual_distribution_2.pdf (europa.eu). Accessed 10 February 2023

European Commission. https://ec.europa.eu/competition/antitrust/legislation/timeline_table_M_AT_final.pdf. Accessed 10 February 2023

European Union (2011a) Guidelines on the applicability of Article 101 of the Treaty on the Functioning of the European Union to horizontal co-operation agreements Text with EEA relevance ("Horizontal Guidelines"), Official Journal 2011/C 11/01. https://eur-lex.europa.eu/legal-content/EN/TXT/PDF/?uri=OJ:C:2011:011:FULL. Accessed 10 February 2023

European Union (2011b) Communication from the Commission No. 2011/C 11/01. https://eur-lex.europa.eu/LexUriServ/LexUriServ.do?uri=OJ:C:2011:011:0001:0072:EN:PDF. Accessed 10 February 2023

Fritzsche A (2011) Die neuen Regeln über horizontale Kooperation im europäischen Wettbewerbsrecht. EuZW 2011:208–213
General of the European Commission (2018) Competition policy brief. https://ec.europa.eu/competition/publications/cpb/2018/kdak18001enn.pdf. Accessed 10 February 2023
Haberer A, Fries H (2021) Entwurf der neuen Vertikal-GVO – Abschied vom "sicheren Hafen"? NZKart 2021:444–449
Hopt K-J (2019) Handelsvertreterrecht, 6th edn. C.H. Beck, Munich
Lübbig T (2011) Die Reform der EU-kartellrechtlichen Regeln über die horizontale Zusammenarbeit. EWS, pp 5–8
Martinek M, Semler F-J, Flohr E (2016) Handbuch des Vertriebsrechts, 4th edn. C.H. Beck, Munich
Rahlmeyer M, Bauer M, Schöner M (2020) Handbuch Vertriebskartellrecht, 1st edn. C.H. Beck, Munich
Rohrßen B (2017) Internetvertrieb in der EU 2018 ff. – Online-Vertriebsvorgaben von Asics über BMW bis Coty. ZVertriebsR 2017:274–281
Rohrßen B (2019) Internetvertrieb 2019/20 – Vertriebsvorgaben, (Best-)Preise & Platform-to-Business-Verordnung. ZVertriebsR 2019, 341, 342
Rohrßen B (2020) Digitale Distribution in der EU – Digital Single Market: Neue Regeln im E-Commerce ab 2022. ZVertriebsR:71–79
Rohrßen B (2021) Online-Vertrieb in der EU – Vertriebskartellrecht: Die neue Vertikal-GVO 2022. ZVertriebsR 2021:293–298
Schultze J-M, Pautke S, Wagener D-S (2019) Vertikal-GVO, Gruppenfreistellungsverordnung für vertikale Vereinbarungen, 4th edn. Deutscher Fachverlag, Frankfurt am Main
Tolkien JRR (1954) The lord of the rings, 1st edn. Klett-Cotta, Stuttgart
Vestager M (2020) "Competition policy: time for a reset?", Speech by EVP Margrethe Vestager at the OECD Global Forum on Competition, 7 December 2020. https://ec.europa.eu/commission/commissioners/2019-2024/vestager/announcements/speech-evp-margrethe-vestager-oecd-global-forum-competition-competition-policy-time-reset_en. Accessed 13 February 2023
Wijckmans F, Tuytschaever F (2018) Vertical Agreements in EU Competition Law, 3rd edn. Oxford University Press, Oxford
Wolf M (2020) I. Freistellung (Art. 101 Abs. 3 AEUV). In: Säcker F-J, Karpenstein U, Ludwigs M (eds) Münchener Kommentar zum Wettbewerbsrecht, vol. 1/2 (Band 1, 2. Teil. Europäisches Wettbewerbsrecht), 3rd edn. C.H. Beck, Munich
Zöttl J (2020) Vertikal-GVO. In: Säcker F-J, Karpenstein U, Ludwigs M (eds) Münchener Kommentar zum Wettbewerbsrecht, vol 1/2, 3rd edn. C.H. Beck, Munich

Articles 3 and 8 VBER: Market Share Thresholds

3

Abstract Vertical restraints may enter the safe harbour of the VBER if they fulfil two requirements: the respective agreement must be free from hardcore restrictions and the parties' market shares must not exceed 30%. Article 3 and Article 8 VBER, together with Chapter 5 of the Vertical Guidelines and the Market Definition Notice, stipulate how to define the relevant market and how to calculate the relevant market shares.

3.1 The Thresholds

For vertical agreements, **three thresholds** matter. The Market Definition Notice provides guidance in how to define the relevant market.[1] It was still subject to a review in 2023 (see Chapter 1.4.3.2).

Rule of thumb for (re)designing vertical agreements: The higher the market shares of the undertakings involved, the higher the requirements for the agreement (or, in other words, the lesser restrictions are lawful)—as shown in Table 3.1.

To determine the market shares: Crucial are the market shares held (i) by the supplier on the market on which the supplier sells the goods or services to its buyers and (ii) the market share held by the buyer on the market on which the buyer purchases the goods or services. The relevant market comprises all those goods or services which are regarded as substitutable (also: "interchangeable") by the consumer by reason of the goods' or services' characteristics, their prices and their intended use in the geographic area in which the companies are involved in the supply of goods or services and in which the conditions of competition are sufficiently homogeneous.

[1] European Commission (1997a).

B. Rohrßen, *VBER 2022: EU Competition Law for Vertical Agreements*, Law for Professionals, https://doi.org/10.1007/978-3-031-35024-5_3

Table 3.1 Requirements for Vertical Agreements due to Market Thresholds

≤ 5%, and	≤15% aggregate share[b] and	15–30% each party[a]	>30% each party
≤ EUR 50 million supplier's aggregate annual EU-wide turnover with products concerned[c,d]	No restriction by object[e]	And no hardcore restriction[f]	
Outside Article 101 TFEU for lack of effect on trade, however national competition law may kick in	Outside Article 101 TFEU due to lack of effect on trade, however national competition law may kick in	Exempt under VBER	Individual assessment under Article 101(3) TFEU

[a]Article 3(1) VBER for two-party agreements and Article 3(2) VBER for multi-party agreements, plus Article 8 VBER on the calculation of market shares
[b]De Minimis Notice, para. II.8. (b)
[c]European Commission (2003, Article 2(1) of the Annex.)
[d]Effect on Trade Guidelines, para. 50
[e]De Minimis Notice, para. I.2
[f]Article 4 VBER

3.2 How to Determine the Relevant Markets

Markets are to be defined by the **goods or services** (i.e. the relevant product market) and the **territory** (i.e. the relevant geographic market).[2] While calculating the market share is dispensable for agreements concluded by SMEs without restrictions by object,[3] the market shares must in all other cases be calculated in order to verify whether the threshold of Article 3(1) VBER of 30% is maintained.

These 30% apply for all parties to the agreement concerned, i.e. in case of a multi-party agreement for each party on the relevant market. If in such a multi-party agreement e.g. a wholesaler is sandwiched between the supplier and the retailer, the market shares of the wholesaler on both the purchasing and the supply market must meet the threshold.

Markets are, according to Article 8 VBER,[4] determined on the basis of value data – or, where unavailable, on substantiated estimates, based on reliable market information at hand, e.g. volume figures. With regard to supplier's market shares, vertically integrated distributors are consequently counted as being one entity with their supplier, which is why a supplier's market share includes also the goods or services supplied to its vertically integrated distributors.[5]

[2]VGL, para. 172.

[3]See above Chapter 1.4.1.

[4]Whose internal order – (a) calculation, (b) relevant time, (c) suppliers' market share, (d) temporarily exceeding the threshold, (e) connected undertakings – could be enhanced by collating (b) and (d) and (c) and (e) together.

[5]Article 8(c) VBER; VGL, para. 176.

Timewise, the preceding calendar year is relevant. If things change, the VBER is still lenient: The VBER's safe harbour continues to be open for undertakings which exceed the market for two consecutive years, provided they have stayed within the 30%-threshold the preceding year.[6]

More details on determining the relevant market—the relevant product market and the relevant geographic market—are given by the Market Definition Notice.[7] As said note dates back to 1997 and stakeholders suggested giving the European Commission more flexibility in assessing the relevant market, also the Market Definition Notice is experiencing a reboot.[8]

In practice, competition analysis is especially needed in cases which are close to exceeding the threshold. This is where the economists' hour has come. Following best practice, they are the ones providing the thorough economic analysis required.

References

Bischke A-H, Brack S (2021) Neuere Entwicklungen im Kartellrecht. Noch zukunftstauglich? – Europäische Kommission stellt wichtige Wettbewerbsregeln auf den Prüfstand. NZG 2021: 191–194

European Commission (1997a) Commission Working Document. Evaluation of the Commission Notice on the definition of relevant market for the purposes of Community competition law of 9 December 1997, SWD(2021) 199 final. https://eur-lex.europa.eu/legal-content/EN/TXT/?uri=CELEX%3A52021SC0199. Accessed 9 Feb 2023

European Commission (1997b) Commission Notice on the definition of relevant market for the purposes of Community competition law, 97/C 372 /03. https://eur-lex.europa.eu/legal-content/EN/TXT/PDF/?uri=CELEX:31997Y1209(01)&from=EN. Accessed 10 Feb 2023

European Commission (2003) Commission Recommendation of 6 May 2003 concerning the definition of micro, small and medium-sized enterprises. https://eur-lex.europa.eu/LexUriServ/LexUriServ.do?uri=OJ:L:2003:124:0036:0041:en:PDF. Accessed 10 Feb 2023

[6] Article 8(d) VBER.

[7] European Commission (1997b).

[8] Bischke and Brack (2021, p. 194).

Article 4 VBER: Hardcore Restrictions—Black Clauses

4

Abstract What must be avoided are hardcore restrictions because they bring severe consequences, as already one hardcore restriction excludes the agreement from the benefits of the VBER.[1] Hardcore restrictions are listed conclusively in Article 4 VBER,[2] which lists groups of restrictions as regards at what price, where and whom to sell the goods or services to.[3] Basically, there are three groups of restrictions, the first two of them restrict the distributor, the last one the supplier: (i) Resale price maintenance, (ii) territory and customer group restrictions (including restrictions of internet sales) and (iii) resale of components as spare parts. They are prohibited, regardless of whether this restriction is direct or indirect, and whether this restriction works alone or combined with others. Therefore, avoiding hardcore restrictions is easier said than done, as indirect obligations require utmost care in contract drafting.

Hardcore restrictions are significant restrictions of competition which are presumed to cause harm to consumers. This presumption of harm to consumers cannot be rebutted within the VBER; instead, the **entire agreement is excluded from the VBER's safe harbour**. If not exempt, there are two main consequences:

First, the agreement loses the benefit of the VBER as the exemption provided for by Article 2 VBER does, according to Article 4 VBER, not apply to vertical agreements containing black clauses. The black clause itself is **void** according to Article 101(2) TFEU **unless** the undertaking can establish it escapes through **Article 101(3) TFEU**.

---

[1] Cf. VGL, para. 177.

[2] By the way, hardcore restrictions under the VBER are always "restrictions by object" (cf. the introductory sentence of Article 4 VBER), while restrictions by object are not always hardcore restrictions in terms of the VBER, cf. Wijckmans and Tuytschaever (2018, para. 6.16).

[3] Cf. the title of Article 4 VBER, first given to it under the Regulation 330/2010 (while its predecessor, Regulation 2790/1999, had no official regulatory headings).

B. Rohrßen, *VBER 2022: EU Competition Law for Vertical Agreements*, Law for Professionals, https://doi.org/10.1007/978-3-031-35024-5_4

The validity of the remaining agreement depends on **two things**: (i) the applicable national law[4] and (ii) on the self-assessment of all other restrictions of the agreement. To "save" agreements, it is best practice in many European jurisdictions to include severability clauses, while care has to be taken if the results will work or if termination and renegotiation would serve better, especially where the competition infringing parts of distribution agreements result in the agreements lacking the essential parts which constituted the respective distribution system.

Second, the door is open to **fines** under Regulation 1/2003. With fines ranging **up to 10%** of the undertaking (or association of undertaking) participating in the infringement's **total turnover** of the preceding business year.[5]

Article 4 VBER contains the black list of once five, now six hardcore restrictions, which in the end boil down to **three different types of restrictions**:

- price fixing (Article 4(a) VBER),
- territory and customer restrictions (Article 4(b)-(e) VBER),
- restriction of supplier to sell components as spare parts (Article 4(f) VBER).

Notably, the structure of Article 4 and 5 differs from the general provisions of Article 2 and 3 of the VBER: While the latter start from what is exempt, Article 4 and 5 start from what is prohibited—and then provide for re-exceptions.

Under the VBER 2022, this structure has changed as the territory and customer restrictions have been split into the three different distribution systems in Article 4 (b), (c) and (d) plus a catch-all clause for online sales restrictions in Article 4 (e). Such splitting has caused the list to grow abundantly (not to say: made it partly redundant): The **blacklist of Article 4** now consists of **+800 words,** instead of +300 under the VBER 2010[6] and the VBER 2790/1999. It is doubtful whether the more detailed differentiation within the territory and customer restrictions has improved the interpretation of Article 4 VBER. While the structure is clear and the single case—exclusive, selective, free distribution—may be more easily allocated to the respective hardcore restriction and its carve-out, Article 4 could overall be shorter.[7]

Not so much an argument against Article 4 VBER's new structure, but for a still more exact translation, is Article 4(d) VBER. Article 4(d)(i) and (ii) VBER contradictorily allow free distributors which neither operate an exclusive nor selective distribution system to restrict sales into exclusive or selective distribution territories. Literally, it reads, (re-)translated e.g. from German into English "(The exemption … in Article 2 shall not apply…) *if* [not, as in English: "where"] the supplier operates

[4] ECLI:EU:C:2006:753 (Brünsteiner, Hilgert/BMW) para. 47 et seq.; ECLI:EU:C:1986:502 (VAG France SA) para. 14 et seq.; ECLI:EU:C:1998:181 (Cabour/Peugeot, Citroën), para. 51.

[5] Article 23(2)(a) Regulation 1/2003.

[6] 862 words 2022 versus 383 words 2010 (including Article 4's heading).

[7] And the wording, at least in the respective German translation, could be more consistent, more closely aligned with the English version. Where for example the English version refers to "*exceptions*", the German version refers to "*Freistellungen*" *(exemptions)* and "Ausnahmen" *(exceptions)*, cf. Article 2(4) and (5) and (6) VBER. Cf. Rohrßen (2021, p. 298 at footnote 96).

neither an exclusive distribution system nor a selective distribution system.[8] The same applies for at least the French ("lorsque"), Italian ("qualora" = when/if), Spanish ("cuando"), Portuguese ("se"), Dutch ("indien") and Swedish ("de fall där") language versions, all of which use a temporal or conditional conjunction instead of a local one.

What is new is the change to extend the protection of a distribution system further down the distribution chain (to "direct customers" as regards exclusive distribution systems and all "customers" as regards selective distribution systems)—while it was explicitly a hardcore restriction in the past, e.g. the restriction of active sales into exclusive territories or to exclusive customer groups "where such a restriction does not limit sales by the customers of the buyer".[9] What is also new is the across-system-protection (also called "reverse protection"[10]) as Article 4 VBER now allows to also restrict sales from buyers outside a selective distribution system into that very territory (Article 4(b)(ii)[11]), not exempt earlier,[12] while the across-system-protection in favour of exclusive distribution systems has already been exempt under Article 4 (b) VBER 2010.[13]

Article 4-restrictions are by definition always restrictions of competition by object, or short "**restriction by object**",[14] as the introductory sentence of Article 4 VBER stipulates[15]: "The exemption provided for in Article 2 shall not apply to vertical agreements which . . . have as their object . . ." any of the restrictions listed therein. They are therefore presumed to harm competition, without the need for assessing their effects in order to be prohibited. As a last resort, however, there is the chance to demonstrate that the respective agreement has overweighing pro-competitive effects and thus can be individually exempt. Accordingly, the ECJ qualifies hardcore restrictions as types of coordination which provide a "sufficient degree of harm to competition that there is no need to examine their effects".[16] They are, thus, not a per se infringement of Article 101 TFEU[17]—but the burden of proof that they comply with competition law is on the undertaking.

---

[8] Haberer and Fries (2021, p. 428); Maritzen (2022, Vertikal-GVO, Art. 4 para. 190).

[9] Article 4(b)(i) VBER 2010.

[10] Distribution Law Center Countdown XX – Selective distribution (Reverse protection) (2022).

[11] Exempting "the restriction of . . . sales by the exclusive distributor . . . to unauthorised distributors located in . . . a selective distribution system".

[12] Because Article 4(b)(iii) exempted only the "restriction of sales by the members of a selective distribution system to unauthorised distributors . . .".

[13] Exempting "the restriction of active sales into the exclusive territory or to an exclusive customer group reserved to the supplier or allocated by the supplier to another buyer", regardless of the type of distributor.

[14] While restrictions by object are not always hardcore restrictions in terms of the VBER, cf. Wijckmans and Tuytschaever (2018, para. 6.16).

[15] Cf. also VGL, para. 179 (where, however, the word "generally" reads suspiciously as if the Commission reserved the possibility of allowing exceptions); European Commission (2014, p. 4).

[16] ECJ ECLI:EU:C:2016:26 ("Toshiba Corporation v Commission") para. 25.

[17] VGL, para. 195 concretely for RPM.

As a consequence, **also SMEs cannot simply include hardcore restrictions** into their agreements. Nor does the De Minimis (up to 15% market share) spare an agreement containing hardcore restrictions. Instead, each agreement with hardcore restrictions can **only** escape Article 101(1) TFEU through the backdoor of an **individual exemption according to Article 101(3) TFEU**.

At the same time, the presence of hardcore restrictions gives a good indication of whether Article 101(1) or Article 101(3) are fulfilled: An agreement with one or more hardcore restrictions likely falls within the scope of Article 101(1) TFEU and will also unlikely fulfil the conditions for individual exemption under Article 101(3) TFEU.[18] To reach the safe harbour, an undertaking must show pro-competitive effects, substantiate that efficiencies are likely, and that they are likely to result from including the hardcore restriction.[19]

4.1 How (Not) to Restrict the Buyer's Sale Price

The wording of Article 4(a) VBER is identical with its predecessor.[20] Buyers must be free to determine their sale prices. Resale price maintenance remains a no-go: No minimum prices, no fixed prices, only maximum prices, these are the principles that Article 101(1) TFEU and Article 4(a) VBER stipulate. Suppliers may impose maximum sale prices or recommend prices, without ending up in fixed or minimum sale prices due to pressure or incentives. Minimum Advertisement Prices remain hardcore restrictions, while the fine line between recommending and binding sale prices remains. Four example cases continue to apply where suppliers may fix the sale prices, however only as an individual exemption under Article 101(3) TFEU.

Among the most "attracting" practices is **resale price maintenance**. The line between recommendation and maintenance is fine and, as the competition practice shows, has been crossed sometimes even by bigger market players, e.g.: Asus, Denon & Marantz, Philips and Pioneer,[21] Casio (United Kingdom[22]), Apple,[23] Bose,[24] Pfizer,[25] or The Netherlands 2021 with Samsung.[26] It is one of the most typical reasons for **fines**.[27]

---

[18] VGL, para. 180.

[19] VGL, para. 181. The example in para. 183, however, seems hard to follow: When is it impractical to specify promotional activities in the agreement to justify cross-supply restrictions?

[20] This is the only hardcore restriction that has remained unchanged. Article 4(e) VBER on online restrictions is completely new; Article 4(f) VBER is extended so that component suppliers are free to sell spare parts also to independent wholesalers.

[21] Commission, Cases 40.465, 40.469, 40.181 and 40.182.

[22] Case 50565-2.

[23] Case 20-D-04.

[24] Case B10-23/20.

[25] Swiss Federal Court, Decision of 4 February 2021, Case No. 2C_149/2018, cf. Stäuber (2022, p. 388 et seq.).

[26] Case 20/040569.

[27] Schultze et al. (2019, para. 567).

Article 101(1) TFEU prohibits the restriction of competition. As one example, it prohibits to "directly or indirectly fix purchase or selling prices".[28] Article 4 (a) VBER seconds that the supplier must not direct the buyer's sale price—neither by establishing a fixed price or a minimum sale price.[29]

4.1.1 What's New for Price Maintenance?

With regard to RPM, the VBER has not changed from 2010 to 2022. There is **no new lenience for suppliers**. RPM and other price fixing measures remain generally prohibited, despite all suggestions to grant suppliers more freedom.[30] RPM remains a hardcore restriction, which may[31] only be permissible by way of the efficiency defence. To this end, the same three examples of possible exceptions as under the 2010 Vertical Guidelines continue to apply (plus a new one). Though the US Leegin case[32] furthered the discussion in Europe whether to retain RPM as a hardcore restriction under the pre-predecessor VBER 2790/99[33] and the discussion, at least with regard to MAPs, has come upon again when updating the VBER 2010, the Commission has maintained its strict view. The Commission's ratio lies in the concerns for competition, split into seven different aspects.[34] As requested by most of the NCAs,[35] the Commission has elaborated more on RPM in the new Vertical Guidelines.

In short: The buyer must not be limited in its ability to determine the lower end of the sale price. The—for suppliers—more attractive lower end of the sale price is a taboo, which the supplier must not influence, neither directly nor indirectly, neither through negative ("pressure"[36]) nor positive ("incentives") measures. With very few, time-limited exceptions. In detail:

[28] Price fixing is one of the examples of Article 101(1) TFEU.

[29] VGL, para. 185.

[30] Rohrßen (2017, p. 281 at footnote 90–92).

[31] Article 4(a) VBER and VGL para. 185 et seq.; cf. also the Draft VGL, para. 152 with regard to franchise agreements as well as para. 180 in general.

[32] US Supreme Court, 551 U.S. 877 (2007). This case overturned the court's decision in Dr Miles (220 U.S. 373) (1911), which held that RPM was prohibited per se, i.e. without the possibility to show that RPM had a pro-competitive effect.

[33] Wijckmans and Tuytschaever (2018, para. 6.54).

[34] VGL, para. 196.

[35] European Commission (2021, para. II.a).

[36] Including other "disincentives", cf. VGL, para. 188.

4.1.2 The Principle: RRP Yes, RPM and MAP No

Article 4(a) VBER prohibits and catches all vertical agreements related to restrict the buyer's (not only resale, but literally any[37]) sale price, both **direct and indirect measures**,[38] as shown in Table 4.1. The measures must neither be directed at the price itself nor the price building factors.[39]

Article 4(a) VBER only covers and prohibits restrictions on the *buyer*'s freedom to set prices in relation to the sale price of contract goods and services. Therefore, restrictions of other goods or services or restrictions of the supplier's freedom to set prices are not covered by the hardcore restriction of Article 4(a)VBER: Such restrictions usually infringe Article 101(1) TFEU, but they may rather easily be exempt[40] and leave the remaining agreement untouched.

What works (is lawful) are **maximum prices**—and **recommended retail price s, as long as** they do **not result in fixing the sale price**, no matter if by negative ("pressure") or positive ("incentives") measures. Imposing maximum prices may make sense especially in case of international customers who may conclude framework agreements with the supplier to which the local affiliates may accede, while they will buy the goods from the local distributors. Scenarios where intra-brand competition is so low that the distributor charges high prices which result in high margins for the distributor (but not for the supplier, whose margin remains the same for every product) occur rather rarely, especially on a European internal market.[41] Nevertheless, it is recommended to foresee a general maximum price clause in distribution agreements to be able to cope with such scenarios when they arise.[42]

What is in principle also allowed is **exchanging views on pricing**. Exchanges of opinions as such are no prohibited means of pressure or incentives within the meaning of Article 101(1) TFEU as long as the pricing autonomy of the buyer is maintained. This applies, for example, to explanations by the supplier on price recommendations, such as the results of market research including price sensitivity analyses.[43]

The following measures are prohibited as **hardcore restrictions** under Article 4 (a) VBER:

---

[37] Usually, Article 4(a) VBER is interpreted as prohibiting only determining the buyer's resale price of contract goods or services—though the provision broadly speaks of the "sale price", hence allows a much wider interpretation, making it a hardcore restriction when dictating the sale price of any product the buyer sells, cf. Schultze et al. (2019, para. 559).

[38] Cf. the introductory sentence of Article 4 VBER ("vertical agreements which, directly or indirectly ...") and VGL, para. 187.

[39] Bechtold et al. (2023, Art. 4 para. 7); Zöttl (2020, Vertikal-GVO Art. 4 para. 24); Baron (2020, Vert-GVO Art. 4 para. 216).

[40] Bechtold et al. (2023, Vertikal-GVO Art. 4 para. 7); Ellger (2019, Art. 4 Vertikal-GVO para. 13).

[41] Example by Wijckmans and Tuytschaever (2018, para. 6.81).

[42] Wijckmans and Tuytschaever (2018, para. 6.81).

[43] Rohrßen (2020, p. 407).

Table 4.1 Direct versus Indirect measures of RPM

Direct measures	Indirect measures
Fixing the resale price[a]—here and below, always including fixing price minimum resale prices or price levels	Fixing the resale margin
Allowing the supplier to fix the resale price	Fixing the maximum level of discount the distributor may grant
	Granting financial advantages (rebates, reimbursements of promotional costs), dependent on observing certain price levels
	Imposing Minimum Advertising Prices ("MAP"[b])
	Linking resale prices to those of competitors
	Any consequence linked to the (non-) observance of specific prices, including refusal to supply

[a]I.e. the price the buyer must charge to its customers, cf. VGL, para. 186
[b]MAP prohibit the distributor from *advertising* (not from selling) below a specific price level. The Commission categorizes MAP as disincentive against lower resale prices, cf. VGL, para. 189

- Fixing the resale price,
- Fixing a minimum price,
- Fixing a price range[44] and
- Setting minimum advertised price policies ("MAPs").

The **following practices are allowed**—always as long as they do not result into fixed or minimum prices "as a result of pressure from, or incentives offered by, any of the parties":

- Recommended resale prices ("RRP"), which also should apply to requiring the distributor to take into account the positioning of products as e.g. a luxury brand)—unless they amount to a fixed or minimum resale price due to pressure or incentives;
- Price monitoring
  The use of price monitoring software continues to be harmless[45] as price monitoring alone does not constitute resale price maintenance. It does not constitute a declaration by the supplier vis-à-vis the buyer to maintain a certain price level.[46] The fine line to prohibited price fixing can quickly be crossed if suppliers go beyond simple monitoring and intervene in the event of price reductions,[47] e.g. identify price-cutting distributors vis-à-vis the distribution network, putting

[44]VGL, para. 185.

[45]VGL, para. 191 (Draft VGL, para. 176).

[46]Lettl (2013, p. 1276 para. 36).

[47]On the fine line between a permissible exchange of views and a prohibited price agreement the case of the Higher Regional Court of Düsseldorf, ECLI:DE:OLGD:2020:0708.U.KART3.20.00, cf. Rohrßen (2020, p. 408).

them in the pillory. Price algorithms that monitor and automatically adjust prices are not regulated by the VBER. Caution needs to be taken as the use of price algorithms may just be an undertaking's independent practice[48]—or a case of merely parallel conduct not covered by Article 101(1) TFEU—or an exchange of information. The fine line drawn here is between independent, parallel conduct of undertakings[49] versus coordination and cooperation which constitutes a concerted practice[50]:

> . . .this requirement of independence does not deprive traders of the right to adapt themselves intelligently to the existing or anticipated conduct of their competitors, it does however strictly preclude any direct or indirect contact between such traders, the object or effect of which is to create conditions of competition which do not correspond to the normal conditions of the market in question, regard being had to the nature of the products or services offered, the size and number of the undertakings and the volume of the said market.[51]

- Price reporting is also harmless in itself.[52]

Generally, measures are allowed "provided that they do not amount to a fixed or minimum sale price as a result of pressure from, or incentives offered by, any of the parties". Pressure in the maximum form may be exercised by threatening to terminate the respective agreement. The supplier remains, however, free to terminate,[53] but must not use such termination as a signal towards the distributors remaining in the distribution network to maintain prices.

Further details—which continue to apply as Article 4(a) VBER is unchanged—have been provided by the German NCA, following an enquiry about the German food retail sector.[54]

In the case of **RPM**, the only way out is to seek an **individual exemption under Article 101(3) TFEU**, with far-reaching consequences[55]: The entire agreement is

[48] Undertakings have the right to adapt their conduct to the established or expected conduct of competitors, cf. ECLI:EU:C:1998:256 (John Deere) para. 87.

[49] Likely especially if the algorithm was developed by or for each undertaking.

[50] In detail: Ong, IIC (2021), p. 189.

[51] ECLI:EU:C:1998:256 (John Deere) para. 87; ECLI:EU:C:1975:174 (Suiker Unie) para. 173; ECLI:EU:C:1981:178 (Züchner) para. 13.

[52] VGL, para. 191.

[53] Bechtold et al. (2023, Art. 4 para. 7).

[54] Bundeskartellamt (2017).

[55] Perfectly pointed out by Wijckmans and Tuytschaever (2018, para. 6.59).

not block-exempt, hence legal uncertainty rises. Therefore, undertakings considering to change from the distributor to the agency model have decided to better be safe than sorry,[56] while others have taken that shot are or about to take it, especially in order to promote a more customer-centric, seamless sales process: While the dealer continues to act as the (familiar) face to the customer, the OEM will face new challenges as contractual partner, thereby however being able to protect the existence of the dealer network, especially in times of crisis.[57] As in the agency model the sales contract is concluded between the buyer and the manufacturer, the seller, i.e. the manufacturer, is responsible for all obligations arising from the contract itself—and also for all associated liabilities in the broadest sense. This includes, for example, discounts, trade-ins of used cars, residual values or the marketing of demonstration cars.

4.1.3 The Exception: Short-Time Measures, Efficiency Gains

By way of the efficiency defence under Article 101(3) TFEU, RPM may be exempt. To this end, the 2022 Vertical Guidelines list four[58] examples of possible exceptions, three of which are already known from the 2010 Guidelines[59]:

- RPM for **short-term promotions** for the purpose of **launching new products**,
- RPM for **coordinated short-term special offer campaigns** of two to six weeks (in particular for uniform distribution formats such as franchising),
- **RPM** for the purpose of **enabling pre-sales services**, **especially for complex products**.[60] Current examples show how rarely such exceptions are permitted. For example, in August 2021 alone the Bundeskartellamt imposed fines of EUR 2 million for RPM concerning school backpacks and school bags under the brands "ergobag" and "Satch"[61] and also investigated against a supplier of guitars, which then provided its distributors with an updated price list, for the first time clearly marked as recommended retail prices ("RRP") and established in

[56] That is also the experience under the VBER 2010 made by Wijckmans and Tuytschaever (2018, para. 6.69–6.70).

[57] Mercedes-Benz and Ford plan to go for "genuine" agency agreements (cf. Plate, Autohaus of 23 May 2022a, p. 12), while others, possibly the majority, consider using non-genuine agency agreement (Plate/Woltermann, Autohaus, 27 June 2022b, p. 12). Some may also consider using agency for new products such as e-vehicles, cf. Autohaus (2022), while others may feel the need to revert to agency agreements as they have market shares beyond 30% and thus cannot rely on the safe harbour of the VBER, e.g. Stellantis on the utility vehicles sector, cf. Plate/Woltermann, Autohaus, 27 June 2022b, p. 12.

[58] In the Draft VGL, para. 182 three examples; the final VGL added MAPs, cf. para. 197.

[59] VGL, para. 223.

[60] While "experience products" as example have been mentioned in the Draft VGL (para. 182(c)), but deleted in the final version (para. 197(d)).

[61] Cf. BKartA, Case B10-26/20 (Fond Of), Case report of 1 October 2021.

a circular that the buyers are free to determine the sale price[62]—and succeeded as the Bundeskartellamt thereupon discontinued its proceedings.

- **Minimum resale prices or MAPs**[63] to prevent a particular distributor from using the product as a loss leader.

Example

The UK case in the commercial refrigerator sector[64]: A division (Foster Refrigerator UK Foster) of ITW Ltd agreed with resellers in its distribution network on a 'discounting policy' which it amended from time to time. Basically, the policy which turned out to be a MAP contained the following:

"Discounting policy (To commence 6th January 2012)

(1) Your existing Trade Dealer discount will be maintained as long as you do not advertise any of the Foster product range at prices below the current Regional Nett price list plus [%] mark up (excluding VAT and installation). . . .
(2) If you do publish or advertise any of the Foster product range at prices below the current Regional Nett price list plus [%] mark-up then we shall deduct [%] of your dealer discount.
(3) Any Dealer that continues to advertise below the current Green Regional Nett price list plus [%] mark-up may lose their Foster dealership . . . .
(4) Foster will monitor . . . .
(5) Foster Refrigerator reserves the right to have full authorisation on Foster Logos, product photographs and any other brand material.
(6) . . . All dealers must respect the principal [sic] of this policy and should not advertise strap lines stating "Ring now for better prices", "Additional Discounts Available" or any other phrase which indicates that the advertised prices do not represent their best offer. . . ." ◀

The UK Competition and Markets Authority imposed a fine of GBP 2.3 million, arguing that the "discounting policy' restricted resellers in their ability to determine their online sales prices at a price below said policy and, as such, amounted to resale price maintenance.

Unlike interpreted into the Draft VGL,[65] the final Vertical Guideline qualify MAPs as indirect form of RPM because they disincentivise distributors from setting

[62] BKartA, press release of 1 October 2021 (Manufacturas Alhambra).

[63] Example added only to the VGL's final version, cf. VGL, para. 187(d), 189 and 197(c), while the Draft VGL still foresaw that MAPs "may also amount to RPM" (but, implicitly, do not automatically have to), cf. Draft-VGL, para. 174.

[64] CMA, Case CE/9856/14, decision of 24 May 2016.

[65] According to the Draft VGL, MAPs could have been allowed if the supplier (i) did not penalize the buyer for selling below the MAP, (ii) not required the buyer not to discount, and (iii) not prevented the buyer from disclosing that the actual price may differ from the MAP, cf. para. 174 of the Draft VGL.

a lower sale price,[66] thus removing a key parameter for price competition between retailers. By way of exception, **MAPs can be exempt** under the—rather rare circumstances of the—**efficiency defence,** if a company can show that MAPs **(i)** contribute to improving the production or distribution/technical or economic progress, **(ii)** consumers receive a fair share of the benefits, **(iii)** the restrictions go not beyond what is indispensable to reach their objectives and **(iv)** do not eliminate competition (Article 101 (3) TFEU). The Commission sees such **pro-competitive effects possibly (not generally) given to prevent** a *particular* distributor **from using a product as a loss leader**—which again shall be the case only "*where a distributor regularly resells a product below the wholesale price*" as such use as loss leader can damage the product's brand image and reduce the overall demand, thus undermine the supplier's incentives to invest in quality and brand image. Considering this explicit statement of the Commission, it is unlikely that courts (in case of dispute with e.g. a distributor) will see this very differently and thus unlikely that courts will allow MAPs on a large scale (and not just with particular distributors in loss leader cases).

A case of MAPs occurred in Germany on the occasion of the new VBER: Orderman GmbH, an affiliate of the US-based NCR Corporation, required the complainant to offer new goods on the internet only at Orderman's RRP, and made further supply conditional on compliance with this requirement. From the outside, it appeared like the company was testing the waters. The company could, however, with help of outside counsel, clarify that there was no systematic infringement of competition law, but just a few, single cases; the company committed to provide compliance trainings to its sales staff and made it clear to its distributors that they were free to determine the sale price. The BKArtA closed the case without decision – but stated in its case report that it clearly considered MAPs as covered by Article 4(a) VBER and thus in principle not exempt. MAPs were a restriction by object, as they aimed at restricting the buyer's possibility to set its sale price.[67]

Beyond these four scenarios, there is—at least theoretically—leeway for other situations where the procompetitive effects of RPM may outweigh the anti-competitive ones because the Vertical Guidelines list the above four explicitly as "examples", hence are not meant to be exclusive.

4.1.4 Special Case: Agency Agreements

Outside of Article 101(1) TFEU and thus also of Article 4(a) VBER is RPM in **agency agreements,** because the agent is considered to form part of the principal's

[66]VGL, para. 187, 189. Before, the UK Competition and Markets Authority had fined for price-fixing companies which operated minimum advertised price policies, cf. Case CE/9856/14 (ITW) and CE/9578/12 (Pride Mobility Products), in the latter called "The Below-RRP Online Price Advertising Prohibition".

[67]BKartA, B7-35/22 (Orderman), case report of 31 May 2022.

undertaking, provided the principal bears all the significant financial and commercial risks of the business (see above).[68] If instead the agent bears any significant risk, any obligation restricting the agent from sharing its commission (fixed or variable) with the customer is an unlawful RPM in terms of Article 4(a) VBER.[69]

4.1.5 Special Case: Fulfilment (Multi-Level Distribution)

Within **fulfilment scenarios**, suppliers may—according to the Vertical Guidelines—impose the "resale[70] price". The Vertical Guidelines, to which the term is new[71], use the term "fulfilment scenario" to describe situations where the supplier first concludes a supply agreement with a specific customer and then selects another buyer to fulfil said agreement. It shall be no RPM where the supplier selects the "fulfilment provider" (i.e. the buyer-reseller), while it may be RPM where the customer selects the "fulfilment provider".[72] Such fulfilment scenarios may especially occur in multi-level distribution. In today's digital age, they occur for example where consumers first come into contact with the supplier online—and then have the products delivered through the local distributor.

The Vertical Guidelines illustrate fulfilment scenarios accordingly by an example of an undertaking within the online platform economy, operated by a group of independent retailers under a common brand, which sells goods to customers and "forwards orders to retailers for fulfilment",[73] i.e. the supplier chooses the buyer-reseller to fulfil the order. So far so unclear, at best: Either, the Vertical Guidelines state the obvious—or they allow the supplier to impose the sale price, which qualifies as RPM.

Under clear scrutiny, there are two abstract fulfilment sub-scenarios where the supplier's action does not constitute an RPM: Either, the supplier acts as agent for the buyer-reseller—or the buyer-reseller acts as agent for the supplier. Understood this way, the expression that the supplier "forwards the order ... for fulfilment"[74] either means that the supplier procures the supply contract as agent for the buyer-reseller (but that does not fit to the Vertical Guidelines' explanations, para. 193)—or it means that the supplier uses the buyer-reseller as vicarious agent (while the buyer-reseller sells the good to the supplier at a price freely agreed). In either case, there is no RPM. In cases where, instead, the supplier actually imposes the sale price at

[68] VGL, para. 192.

[69] VGL, para. 192.

[70] Notably, the Commission here specifically refers to the "resale" price, not the "sale" price, as in Article 4(a) VBER.

[71] The guidance on fulfilment scenarios has only been inserted in the final version of the VBER.

[72] VGL, para. 193.

[73] VGL, para. 193.

[74] VGL, para. 193.

which the buyer-reseller must sell the product to the customer, there is RPM[75]—unless the fulfilment service provider acts as agent, i.e. without bearing any significant risk. In the latter scenario, the fulfilment service provider could be an atypical agent under distribution law (for being a distributor), but a "genuine" agent under competition law (for bearing no significant risks).

Accordingly, the Vertical Guidelines shed light onto fulfilment scenarios, however, that light could be more focused and clearer, because the Vertical Guidelines may be interpreted to open up the RPM hardcore restriction—without any basis in the VBER, and without any need—as the supplier may use third persons acting as agent or logistics provider in order to fulfil the sale to the specific customer at the price agreed with said customer. Moreover, suppliers who are faced with customers that negotiate with the supplier but buy the goods from the (local) distributors have the option to impose maximum sale prices to the distributors.

4.1.6 Practical Tips for the Exchange on Pricing

There is a fine line between **a lawful exchange of opinions and a prohibited price agreement**. Practical tips:

- The exchanging of views on price formation is very sensitive. In general, such exchange is lawful as far as the parties stay away from any agreement and retain the buyer's pricing autonomy. Lawful is, for example, the supplier's explanations on price recommendations, such as the results of market research including price sensitivity analyses.
- Requesting information from the buyer about its pricing policy is also lawful.
- The limit is, however, reached where the supplier gives advice on the buyer's pricing, such as
  - "why the distributor applies very aggressive prices",
  - "asking the distributor to reconsider the pricing policy",
  - "drawing attention to possible miscalculations".[76] While the Higher Regional Court of Düsseldorf considered such advice still within the limits as it was not accompanied by envisaging a dealer-delisting if the distributor did not raise the resale prices, especially the request to "reconsider the pricing policy" can also be understood as a request to increase prices. And pressure can also be expressed subtly. This goes especially in the light of potential national laws as Section 21(2) of the German Act on Restraints against Competition which prohibits inducing another party to unlawful conduct through pressure or incentives, hence covers already conduct preliminary to anti-competitive agreements. The line is crossed if the supplier expects a certain price-setting

[75] Cf. Schultze et al. (2019, para. 586).

[76] ECLI:DE:OLGD:2020:0708.U.KART3.20.00 (Model making and toys), with comment by Rohrßen (2020, p. 408).

behaviour and (ii) the buyer understands it has to expect a disadvantage in case of non-compliance ("quantity management", termination of delivery) or an advantage in case of compliance (e.g. "price maintenance discount").

- The line is also crossed where the exchange of views turns into an agreement or concerted practice (e.g. in the case of data exchange not only of past, but also of future pricing or recourse to the data sets of the same third party supplier).
- A supplier may also prohibit the use of images and data (here limited to the extent that the trader did not stock the products.[77]
- Suppliers may also terminate distributors for whatever reason, provided, however, that such termination does not have as effect or object to streamline the existing distributors, making an example out of said distributor with signalling effect to the others, thereby amounting to RPM.[78]
- Documentation can protect—namely if it shows that it is not a question of compliance with certain (minimum) prices. The written (e-mails!) communication of the parties often serves as circumstantial evidence.

4.2 Exclusive Distribution Systems

Exclusive distribution systems are defined by the VBER as follows:

▶ **Definition** "a distribution system where the supplier allocates a territory or group of customers exclusively to itself or to a maximum of five buyers and restricts all its other buyers from actively selling into the exclusive territory or to the exclusive customer group".[79]

The definition itself is new to the VBER. So far, exclusive distribution had only been indirectly defined within the hardcore restrictions in Article 4(b)(i) VBER 2010, which allowed "the restriction of active sales into the exclusive territory or to an exclusive customer group reserved to the supplier or allocated by the supplier to another buyer, where such a restriction does not limit sales by the customers of the buyer". Essential for exclusive distribution is that the supplier protects its exclusive distributors necessarily[80] against active sales by all of the supplier's other customers, including specifically (i) exclusive distributors from another territory (Article 4(b)(i) VBER), (ii) selective distributors (Article 4(c)(i) VBER) and (iii) all other buyers (Article 4(c)(i) VBER). Moreover, Article 4(b)(iv) on restricting wholesalers from

[77] ECLI:DE:OLGD:2020:0708.U.KART3.20.00 para. 87.

[78] Considering also that suppliers in a dominant position may face further restrictions before terminating a distributorship agreement, especially where the distributor depends on the supplier, cf. under German law Sections 19, 20 German Competition Act.

[79] Article 1(1)(h) VBER.

[80] This protection against third party intrusion into the exclusive territory is constitutive of exclusive distribution systems, cf. its definition in Article 1(1)(h) VBER.

direct supplies to end-users is unchanged[81]; the same goes for Article 4(b)(v) exempting the restriction on component supplies to the supplier's competitors.[82]

There are two new issues for exclusive distribution: While "exclusive distribution" may be watered down by allocating a territory or customer group to five exclusive distributors, such distributors can be better protected through passing on the exclusivity. Such passing on works where the distribution chain goes down one or maximum two further levels.

However, it hardly works beyond further levels, because the supplier must not pass on the territory/customer restrictions further down, not beyond the direct customers of the supplier's buyer. Therefore, suppliers need to be aware that they cannot protect the exclusive distribution system in multi-level distribution which goes beyond three levels, while they can pass on customer/territory restrictions further down within selective distribution.

4.2.1 What's New for Exclusive Distribution?

Four aspects of exclusive distribution have changed—a formal, **three material ones**, in favour of the suppliers who have more freedom to design their distribution systems: First, the definition of "active sales" now binds all courts and authorities as it has been moved from the Vertical Guidelines into the Vertical Block Exemption Regulation. Second, "active sales" now include using top-level domains or offering language options different from the country of distribution. Third, the supplier may assign a territory "exclusively" not just to one, but up to five distributors exclusively. Fourth, the supplier may agree with its buyers to pass on the territory or customer restrictions down to the next level within the distribution chain.

4.2.2 Restricting Active Versus Passive Sales

What is new is not so much the definition of "active sales" itself, but the "**sedes materiae**": While it had so far been defined only in the Vertical Guidelines,[83] it is now defined in the regulation itself, in Article 1(1)(l) VBER. Accordingly, the definition now binds according to Article 288(2) TFEU[84] all EU courts and authorities.

[81] Except for now explicitly mentioning "active and passive sales", while Article 4(b(ii)) before simply referred to "sales"; cf. on the details Bortolotti and Bortolotti (2023, p. 51 seq.).

[82] Previously laid down in Article 4(b)(iv) VBER 2010/330.

[83] VGL 2010, para. 51, whereas the concept of active sales was born in Article 2(B) of the Regulation No 67/67/EEC on exclusive dealing agreements.

[84] Article 288(2) TFEU: "A regulation shall have general application. It shall be binding in its entirety and directly applicable in all Member States."

▶ **Definition** Active sales are defined by Article 1(1)(l) VBER as:

> actively targeting customers by visits, letters, emails, calls or other means of direct communication or through targeted advertising and promotion, offline or online, for instance by means of print or digital media, including online media, price comparison services or advertising on search engines targeting customers in particular territories or customer groups, operating a website with a top-level domain corresponding to particular territories, or offering on a website languages that are commonly used in particular territories, where such languages are different from the ones commonly used in the territory in which the buyer is established.

Compared to the previous definition, the new one clearly differs between direct (visits, letters, emails, calls) and indirect (advertising and promotion) communication, all of which are only active if targeted at a specific customer or customer group or territory. New is the chance for suppliers to restrict as active sales the following measures because they are now considered as active sales by the Vertical Block Exemption Regulation itself[85]:

- Operating online stores with specific national or regional top-level domains. The VBER 2010 and the Guidelines did not answer whether restricting country-/region-specific top-level domains was exempt, though there have already been good arguments considering them as active sales.[86]
- Offering language options in online stores (except the ubiquitous English[87]) which are different from those commonly used in the territory the buyer is established.[88]
  Under the VBER 2010, offering online shops with different language options qualified as non-restrictable passive sales[89]: The VBER 2022 allows restricting as active sales the offering of different language options "where such languages are different from the ones commonly used in the territory in which the buyer is established". [90] The territory where the buyer is established may not necessarily coincide with the registered place of business. The term "territory in which the buyer is established" needs, however, to be read together with the rationale of restricting active sales in/to exclusive territories / customers, and with the "place

[85] Article 1(1)(l) VBER. Cf. also VGL, para. 213.

[86] First, the European Commission generally considered "online advertisement specifically addressed to certain customers as a form of active selling to those customers. For instance, territory-based banners on third party websites ..."; second, the VGL 2010, para. 53 already allowed restricting "paying a search engine or online advertisement provider to have advertisements displayed specifically to users in a particular territory".

[87] VGL, para. 213.

[88] Thereby implementing critical remarks from many practitioners, e.g. Rahlmeyer (2015, p. 146); Schultze et al. (2019, para. 860); Rohrßen (2018a, p. 39).

[89] VGL 2010, para. 52: "Offering different language options on the website does not, of itself, change the passive character of such selling."

[90] Article 1(l) VBER.

of establishment" referred to in Article 4",[91] i.e. as the place where the buyer physically operates the distribution. Article 1(1)(l) VBER should therefore read as follows (wording to be deleted crossed out, additional wording for interpretation underlined): ". . . offering on a website languages that are commonly used in particular territories, where such languages are different from the ones commonly used in the territory ~~in~~ which the supplier has exclusively allocated to the buyer ~~is established~~;".

Accordingly, suppliers are able to better delimit their exclusive distribution systems and the distributors operating in the respective territories as suppliers will be allowed to specify the website language options the distributors offer.

Passive sales, in contrast, may not be restricted. In other words: ". . . the protection of such exclusively allocated territories or customer groups is not absolute, as the supplier may not restrict passive sales into such territories or customer groups".[92] Therefore, the respective wording may be:

Example

Short Version of Updating the "Active Sales" Restriction:

The Distributor refrains from actively promoting sales (e.g. through advertising, or by establishing branches or distribution depots) into any territory the Supplier has reserved exclusively to itself or allocated to other exclusive distributors or buyers and to extend such restriction also to its direct customers. ◀

Example

Long Version of Updating the "Active Sales" Restriction:

The distributor shall not make active sales of the contract goods into territories or to customer groups reserved exclusively to the Supplier or allocated by the Supplier exclusively to a maximum of five distributors. For these purposes, active sales shall be understood to include the following actions:

- actively targeting such customers outside the Territory by visits, letters, emails, calls, or other direct means of communication;
- targeted indirect means of communication, such as advertising and promotion, offline or online, by means of print or digital media, including online media, price comparison services or advertising on search engines targeting such customers, operating a website with a top-level domain corresponding to such territories, or offering on a website languages that are commonly used in such territories (unless they are commonly used in the Territory);
- advertisement or promotion that is only attractive for Distributor if it (in addition to reaching other customers) reaches such customers;

[91] Cf. "distributor's place of establishment" in Article 4(b)(iii), "place of establishment of the members of the selective distribution system" in Article 4(c)(i)(3) or "the buyer's place of establishment" in Article 4(d)(iii) VBER.

[92] VGL, para. 229, 240.

- offering on a website language options different from the ones commonly used in the Territory; and
- using a domain name corresponding to a geographical area other than the Territory. ◀

Additionally, or alternatively, the—unrestricted—passive sales can be contractually defined closely to the definition in the VBER:

Example

Updating the Non-Restrictable "Passive Sales":

Into territories or to customers which are reserved exclusively to the Supplier or allocated by the Supplier exclusively to a maximum of five distributors, the Distributor may make only passive sales of the contract goods. For these purposes, passive sales shall be understood to include the following actions:

- responses (including delivery of the contract goods) to unsolicited requests from individual customers, without having been initiated by actively targeting such customer, customer group or territory,
- including sales resulting from participating in public procurement or responding to private invitations to tender. ◀

4.2.3 Shared Exclusivity

Under the VBER 2010, exclusive distribution systems meant excluding every other independent distributor but one.[93] Under the VBER 20222, exclusivity has become less exclusive as Article 4(b)(i) VBER allows allocating a territory or customer group "to a **maximum of five other exclusive distributors**". [94]

Where does this "party of five" come from? Originally, the 2021 Draft VBER started off more flexible (and has thus been criticized as less clear): It allowed sharing exclusivity with "one or a limited number of other buyers".[95] Said "limited number of buyers" was intended to provide flexibility, but would have opened up room for interpretation and thus created legal uncertainty because the "number of appointed distributors should be determined in proportion to the allocated territory or

[93] "...allocated by the supplier to another buyer", cf. Article 4(b)(i) VBER 2010.

[94] Where, as "another" under the VBER 2010, "other" allows also the supplier itself to sell in the exclusive territory if the agreement provides for such sales.

[95] Article 4(b)(i) Draft VBER: "reserved to the supplier or allocated by the supplier exclusively to one or a limited number of buyers".

customer group in such a way as to secure a certain volume of business that preserves their investment efforts."[96]

Supplier welcome this extended concept of "exclusivity" as it gives them more options in designing their distribution systems. Even if the criterion of "limited number of buyers" has been replaced by the clear number of "five", suppliers should consider the size of the territory/customer group when deciding about the number of distributors to be allocated—not such much for competition law[97] (as Article 4(b)(i) VBER explicitly allows up to five exclusive distributors), but for competition itself: Shared exclusivity may lead to hold-up issues and free-riding of exclusive distributors amongst each other—and thus bears the risk of losing acceptance required for the functioning of the system. Furthermore, shared exclusivity exposes distributors to claims under the applicable distributorship laws, which might claim damages for exactly what the Draft VBER wanted to protect against: That the allocated territory or customer group did not secure a sufficient business volume.

4.2.4 Passing on the Sales Restrictions

Suppliers may now also agree with their buyers—exclusive distributors (Article 4(b)(i)), selective distributors (Article 4(c)(i)(1)) and any other buyer (both free distributors and all other buyers) (Article 4(d)(i) VBER)—**to pass on** (practically: to forward) **the restriction of active sales** into exclusive territories/towards exclusive customer groups, to the buyer's "direct customers". Passing on sales restrictions thus enables further protection of the distribution system up to a maximum of two further levels of the distribution chain, as shown in Fig. 4.1.

Therefore, suppliers cannot protect the exclusive distribution system in multi-level distribution beyond the third level (beyond the buyer's direct customers). Such extended protection, however, works for selective distribution.

Fig. 4.1 Multi-level Distribution Chain

Supplier
↓
Wholesaler/Distributor
↓
Retailer
↓
Final Customer

[96]Draft VGL, para. 102. Critical e.g. Haberer and Fries (2021, para. 445 at II.1.a); Rohrßen (2021, p. 298).

[97]Though one might argue that the rationale of the Draft VBER for limiting the number of exclusive distributors ("should be determined in proportion to the allocated territory or customer group in such a way as to secure a certain volume of business that preserves their investment efforts", Draft VGL, para. 102) continues to apply, neither the VBER nor the VGL provide any hint into that direction.

This new term "direct customers" may not be self-explaining as it has so far rather been used in agency agreements for those customers to which the principal sells the contract goods or services without the agent's action (and commission), i.e. directly.[98] Whereas the VBER uses the term in order to distinguish the different levels of the distribution chain below the buyer: The "direct customers" are to be distinguished from the "customers further down the distribution chain".[99] Accordingly, suppliers may pass on sales restrictions with regard to exclusive territories/ customer groups **only one level** further down the distribution chain. As a result, the VBER allows suppliers to require their distributors and other buyers to restrict their (so-called "direct") customers from actively selling into territories or to customer groups that the supplier has exclusively allocated to other distributors, other buyers, or reserved to itself.

The ratio behind allowing the passing on is that sales by customers of an exclusive distributor into exclusive territories discourage the exclusive distributors there from investing in quality or demand-enhancing services.[100] Whereas under the VBER 2010, suppliers were explicitly not allowed to "*restrict sales by the buyer's customers*" (Article 4(b)(i) VBER 2010[101]), i.e. they were not allowed to impose any requirements on downstream levels of trade. Accordingly, manufacturers could so far at most—in practice probably hardly used[102]—conclude corresponding agreements with the further trade levels (possibly as multi-party agreements[103]). Under the VBER, an exclusive distribution system may be set up as shown in Fig. 4.2.

If a supplier opts for the **new, broad concept of shared exclusivity**, the respective clause in the exclusive distributorship agreement could be as follows:

Example

Short version, language close to Article 4 VBER [104]:

The Distributor refrains from actively promoting sales (e.g. through advertising, or by establishing branches or distribution depots) of the contract goods into any territory (or to a customer group) the Supplier has either reserved exclusively to itself or allocated exclusively to other exclusive distributors and to extend such restriction also to its direct customers. ◀

[98] E.g. § 3.2 of the international agency agreement template by Spenner (2021, 2nd Chapter, § 5.II).

[99] VGL, para. 220.

[100] Cf. VGL, para. 220; see already Draft VGL, para. 206.

[101] Article 4(b)(i) VBER 2010 explicitly prohibited passing on such territory or customer restrictions as territory or customer restrictions were only lawful "where such restriction does not limit sales by the customers of the buyer".

[102] Schultze et al. (2019, para. 753 et seq.).

[103] Cf. Art. 3(2) VBER as well as Schultze et al. (2019, para. 753 et seq.).

[104] Combining the distributor's obligation to refrain from active sales into exclusive territories/ customer groups with passing the restriction on to the direct customers.

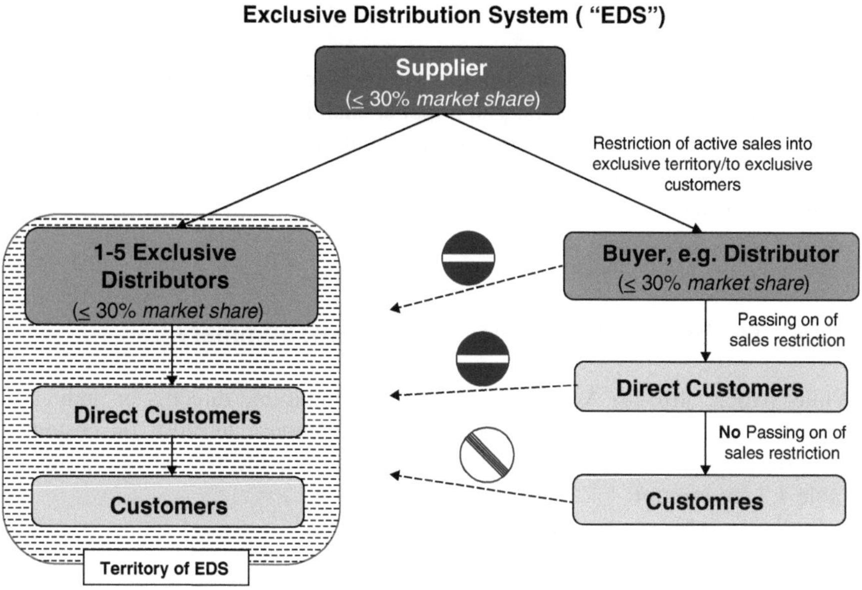

Fig. 4.2 Exclusive distribution systems

Example

Short version, alternative, drafted with "positive expressions":

The Distributor shall only actively promote sales (e.g. through advertising, or by establishing branches or distribution depots) of contract goods only into territories (or to customer groups) the Supplier has neither reserved exclusively to itself nor allocated exclusively to other exclusive distributors and to extend such restriction also to its direct customers. ◄

Example

Long version:

The Distributor must not actively sell the contract products into such territories or to such customer groups which the Supplier has reserved to itself or allocated exclusively to one or a maximum of five other exclusive distributors. The Distributor shall pass on such restriction to its direct customers. ◄

However, the Distributor is entitled to sell passively, i.e. serve customer enquiries from customers in these customer groups as well as from customers outside the contract territory. The same applies to online sales.

In any case, the **supplier should inform the distributor** (and the distributor again its direct customers) about the exclusive territories and customers:

Example

At present, the territories and customer groups listed in Annex [•] are exclusively allocated to other distributors. The Supplier shall inform the Distributor (and the Distributor its direct customers) of any changes, in particular of which exclusively allocated territories and customer groups have been added or dropped after the conclusion of this contract. ◀

4.2.5 Territory and Customer Restrictions: Summary

While Article 4(b)-(e) VBER in principle prohibit to, directly or indirectly, standalone or combined with other factors, to impose territory or customers restrictions on their buyers (distributors and others), the restrictions shown in Table 4.2 are **exempt**:

Further, working in the other direction, however,

- restricting any sales by the supplier of components as spare parts to end users or service providers not entrusted by the buyer.

Direct measures are the easiest to detect—prohibiting sales, requiring approval, or obliging the distributor to forward orders.[105] In practice, however, indirect measures are most relevant and require most scrutiny as their objective often depends on the context whether they aim at controlling the destination of the goods. Distributor audits and other control measures may amount to indirect measures, when they aim to control the destination of goods.

The Commission's twelve examples[106] of indirect restraints can actually be refined to the following **six categories of indirect restraints**:

- granting/raising or refusing/reducing remuneration (bonus, discount, margin, etc.) if the buyer sells to or refrains from selling to specific customers/territories. This includes dual pricing (higher prices for goods resold into such territory/to such customers) and obliging the buyer to pass on profits from such customers to the supplier;
- limiting supply volumes;
- limiting the use of additional languages on the packaging or in advertising;
- excluding such customers from the supplier's Union-wider guarantee service; within the distribution system, additional services such can however be used as a tool to attract and bind customers to the distribution system. The Swiss watchmaker Rolex since end of 2022 also issues certificates of authenticity and an extra

[105] Listed by the Vertical Guidelines as indirect measure, cf. VGL, para. 204(a), though it, even if implicitly, works as direct measure.

[106] VGL, para. 204.

Table 4.2 Territory and customer restrictions in exclusive distribution

Restriction of	Passing on?	Sample clause
Active sales into exclusive territories or to exclusive customer groups	Yes, block exempt, to the buyer's "direct customers"	The Buyer shall not actively sell the contract products into such territories or to such customer groups that the Supplier has reserved for itself or has exclusively allocated to one or up to five other distributors.[a]
Sales (active and passive) to unauthorized distributors in territories where a selective distribution system for these goods/services is operated	Yes, block exempt, to the buyers "and its/their customers", i.e. all customers down the distribution chain	The Buyer shall not sell the contract products to unauthorised distributors in territories where the Supplier operates a selective distribution system for the contract goods.
The buyer's place of establishment[b]	No	The Buyer shall have at least one physical outlet[c] (OPTIONAL: and warehouse[d]). Such physical outlet (OPTIONAL: and warehouse) shall be located at the address or territory specified in Annex [•].—"location clause"[e]
Sales (active and passive) by wholesalers to end users[f]	No	The Buyer, being a wholesaler, shall only sell the contract goods to other wholesalers and retailers,[g] but not to end users. [OPTION: but not to end users, except those listed in Annex [•].[h]
Sales (active or passive) of components[i] deemed for incorporation,[j] to the supplier's competitors[k]	No	The Buyer shall not sell the contract goods, being components deemed for incorporation, to customers who would use them to manufacture goods which compete with goods by the Supplier.
Online sales, including online advertising, as far as this does not prevent the effective use of the internet for selling nor have as object closing the entire online advertising	No, explicitly prohibited ("effective use of the internet by the buyer or its customers")	The Distributor may advertise the contract products on the Internet and in particular on its homepage and sell them via the Internet in accordance with the criteria in Annex [•].[l] The Distributor shall sell at least [value/quantity] of the contract products via his physical store(s).

(continued)

Table 4.2 (continued)

Restriction of	Passing on?	Sample clause
		Selective Distribution: The Distributor must not sell the contract products via third party websites discernible as such.[m]

[a]To be amended by restrictions on online sales, e.g.; "This restriction of active sales includes active sales via the internet, whereby active means . . ." (see the explanations on active sales above)
[b]Referring to "outlets where direct sales take place" (ECJ, EUCLI:C:2011:649 (Pierre Fabre), para. 56 re Article 4(c) VBER No 2790/1999), specifically only to "physical", not to virtual outlets (cf. VGL, para. 231), i.e. suppliers must not restrict online sales beyond what Article 4(b), (c) or (d) allow for. Suppliers may, however, specify an area where to operate mobile outlets (VGL, para. 224, 231, 242)
[c]If the supplier may determine from which physical outlet the buyer resells, then the supplier may—a fortiori—also determine that the buyer resells from a physical outlet at all, cf. Bechtold et al. (2023, Vertikal-GVO Art. 4 para. 22: even though this right of the supplier is not the "mirror image" of Article 4(b)(iii) VBER)
[d]Instead of the distribution outlet, the supplier may also determine the place of the warehouse, cf. VGL, para. 224, 231, 242
[e]VGL, para. 224 (for exclusive distribution), para. 162, 231, 236 (for selective distribution) and para. 242 (for free distribution). This can be further amended, e.g. with an escape clause as "Opening a new outlet in a different location requires the Supplier's consent."
[f]Wholesalers may seek to escape such restriction imposed by suppliers through vertical integration, cf. for the vastly identical Article (c)(i)(4) Dohrn (2022, Art. 4 para. 107), for Article 4(d)(iv) Maritzen (2022, Art. 4 para. 201)
[g]Cf. ECJ, ECLI:EU:C:1977:167 (Metro) para. 23 and 28, while limiting the clause to prohibiting sales to end users would be closer to Article 4 VBER
[h]Suppliers do not have to make an "all-or-nothing" decision; different view, at least for Article 4(c)(i)(5): Bechtold et al. (2023, Vertikal-GVO, Art. 4 para. 30): They may allow wholesalers to sell to specific end users and block others, cf. VGL, para. 225, 232 and 243, observing, however, Article 6 Geo-blocking Regulation
[i]I.e. any intermediate goods (VGL, para. 226), i.e. any goods "for use as an input to produce other goods (. . .) [and that] are generally not recognisable in the final goods" (VGL, para. 287)
[j]It does not cover the supply of spare parts, cf. German Federal Court, decision of 6 October 2015, Case No. KZR 87/13 ("Porsche-Tuning"), para. 94
[k]This exception concerns multi-level-distribution. The exception's rationale is to foster inter-brand competition, respectively avoid hold-up issues which might arise if distributors would also supply the supplier's competitors and at the same time make best use of the supplier's production capacities, cf. Wijckmans and Tuytschaever (2018, para. 6.228). Care must be taken to comply also with Article 2(4) VBER, cf. Maritzen (2022, Art. 4 para. 205)
[l]Possibly amended e.g. by "provided that it also operates at least one physical outlet" ("brick and mortar clause"), which suppliers may impose regardless of the type of distribution system, cf. VGL, para. 208(d)
[m]Cf. VGL, para. 208(c) and para. 332–342 on online marketplace bans, taking up the Coty decision by the ECJ, ECLI:EU:C:2017:941 para. 62 et seq., 69, and para. 343–353 on restrictions on the use of price comparison services

guarantee service for used watches. As, however, only the selected distributors can have their watches certified, this aims at guiding the second-hand business in an official direction.[107]

- "terminating the supply of products" or "threatening to terminate the agreement",[108] at least according to the Vertical Guidelines; before amounting to an agreement or concerted practice in the meaning of Article 101(1) TFEU, such acts require additional elements. Said line will be crossed if the distributor objectively understands that (i) the supplier expects a certain price-setting behaviour, (ii) the distributor must expect a disadvantage in the event of non-fulfilment ("managing volumes differently", "cancelling orders") or an advantage in the event of fulfilment (e.g. "price maintenance discount", margin guarantee) and (iii) the distributor follows such expectations, or if the communication or other exchange of opinions turns into an agreement or concerted practice (e.g., in the case of data exchange not only of past but also of future pricing or recourse to the data records of the same third-party provider).[109]

All in all, the territory or customer restrictions **must avoid the blacklisted provisions** in order to be block exempt.

All these restrictions can be introduced into any vertical agreement where the parties' market shares fall short of or equal 30%—as the respective rules occur repeatedly throughout Article 4(b)-(d) VBER. Hence though Article 4 VBER has been split, distinguishing the territory and customer restrictions per each distribution system, the exemptions can be summarized for all—which might consider shortening Article 4 VBER again when creating the next update.

4.3 Selective Distribution Systems

Selective distribution systems are defined by the VBER as follows:

Definition "distribution system where the supplier undertakes to sell the contract goods or services, either directly or indirectly, only to distributors[110] selected on the basis of specified criteria and where these distributors undertake not to sell such goods or services to unauthorised distributors within the territory reserved by the supplier to operate that system".[111]

[107] Martel (2022).

[108] VGL, para. 204(c) and (e).

[109] Rohrßen (2020, p. 408).

[110] Ideally, this is read as "... only to such distributors ..." as it would otherwise restrict suppliers to sell also to end customers.

[111] Article 1(1)(g) VBER 2022.

The definition is the same as before in the VBER's predecessor of 2010[112] and largely the same as in the VBER 2790/1999.[113] Just its "location" has been shifted from Article 1(1)(e) to Article 1(1)(g).[114] As before, the selective distribution system (or "SDS") **has three requirements**: (i) while the supplier only sells to selected distributors, (iii) with the selection taking place according to specified criteria,[115] (iii) the distributors in turn must cross-supply only other selected distributors.

As before, the definition includes both quantitative and qualitative selective distribution, i.e. distribution systems whose selective criteria are of quantitative (imposing a maximum number of distributors) or qualitative (imposing substantive requirements) nature.[116] Also, as before, the hardcore restrictions (Article 4 VBER[117]) as well as the excluded restrictions in form of non-compete clauses tailored to certain competing suppliers (Article 5(1)(c) VBER) continue to apply.

4.3.1 What's New for Selective Distribution?

Under the VBER 2022, suppliers

- may[118] now **pass on active and passive sales restrictions further down the distribution chain** to protect the selective distribution system—not limited only to the distributor's customers, but all the way down the distribution chain (and thus different from exclusive distribution systems).
- may **impose different criteria for online/offline sales** in selective distribution systems, provided the criteria do not aim at preventing the effective use of the internet. Thus, suppliers may for example require specific quality standards for online sales, such as setting up an online after-sales helpdesk or require secure payment systems.

---

[112] Article 1(1) (e) VBER 2010.

[113] Article 1(d) VBER 1999, compared to which the VBER 2010 specified that distributors undertake not to sell to unauthorised distributors "within the territory reserved by the supplier to operate that system".

[114] The definition in Article 1(1)(d) VBER 1999 was almost the same; the VBER 2010 added the last part "within the territory reserved by the supplier to operate that system" to clarify that restricting cross-supplies is only exempt concerning unauthorised buyers within the territory; cf. Bechtold et al. (2014, Vertikal-GVO Art. 1 para. 33; in the subsequent 2023 edition, para. 35 accidentally still called "new"). The clause also confirms that suppliers may operate different distribution systems in parallel in the European market.

[115] Regardless of what the criteria relate to, also sustainability criteria that do not necessarily relate directly to the goods—thus in contrast to the stricter definition of qualitative selective distribution systems in Article 5(2) Swiss VertBek.

[116] VGL, para. 144.

[117] Which continue to refer to the "restriction of . . . the customers", while the Draft VBER foresaw to change it—as in the VBER 2010 German version—to "restriction of . . . the customer groups".

[118] Actually: shall pass on as the definition of selective distribution systems requires the supplier not to sell directly or indirectly to non-selected distributors.

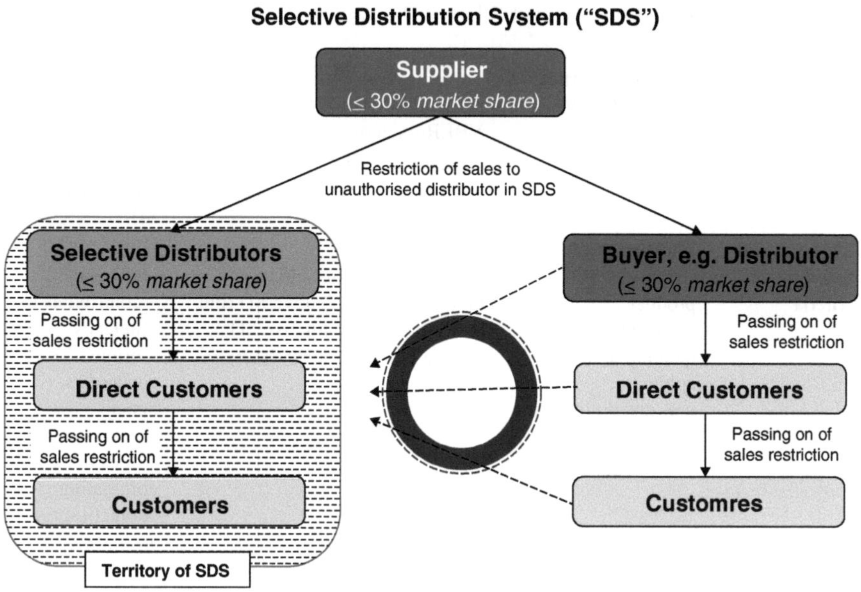

Fig. 4.3 Selective distribution systems

A selective distribution system can therefore be built up as shown in Fig. 4.3.

4.3.2 How to Escape Article 101 TFEU Under the Metro Criteria

If selective distribution systems fulfil the so-called "Metro criteria" of the ECJ,[119] they already do fall outside Article 101(1) TFEU[120]—because they are presumed to enhance inter-brand competition and thus outweigh the restriction of intra-brand competition arising out of selective distribution. The overview in Table 4.3 shows the options for suppliers under both regimes, the "Metro criteria" and the VBER:

Attention must be paid—and therefore it is always worth looking left and right—to the market structure because the benefit of the VBER may be withdrawn, especially in cases where cumulative effects of parallel networks of similar agreements **restrict and/or foreclose the market.**[121] This may explicitly be the case where several suppliers in one market apply selective distribution.[122] As a **rule of thumb**: The stronger the position of the competitor(s) without selective distribution, the less likely market foreclosure will occur.

[119] See above and, specifically on selective distribution and online sales restrictions in the light of the "Coty" case, Rohrßen (2016, p. 279 et seq.); Rohrßen (2018c, p. 306); Rohrßen (2018a, p. 41).

[120] As the Vertical Guidelines reconfirm, VGL, para. 148.

[121] Article 6 VBER.

[122] VGL, para. 155.

Table 4.3 Competition Compliance of Selective Distribution

	SD outside Article 101 TFEU ("Metro" criteria)	SD inside Article 101 TFEU, VBER-exempt	SD inside Article 101(1) TFEU, efficiency defence
Scope	Qualitative SD	– Qualitative SD – Quantitative SD	– Qualitative SD – Quantitative SD
Requirements for selection criteria	Three requirements: – required by product – objectively qualitative and applied non-discriminatorily – necessary	One requirement: – applied non-discriminatorily, otherwise no qualitative SD (but possibly still quantitative SD[a]); criteria need not be necessary	Four requirements[b]: – contributes to efficiency – brings consumers benefit – necessary – does not allow eliminating competition
Market share	Allowed from the outset	Maximum 30%[c]	No limits
Consequence	Allowed from the outset	Block-Exempt, provided no hardcore restriction[d]	Individually Exempt

[a]Bechtold et al. (2023, Vertikal-GVO, Art. 1 para. 43)
[b]For guidance on the individual assessment of selective distribution agreements, see VGL, para. 153–164. Most importantly, cumulative effects of which lead to market foreclosure must be considered and avoided
[c]Article 3(1) VBER
[d]Whose overarching principle for selective distribution systems is not to restrict sales to end users, cf. Article 4(c)(i) and (iii), cf. Bechtold et al. (2023, Vertikal-GVO, Art. 1 para. 25)

Accordingly, the exemption under the VBER has a **broader scope** as it exempts selection distribution agreements regardless of the need of the criteria, as long as they are applied in a non-discriminatory manner. Also, the criteria may relate to other issues than the product, e.g. sustainability of services related.

4.3.3 How to Set Up Selective Distribution?

Selective distribution systems have been trending much under the previous VBER because they allow suppliers to exert control over their distributors, keeping them on a short leash by establishing clear criteria for sales. Controlling said criteria is key—not only because it usually takes years to build a reputation, but minutes to ruin it,[123]

[123] A quote often attributed to Warren Buffett, however without a clear source.

but especially because a discriminatory selection may lead to **losing the benefit of the VBER**.[124]

As a "collateral" consequence, selective distribution often comes along with **higher costs** for the distributors arising from compliance with the criteria, e.g. maintaining a brick and mortar store, possibly even in a high street, employing and training staff on the products, ensuring the quality of sales and after-sales, etc.

The selective distribution system must be[125] protected against active and passive sales to unauthorised distributors by the supplier's selective distributors (Article 4(c)(i) second hyphen VBER), (ii) exclusive distributors[126] (Article 4(b)(ii) VBER) and (iii) all other buyers (Article 4(d)(ii) VBER). In order to further ensure the "closed nature of selective distribution systems",[127] the VBER now allows the supplier to **pass on** such customer restriction to the distributor's direct and indirect customers, i.e. the entire supply chain downwards (unlike in exclusive distribution systems, see above). Though beyond the wording of Article 4(c) VBER but in line with the definition of selective distribution systems, suppliers are not only entitled but also obliged to "**close the system**"[128] downwards. This interpretation is based on two reasons: First, on a literal interpretation of Article 1(1)(g) VBER ("...the supplier undertakes to sell, either directly or indirectly, only to distributors selected ...") and second, on a purposive interpretation of selective distribution.

In a multilevel-distribution system, the selection criteria do not need to be identical on each level[129]—and usually, they will not be either: While the importer or wholesaler will have a rather small set of criteria, focusing on the experience in the specific sector, the retailer will be the one with the most specific criteria, from presentation of the goods to after-sales services. The checklist in Table 4.4 shows how to ensure that a selective distribution system complies with competition law:

4.3.4 Sustainability as Selection Criterion

Sustainability is, along with digitalisation and a "resilient Single Market", "a **core principle**" and "a priority objective for the policies of the Union".[130] Whereas sustainability includes climate change, a limited use of natural resources, reduced

[124] Bechtold et al. (2023, Vertikal-GVO, Art. 1 para. 43).

[125] This very protection against active sales intruding into the exclusive territory is constitutive for exclusive distribution systems, cf. its definition in Article 1(1)(h) VBER.

[126] Which per definition must be from another territory; establishing a mixed selective-exclusive distribution system in the same territory/vis-à-vis the same customers covering the same products/services continues to be not block-exempt, cf. VGL, para. 236.

[127] Cf. VGL, para. 223.

[128] Cf. Bechtold et al. (2023, Vertikal-GVO, Art. 4 para. 27) as regards cross-supplies; the same argument applies to the passing on of customer restrictions.

[129] Schultze et al. (2019, para. 273) (in relation to Article 1(e) VBER 2010).

[130] VGL, para. 8.

Table 4.4 Checklist selective distribution

Step	Selective distribution
1	Restriction of competition?
	• **Qualitative criteria:** Lawful because no restriction of competition if required by product, objective, applied non-discriminatorily and necessary ("Metro" criteria)—see the checklist in Chapter 9
	• **Quantitative criteria:** Generally prohibited because (intended) restriction of competition.
2	**Appreciable restriction of competition?**
	Appreciable if restriction by object, if not of minor importance
3	**Appreciable effect on trade?**
	Not appreciable if not affecting trade: ≤5% market share and turnover ≤EUR 40 million (if not appreciable, test national competition law).
4	**Exemption under Vertical Block Exemption Regulation orMotor Vehicle Block Exemption Regulation (aftermarket[a])?**
	In particular: • Market shares ≤ 30% • Absence of hardcore restrictions Article 4 VBER) Especially the following principles apply: – Cross-supplies in the selective distribution system ("SDS") must remain free, – supplies outside the SDS can be prohibited, supplies to end users must not be restricted (except for wholesalers[b])
5	**Individual exemption under Article 101(3) TFEU as last resort?**
	Efficiency benefits, whereof consumers participate, restrictions of competition indispensable and no elimination of competition

[a]Cf. Article 5 MVBER prevails
[b]Article 4(c)(i)(4) VBER

waste and animal welfare.[131] Suppliers may include selection criteria which strive to achieve said objectives[132]—which is already clear from the definition of selective distribution systems in Article 1(3) VBER as it does not require the selection criteria to be based on the product in question.

Regardless of selective distribution, the benefits derived under a vertical agreement may be taken into consideration within the efficiency defence under Article 101(3) TFEU. This may e.g. be the case where a supplier requires a non-compete exceeding the basic five years of Article 5(1)(a) VBER because it is indispensable for the supplier to make its investment and thus avoid the—otherwise existing—hold-up problem.[133]

[131]VGL, para. 8.
[132]VGL, para. 144.
[133]VGL, para. 316.

4.3.5 Restricting Cross-Supplies: How to Reduce Grey-Market Sales

Selective distribution systems, to be outside Article 101(1) TFEU or exempt under the VBER, require the supplier to sell the contract goods or services only to authorised (selected) distributors, who in turn undertake not to sell such goods or services to unauthorised distributors within the territory reserved by the supplier to operate that system.[134]

At the same time, cross-supplies between the members of the selective distribution system (regardless at which level of trade they operate) must not be restricted,[135] both by other selected distributors—and possibly by the supplier. This is at least what the new wording on the freedom of system-internal cross-supplies suggests[136] as it now refers to cross-supplies between the members of the selective distribution system, while its predecessor referred to cross-supplies "between distributors within a selective distribution system".[137] The Commission, however, reads its Article 4 VBER as relating to its "selected" members, i.e. the distributors only: It actually defines the "members of a selective distribution system" as 'authorised distributors'.[138] That means that suppliers may under the VBER agree with distributors that the suppliers refrain from direct deliveries to retailers.

If a supplier opts for the new, extended concept of selective distribution, the respective clause in the exclusive distributorship agreement could be as follows:

Example

Negative Version:

The Distributor shall not sell the contract goods to resellers not authorised by the Supplier.[139] The Distributor shall pass on this restriction to its customers and shall oblige each customer to pass on this restriction itself along the distribution chain, including the obligation to pass on this obligation, except to the end user who is a consumer. ◀

[134] Cf. the "Metro" criteria in ECLI:EU:C:1977:167 (Metro) para. 27 ("To be effective, any marketing system based on the selection of outlets necessarily entails the obligation upon wholesalers forming part of the network to supply only appointed resellers ...."), respectively the definition of "selective distribution system" in Article 1(1)(g) VBER.

[135] Article 4(c)(ii) VBER.

[136] Cf. Dohrn (2022, Art. 4 para. 116).

[137] Article 4(d) VBER 2010.

[138] VGL, para. 227.

[139] The clause may be preceded by a clarification on the non-exclusive character of the distribution system, e.g. "The Supplier grants the Distributor the non-exclusive right to distribute the contract goods in the Territory. Non-exclusive means that the Supplier remains entitled to sell the contract goods through other authorized distributors or, in the Supplier's own name, through other sales intermediaries in the Territory."

Example

Positive Version:

The Distributor shall sell the contract products only to end customers and other members of the selective distribution system within the territory where the system is operated. ◀

Example

Long Version. Authorised and Unauthorized Sales:

The Authorised Distributor shall sell[140] the contract goods exclusively to end customers or other Authorised Distributor in the EEA, the UK and Switzerland.

In particular, the Authorised Distributor shall therefore neither directly nor indirectly sell contract goods to

- a reseller, unless the reseller is an Authorised Distributor; or
- a customer using the services of an intermediary, unless the intermediary provides the Authorised Distributor with (i) the original power of attorney issued and signed by the customer prior to the purchase authorising the intermediary to purchase and, if applicable, collect and store the contract good on behalf of the customer, and (ii) such other information as Supplier may reasonably request. The Authorised Distributor shall keep at its place of business all originals of written powers of attorney and all other information relating to contract goods supplied to resellers or through intermediaries to end users during the current calendar year and the three' preceding calendar years.

If the Supplier has factual indications that sales to unauthorised resellers or through unauthorised intermediaries have taken place or will take place, the Authorised Distributor shall provide the Supplier with all information and documents requested by the Supplier which are necessary to enable the Supplier to verify this. If the Supplier so requests, the Authorised Distributor shall discuss all such information with the Supplier.

To the extent that the Authorised Distributor has sold the contract goods to unauthorised resellers or through unauthorised intermediaries, the Supplier may, without prejudice to its right to terminate the contract pursuant to Article [•], require the Authorised Distributor to pay the Supplier:

(a) the total value of the remuneration (including bonuses, if any) received by the Authorised Distributor in connection with such unauthorised sales transactions; and
(b) all remuneration received from programmes in connection with such unapproved sale.

[140] Where required to be combined with single branding, e.g. "… will purchase contract goods from the Supplier and/or another Authorised Distributor in the EEA, the UK and Switzerland, …".

Without the Supplier's prior approval, the Authorised Distributor will not directly or indirectly sell contract goods to:

(a) purchasers established outside the EEA, UK and Switzerland; or
(b) purchasers of which the Authorised Distributor knows or should know by reason of the circumstances that they are exporting or attempting to export, directly or indirectly, contract goods for resale outside the EEA, UK and Switzerland. ◄

4.3.6 Restricting Passive Sales: How to Comply with the Geo-Blocking Regulation

Restrictions of cross-border B2C sales also have to **comply with the Geo-blocking Regulation.**[141] While Article 101(1) TFEU and Article 4(b) VBER prohibit agreements between supplier and buyer to restrict passive sales, the Geo-blocking Regulation deals in principle with unilateral restrictions of access[142]—and in one article also tackles agreements that impose restrictions on passive sales. The Geo-blocking Regulation **prohibits discriminating end users**—both consumers and undertakings[143]—against local customers for nationality, residence or establishment as regards access to online stores and other online interfaces, general terms and conditions, and means of payment (not: the price). In short, end customers shall be able to "**shop like a local**".[144]

The VBER changes the Geo-blocking Regulation insofar as Article 6-(2) Geo-blocking Regulation refers to "passive sales within the meaning of Regulation (EU) No. 330/2010—which, if read as a dynamic reference, now refers to the narrower definition of passive sales under Article 1(1)(l) VBER, compared to the broader definition under the previous Vertical Guidelines.[145] In favour of reading it as a dynamic reference speak both recital no. 34 and Article 6(1) Geo-blocking Regulation as they state that the Geo-blocking Regulation shall leave the EU rules on competition unaffected—which only works if the currently applicable competition rules are applied.[146]

---

[141] Regulation (EU) 2018/302.

[142] Bernhard (2019, p. 472).

[143] Cf. the definition of "customer" in Article 2(13) Geo-blocking Regulation.

[144] E.g. European Commission (2020, IP/20/156).

[145] VGL 2010, para. 51: "responding to unsolicited requests from individual customers including delivery of goods or services to such customers", including, according to the Commission, the situation "where a distributor uses a website to sell products" (para. 52), which under the VBER 2022 also the Commission considers active selling where the website uses languages foreign to the distributor's country.

[146] Siegert and Schneider (2022, Art. 6 Geoblocking-VO para. 1).

The Geo-blocking Regulation therefore additionally prohibits agreements on passive sales which "impose obligations on traders to act in breach of the prohibitions laid down in this Regulation regarding access to online interfaces, access to goods or services and payment"[147]—which under the EU competition rules will only work in selective distribution[148] and by way of exception to Article 101(1) TFEU, possibly in the case of so-called genuine testing where suppliers test a new product on a limited market.[149] The example given by the EU is a contractual restriction "that prevent(s) a trader from responding to unsolicited requests from individual customers for the sale of goods, without delivery, outside the trader's contractually allocated territory for reasons related to customers' nationality, place of residence or place of establishment."[150] This means that suppliers and buyers must not rely only on the VBER; vertical agreements imposing restrictions on passive sales must—**additionally**[151]—comply with the Geo-blocking Regulation.

As a result, suppliers can continue to set up or have their distributors or other distribution intermediaries set up local online stores, in local languages and local currency. They may reroute customers—with their consent. However, they **must not block** nor require their distributors or other distribution intermediaries to block the access to such **store because of any of the three aspects: nationality, residence or establishment**.

4.3.7 Territory and Customer Restrictions: Summary

As regards territory and customer restrictions vis-à-vis selective distributors in general, the same rules apply (see above). **Exempt** are only the restrictions listed in Table 4.5.

4.4 Free Distribution

Free distribution systems are defined by the Vertical Guidelines as follows:

▶ **Definition** Any other type of distribution than selective and exclusive distribution.[152]

[147] Geo-blocking Regulation, Recital no. 34.

[148] Cf. Article 4(b)(ii), (c)(i)(2) and (d)(ii) VBER.

[149] VGL, para. 184 – where, however, the Commission sees genuine testing as falling outside Article 101(1) if the distributor's *active* sales outside the territory are restricted.

[150] Geo-blocking Regulation, Recital no. 34.

[151] Siegert and Schneider (2022, Art. 6 Geoblocking-VO para. 2); Maritzen (2022, Vertikal-GVO, Art. 4 par. 69).

[152] VGL, para. 116; see also Article 4(d) VBER ("where the supplier operates neither an exclusive distribution system nor a selective distribution system").

Table 4.5 Territory and Customer Restrictions in Selective Distribution

Restricting ...		Passing on?
The buyer's	Active sales into exclusive territories or to exclusive customer groups,	The buyer's direct customers
	Sales (active and passive) to unauthorized distributors in territories where a selective distribution system for these goods/ services is operated,	The buyer's customers, all down the distribution chain
	The buyer's place of establishment,[a]	No
	sales (active and passive) by wholesalers to end users,[b]	No
	Sales (active or passive) of components[c] deemed for incorporation, to the supplier's competitors,	No
	Online sales, including online advertising, as far as this does not prevent the effective use of the internet for selling nor have as object closing the entire online advertising.	No, explicitly prohibited ("effective use of the internet by the buyer or its customers")
The supplier's	Sales of components as spare parts to end users or service providers not entrusted by the buyer.	No

[a]Referring only to "outlets where direct sales take place" (ECJ, EUCLI:C:2011:649 (Pierre Fabre), para 56), specifically only to "physical" and not to virtual outlets (cf. VGL, para. 231)
[b]Thus, keeping the wholesale and retail levels separate, cf. VGL, para. 225, following the practice of the Commission and the ECJ in the Metro case. Schultze et al. (2019, para. 755). At least within selective distribution, this reads as an ancillary restraint, cf., ECLI:EU:C:1977:167 (Metro) para. 27
[c]I.e. any intermediate goods (VGL, para. 226), i.e. any goods "for use as an input to produce other goods (...) [that] are generally not recognisable in the final goods" (VGL, para. 287)

The Vertical Guidelines insofar simply stress the supplier's freedom if and which distribution system to set up: "A supplier is free to organise the distribution of its goods or services as it sees fit."[153] This goes from selling through the supplier's own salesforce (employees) over vertically integrated distributors (which, as connected undertakings in terms of Article 1(2) VBER are outside of Article 101 TFEU) to commercial agents (again, free from Article 101 TFEU if "genuine", i.e. bearing no significant risks) and independent distributors—which are subject to Article 101 TFEU and agreements with which can be exempt under the VBER.

[153]VGL, para. 115.

Table 4.6 Exceptions from hardcore restrictions in free distribution

Restricting . . .		Passing on?
The buyer's	Active sales into exclusive territories or to exclusive customer groups,	The buyer's direct customers
	Sales (active and passive) to unauthorized distributors in territories where a selective distribution system for these goods/ services is operated,	The buyer's customers, all down the distribution chain
	The buyer's place of establishment,[a]	No
	Sales (active and passive) by wholesalers to end users,[b]	No
	Sales (active or passive) of components[c] deemed for incorporation, to the supplier's competitors,	No
	Online sales, including online advertising, as far as this does not prevent the effective use of the internet for selling nor have as object closing the entire online advertising.	No, explicitly prohibited ("effective use of the internet by the buyer or its customers"[d])
The supplier's	Sales of components as spare parts to end users or service providers not entrusted by the buyer.	No

[a]Referring only to "outlets where direct sales take place" (ECJ, EUCLI:C:2011:649 (Pierre Fabre), para 56), specifically only to "physical" and not to virtual outlets (cf. VGL, para. 231)
[b]Thus, keeping the wholesale and retail levels separate, cf. VGL, para. 225, following the practice of the Commission and the EJC in the Metro case, cf. Schultze (2019, para. 755)
[c]I.e. any intermediate goods (VGL, para. 226), i.e. any goods "for use as an input to produce other goods (. . .) and [that] are generally not recognisable in the final goods" (VGL, para. 287)
[d]Article 4(e) VBER

4.4.1 What's New for Free Distribution?

Free distribution now has its own paragraph of hardcore restrictions in Article 4 (d) VBER. As free distribution is defined negatively by not being exclusive or selective distribution, it lacks a characteristic set of restrictions which make free distribution stand out from other distribution systems. Therefore, the five hardcore restrictions Article 4(d) VBER stipulates are but a repetition of the two hardcore restrictions which are specific for exclusive (i) and selective (ii) distribution respectively plus the three general hardcore restrictions (place of establishment, wholesaler's sales to end users and buyer's sales of components as spare parts).

4.4.2 Which Hardcore Restrictions to Avoid in Free Distribution?

As regards territory and customer restrictions vis-à-vis selective distributors in general, the same rules apply (see above). **Exempt** are only the restr4-6.ictions listed in Table 4.6:

4.5 Internet Sales and Advertising Restrictions

As expected, the VBER 2022 and the accompanying Vertical Guidelines address the platform economy.[154] The VBER now explicitly covers **restrictions on online sales**. As a **rule of thumb**, the primary guideline remains: Manufacturers/suppliers must not prevent the "effective use of the internet" as sales or advertising channel. For online marketplace restrictions, the hardcore restriction now codifies, according to the Vertical Guidelines, the Coty decision by the European Court of Justice,[155] hence the discussions as to whether third party platform bans are exempt appears to be "dead", while discussions will continue to with regard to advertising restrictions: Which restrictions are exempt – and which are not because they have the object of preventing the use of an entire online advertising channel?

4.5.1 What's New for Digital Distribution?

The **entire hardcore restriction** on internet advertising and sales restrictions is new. So far, restrictions of digital distribution were reviewed against the existing hardcore restrictions, which applied regardless of the sales channel used.

The new hardcore restriction, which focuses on the "effective use" is to be read with Recital 15, which does not require an effects analysis ("shall not depend on the market-specific circumstances or the individual characteristics of the parties"[156]). Such effects analysis would also go beyond the scope of the block exemption. Instead, the hardcore restriction is to be measured solely against the content and context of the restriction: It must neither prevent the effective use of the internet for advertising or sales—in other words, the use of internet must not, neither legally nor "de facto", be prohibited.[157] Example for such "de facto" or indirect prohibition has been the French supplier of cosmetics and personal care products Pierre Fabre, where "the requirement that a qualified pharmacist must be present at a physical sales point de facto prohibits the authorised distributors from any form of internet selling."[158] Whereas dual pricing—i.e. setting different wholesale prices for goods sold online versus offline—may now be exempt, especially where it shall support investments in one or the other sales channel.

The new hardcore restriction is also to be read together with the new, broader definition of active sales in Article 1(1)(l) VBER, according to which "operating a website with a top-level domain corresponding to particular territories, or offering on a website languages that are commonly used in particular territories, where such languages are different from the ones commonly used in the territory in which the

[154] Cf. Rohrßen (2019, p. 345 at footnote 88 et seq.).

[155] VGL, para. 208 footnote 133; para. 332 et seq.

[156] VBER, Recital 15.

[157] VGL, para. 203.

[158] Cf. ECJ, ECLI:EU:C:2011:649 (Pierre Fabre) para. 14, 37, 38, 42, 54, 58, 59.

buyer is established" are active sales—which can be restricted especially in exclusive distribution. Accordingly, suppliers may in principle also restrict the use of third-party websites and language options on the distributors' own websites.

Finally, the new hardcore restriction is to be read also with the new Vertical Guidelines, especially para. 203 et seq. with their overview of Article 4(e) VBER (para. 203), examples of indirect obligations which may result in hardcore restrictions, both in general (para. 204–205) and concretely for online sales (para. 206), quality requirements, both in general (para. 207) and online (para. 208, 222, 235 with focus on selective distribution), dual pricing (para. 209), online advertising restrictions (para. 210), online stores as passive sales (212), online language options as active sales (para. 213–214), restrictions on the use of online marketplaces (para. 332–342), and restrictions on the use of price comparison services (para. 343–355). Together with the Vertical Guidelines, the new hardcore restriction provides more legal certainty than before for assessing online sales and advertising restrictions.

4.5.2 The Principle: Maintain the Effective Use of the Internet

Article 4(e) VBER prohibits the supplier to prevent the effective use of the internet by the buyer or its customers to sell the contract goods or services—"as it restricts the territory into which or the customers to whom the contract goods or services may be sold within the meaning of points (b), (c) or (d)". Article 4(e) VBER thereby reveals both

- its **rationale**, which is to avoid territory or customer restrictions by blocking the internet as an advertising and sales channel, which would be the effect of internet sales restrictions.[159]
- its **material scope**: The hardcore restriction applies to all types of distribution, exclusive, selective or free.

Article 4 **blacklists** any vertical agreements "which, directly or indirectly, in isolation or in combination with other factors under the control of the parties, have as their object" to restrict the effective internet use. "Direct" restraints are the most obvious ones, especially prohibiting (i) the use of internet as sales channel, as in the Pierre Fabre case where the supplier required that "sales must be made exclusively in a physical space, in which a qualified pharmacist must be present",[160] prohibiting to operate through online stores or requiring the supplier's prior authorization. Or (ii) generally prohibiting the use of search engines or price comparison services.

Blacklisted as **"indirect" restraints** are especially[161] vertical agreements which:

[159] VGL, para. 202, which sums up the territory and customer restrictions of Article 4(b), (c) and (d) VBER.

[160] ECJ, ECLI:EU:C:2011:649 (Pierre Fabre) para. 12.

[161] Examples from VGL, para. 206. Further examples in the overview by Bortolotti and Bortolotti (2023, p. 85 et seq.).

- have the object of significantly diminishing the aggregate volume of online sales of the contract goods or services;
- prevent the use of one or more entire online advertising channels (e.g. "no search engines", "no price comparison services", "no own online store").[162]

Examples of indirect restraints include:

- obliging the buyer to geo-block or reroute customers (including blocking or terminating payment transactions);
- prohibiting the buyer to use the supplier's trademarks or brand names on its website or online store, as in the case of the fashion brand Guess, fined for competition law infringements by the Commission,[163]
- prohibiting the buyer to use an entire online advertising channel, by prohibiting the use of the supplier's trademark or brand names for engaging in search engine optimization or other marketing or providing price-related information to price comparison services.

Article 4(e) VBER nevertheless provides for two exceptions, one for online sales and one for online advertising.

4.5.3 First Re-exception: Restrictions of Online Sales

Suppliers may impose "other restrictions of online sales" as they may be exempt according to Article 4(e)(i) VBER. The line between exempted and non-exempted restrictions, which must not be crossed, is the "**effective use of the internet**" by buyers and their customers.

Whitelisted and thus **exempt** are regularly the following agreements (whereby it must be ensured in the single case that the above line is not crossed, especially in combination with other restrictions):

- **Quality requirements**:
  Suppliers may set up quality requirements relating to offline and online sales, including on the appearance of an online store or the display of contract goods or services in the online store, the supplier's trademark etc.

[162] Cf. VGL, para. 206, listing seven examples of obligations that indirectly have the object of preventing the effective use of the internet.

[163] European Commission, Case AT.40428 (Guess), 17 December 2018, para. 45: Guess Europe systematically banned its authorised retailers, both mono-brand and multi-brand retailers, from using or bidding on Guess brand names and trademarks as keywords in Google AdWords in the EEA, thus restricting the distribution intermediary's findability, maximizing traffic on the supplier's website(s) and minimizing its advertising costs.

- **Online marketplace bans**:
  What has been discussed and disputed for many years,[164] shall now be exempt, regardless of which goods are concerned (luxury [165] or other) and regardless of which distribution system is operated. However, the Vertical Guidelines keep a tiny door open as they stipulate that the general ban of online marketplaces "can", [166] in principle, benefit from the exemption" of Article 2(1) VBER. This goes as far as other online sales channels including an own online store are available as means of internet sales to the buyer. The Commission insofar recognises that search engine optimisation together with the—necessarily[167]—open online advertising allows to increase visibility[168] and thus safeguards the effective use of the internet for sales. Therefore, general marketplace bans are generally exempt.

  Online marketplace bans may already fall out of the scope of Article 101 TFEU (if selective distribution complies with the "Metro criteria") or may be block exempt, irrespective of the distribution system (if the ban does not have the object of preventing the effective use of the internet as sales channel, which "in principle" (VGL, para. 336, i.e. with exceptions is not the case where the buyer remains free to operate its own online store and advertise online), cf. VGL, para. 150 and para. 208, 334 et seq.
- **Brick and mortar clauses**:
  Requiring one or more physical stores is, as before,[169] exempt, including the requirement to sell a certain minimum absolute amount (no proportion of the total sales).
- **Dual pricing**:
  Dual pricing refers to wholesalers have to pay a different price to their suppliers, depending on whether they resell the goods offline or online.[170] In contrast to the VBER 2010, such dual pricing is now exempt—always minding not to cross the line that such dual pricing does not have the object of restricting sales to particular territories or customers. Moreover, the boarder not to cross: the wholesale price must not make selling online unprofitable or unsustainable,[171] as it would otherwise have the same object as a total internet sales ban.

---

[164] Cf. Rohrßen (2019, p. 343); Rohrßen (2018b, p. 282); Rohrßen (2017, p. 281); Rohrßen (2016, p. 284).

[165] As the position taken by the German Bundeskartellamt after the Coty case, cf. Rohrßen (2018b, p. 278); Wegner et al. (2022, p. 273).

[166] VGL, para. 208, 335.

[167] Article 4(e)(ii) VBER, see below.

[168] VGL, para. 336.

[169] VGL 2010, para. 52(c) and para. 54.

[170] VGL, para. 209.

[171] VGL, para. 209.

4.5.4 Second Re-Exception: Restrictions of Online Advertising

Suppliers may also impose "**restrictions of online advertising**" as they may be exempt, too, according to Article 4(e)(ii) VBER, provided they do not have the object of preventing the use of an entire advertising channel.

Whitelisted and thus **exempt** are regularly the following agreements:

- **Quality standards:**
  As suppliers may set up quality standards in general, they may all the more set up quality standards for advertising online.
- **Prohibiting the use of particular online providers:**
  Suppliers may have buyers refrain from using a concrete online advertising provider (e.g. a search engine, price comparison tool, social media service or influencer [172]). This goes, according to the Vertical Guidelines, at least where such provider fails to meet specific quality standards. However, the wording of Article 4(e)(ii) VBER does not set up such requirement so that suppliers may in principle, also without referring to specific quality standards, prohibit the use of one (or more) particular providers—provided that the concrete providers do not make up a large part of the market since the above line of not "preventing the use of an entire online advertising channel" may be crossed. As a rule of thumb: the more providers are prohibited or the higher their market share is, the closer such prohibition comes to crossing the line to the hardcore restriction. In an extreme case, where one provider dominates the market, the line will therefore arguably already be crossed where the supplier prohibits the use of that provider.

Contract Drafting Advice
Such rationale should be explicitly stipulated in the contract or annex containing the online sales and advertising guidelines as giving the reasoning makes any prohibition more acceptable to the buyer. Suppliers will anyway rely on specific rationale in the single case when deciding for such a restriction.

- Domain name restrictions:
  Suppliers may require the buyers not to use the suppliers' brand name as part of the domain name of its online store. The line to the hardcore restriction would be crossed where suppliers prohibit any use of the brand name, on the website and anywhere else.

[172] As to the legal quality of influencer marketing in terms of German distribution law cf. Höving (2023).

Fig. 4.4 Aftermarket Scenario

Supplier
↓
Buyer
(OEM or other[616])
↓
Customer

4.5.5 Third (Unwritten) Re-Exception: System-Specific Restrictions

Finally, suppliers are free to establish restrictions along the hardcore restrictions of the respective distribution system. This follows from a systematic interpretation of the single hardcore restrictions and also follows from Article 1(1)(l) which defines "active sales" as including operating websites with top-level domains or in languages for particular territories or customers. As far as the supplier has set up exclusive territories or customer groups, the supplier may restrict active sales into exclusive territories/to exclusive customer groups—and thereby restrict online sales, too (see above Sect. 4.2.2).

4.6 Aftermarket Restrictions: Sale of Components as Spare Parts

Finally, Article 4(f) VBER **blacklists** also a restriction imposed on (not: by) the supplier: Suppliers of components[173] and their buyers who incorporate said components, must not agree to restrict suppliers in selling the components as spare parts to end users and independent[174] repairers, wholesalers or other service providers. Such aftermarket scenario is shown in Fig. 4.4.

In practice, this hardcore restriction is relevant especially in the automotive industry.[175] For the automotive aftermarket, however, the industry-specific hardcore restriction in Article 5(b)[176] of the Motor Vehicle Block Exemption Regulation ("MVBER") prevails,[177] which is more restrictive than Article 4(f) VBER as the effective competition on the markets for purchase and sale of automotive spare parts requires, according to the Commission, an unrestricted access to essential inputs such as spare parts and technical information.[178]

[173] Any kind of suppliers, both manufacturers and resellers, cf. Ellger (2019, Art. 4 para. 114 on the VBER 2010).

[174] Independent because "not entrusted by the buyer".

[175] Bechtold et al. (2023, Vertikal-GVO, Art. 4 para. 49).

[176] "The exemption provided for in Article 4 shall not apply to vertical agreements which, . . . have as their object: . . . (b) the restriction, agreed between a supplier of spare parts, repair tools or diagnostic or other equipment and a manufacturer of motor vehicles, of the supplier's ability to sell those goods to authorised or independent distributors or to authorised or independent repairers or end users; . . .".

[177] Cf. Article 2(7) last sentence VBER together with Article 4(1) MVBER.

[178] Recital 13 MVBER.

4.6.1 What's New for Aftermarket Restrictions?

The answer to the above question is short: not much—only "**wholesalers**" have now been explicitly added to Article 4(f) VBER. That means: The VBER now also blacklists the restriction of supplier's sales to wholesalers for the mere resale.[179] This general hardcore aftermarket restriction has thus been aligned closer to the corresponding automotive-specific hardcore restriction in Article 5(b) MVBER which prohibits to restrict sales to distributors or repairers (both regardless if authorised or independent[180]) and end users.

Already the VBER 1999 contained almost the same hardcore restriction in its Article 4(e).[181] Since Article 4(e) VBER 2010, which was subject to mere grammatical changes,[182] it has been existing in its current wording. Its objective also remains the same: it shall protect "independent repairers, wholesalers and service providers"[183] and ensure their chance to procure original spare parts. It therefore aims at protecting inter-brand competition,[184] avoiding foreclosure in the spare parts aftermarkets.

Corresponding to the unchanged hardcore restriction on spare parts, the Vertical Guidelines deliver only one paragraph,[185] which is almost the same as under the previous Guidelines. Therein, the Vertical Guidelines emphasise again that both direct (e.g. exclusive supply obligations) and—most importantly in practice—indirect restraints fall under this hardcore restriction (e.g. restricting the supply of technical information or special equipment required for the use of spare parts or upfront access payments[186]). Already the introductory sentence of Article 4 VBER makes clear that all hardcore restrictions, including aftermarket restrictions, are prohibited, regardless if direct or indirect.

---

[179] While a restriction on the sale of components to mere resellers was not covered by the hardcore restriction under VBER 2010, cf. Siegert (2022, Vertikal-GVO, Art. 4 para. 221 with further references).

[180] Insofar, Article 5(b) MVBER still reaches further as it (i) covers all kinds of distributors (wholesalers and retailers) and (ii) also prohibits restrictions of sales to the buyer (OEM)'s authorized distributors.

[181] "The exemption ... in Article 2 shall not apply to vertical agreements which ... have as their object: ... (e) the restriction agreed between a supplier of components and a buyer who incorporates those components, which limits the supplier to selling the components as spare parts to end-users or to repairers or other service providers not entrusted by the buyer with the repair or servicing of its goods".

[182] Schultze (2019, Art. 4 para. 956).

[183] VGL, para. 245.

[184] Nolte (2022, Nach Art. 101 para. 580).

[185] VGL, para. 245.

[186] VGL, para. 380.

Table 4.7 Restrictions on suppliers of components

	Subcontracting = Outside Article 101(1) TFEU[a]	No subcontracting = Vertical restraints can be exempt under the VBER
Preconditions	• Supplier entrusted to manufacture goods/services under buyer's instructions • Technology (industrial property rights, secret know-how, studies, plans or documents beyond general information or description) or equipment (dies, patterns or tools or accessory equipment making the goods differ in form, function or composition from competitor' goods) provided by customer for manufacturing, • Technology or equipment provided by customer necessary to enable the supplier under reasonable circumstances to manufacture	• Supplier entrusted to supply components which buyer incorporates • Parties' market shares ≤30% • No hardcore restrictions, especially: – No restriction of the supplier's sales of the goods as spare parts to end users, repairers, wholesalers or other service providers not entrusted by the buyer with repair or servicing
Consequences	The following obligations are outside Article 101(1) TFEU: • to use technology or equipment only for subcontracting, • to keep secret the technology or equipment, during the negotiations, performance of the agreement and after its expiry, as long as not public knowledge, • to supply the goods manufactured by the technology or equipment only to the customer • to pass on any technical improvements made during the term of agreement, including granting a licence on inventions, – non-exclusively if the improvements/inventions can be used independently, – exclusively if the improvements/ inventions can be only used with the customer's secret know-how or patent • to use the customer's trademarks or trade names or get up only for goods supplied to the customer Other obligations: If vertical restraint, see right hand column.	• Vertical restraints are exempt if above preconditions are observed

[a]For the ease of understanding and comparison, the terms in this table have been aligned with the current use of terms under the VBER (e.g. supplier instead of subcontractor, customer instead of contractor)

4.6.2 Aftermarket Hardcore Restriction vs Restriction of Subcontracting

Suppliers of components and their buyers who incorporate said components, must not agree to restrict suppliers in selling the components as spare parts to end users, repairers, wholesalers or other service providers. Such restrictions—specifically obliging the supplier to supply the components only to the very customer may, however, already fall outside Article 101(1) TFEU, provided that the technology or equipment provided by the customer (which must be more than general information/ descriptions of the goods) is necessary to enable the supplier under reasonable circumstances to manufacture the goods. By providing this opportunity, EU competition law solves a hold-up problem, as otherwise undertakings might be reluctant to share their technology or equipment with sub-suppliers unless they could protect such technology or equipment.[187] Such agreements may, however already fall out of Article 101(1) TFEU[188] where the supplier qualifies as a subcontractor and thus is not considered an independent undertaking. The different treatment of restrictions imposed on suppliers is shown in Table 4.7.

4.6.3 Aftermarket Restrictions: Details on Article 4(f) VBER

The hardcore restriction of Article 4(f) VBER aims at ensuring the free supply of end users, independent repairers or other service providers and—new under the VBER 2022—**wholesalers**. In other words: it aims at a free aftermarket for the supply of components as spare parts.

The hardcore restriction broadly **protects** all "**suppliers of components**", i.e. manufacturers and resellers[189] of components. Components include any "intermediate good",[190] while "incorporate" covers any use of any input to produce goods.[191] The supplier must, thus, be free to sell the components as spare parts—also for resale[192]—to independent buyers as far as they act as end users, repairers, wholesalers or other service providers. The rationale behind this is to protect the aftersales market.

The hardcore restriction is addressed to all buyers who incorporate said components—so-called "industrial buyers",[193] often OEMs. They must not restrict their component suppliers to supply the components as spare parts "to end users or to repairers, wholesalers or other service providers not entrusted by the buyer with the

[187] Kerber and Schwalbe (2020, para. 494).
[188] Subcontracting Notice, para. 2.
[189] Ellger (2019, Art. 4 para. 114 on VBER 2010).
[190] VGL, para. 244.
[191] VGL, para. 244.
[192] As Article 4(f) VBER now blacklists also restricting the supplier's sales to wholesalers.
[193] Nolte (2022, Nach Art. 101 para. 585).

Table 4.8 Hardcore restrictions on the aftermarket

General Aftermarket	Difference in scope	Automotive Aftermarket
Sale of components (incorporated by the buyer) as spare parts	<	Sale of equipment (spare parts, repair tools or diagnostic or other equipment)
to • end users • independent[a] – repairers, – wholesalers, – other service providers	<	to • end users • authorised or independent – repairers, – distributors.

[a]Article 4(f) VBER: "... not entrusted by the buyer"

repair or servicing of its goods". This means: Industrial buyers must not require their component suppliers to exclusively supply them (and their authorised service partners). Rather, component suppliers must be free to sell to any end user, repairer, wholesaler or other service provider other than those of the buyer, which includes also service providers authorised by the buyer's competitors. Reversely, the hardcore restriction **allows**:

- restricting sales to third party manufacturers (because they are others than "end users, repairers, wholesalers or other service providers" listed in Article 4(f)) and
- restricting sales to the buyer's authorised service partners (because they have been "entrusted" by the buyer). This is contrary to the automotive aftermarket, where buyers may restrict the suppliers in their sales of spare parts to the industrial buyer's authorised service providers[194] or authorised distributors[195]: The industrial buyers may therefore have their distribution intermediaries commit to an exclusive purchasing obligation—and safeguard it by obliging the spare parts supplier to refrain from supplying the industrial buyer's distribution intermediaries as they are served by the industrial buyer (regularly: the OEM) exclusively. As the following table shows, the spare parts hardcore restriction is stricter in the automotive sector as it encompasses more types of goods and covers more types of customers to whom sales must not be restricted.

The comparison in Table 4.8 between the restriction on spare parts in general versus the restriction on automotive spare parts shows the different scope (whereby "<" means less scope, i.e. more leeway for the agreements; additional elements for the automotive aftermarket are underlined).

A question which frequently comes up: May component suppliers also sell components which are identical with the ones manufactured for the OEM (or other

[194]VGL, para. 245.

[195]Because (i) Article 4(f) VBER does not cover restrictions of spare part sales to the customers' authorised service partners and (ii) it anyway only covers wholesalers, not retailers, compared to the wording of Article 5(b) MVBER, see above.

buyer), made on another production line than the original component, but with a "matching quality" (so-called "identical parts" or "matching quality parts"[196]), provided they do not infringe any intellectual property rights? Or may the buyer (OEM) prohibit the sales of such matching quality parts? The wording of Article 4 (f) VBER just refers to "the components as spare parts"—which may be interpreted as referring only to "the" original components as only those will be incorporated by the buyer (OEM). This is not sufficiently clear. In the light of the hardcore restriction's objective to protect the aftermarket, it makes rather sense to interpret "components" as any kind of such component, as far as it can be used as a spare part.[197]

What buyers may ask from suppliers under Article 4(f) VBER is to refrain from selling to competitors as they do not qualify as repairers, wholesalers or other service providers.[198]

Example

The supplier must not sell the contract products to competitors of the Buyer. ◀

Example

Where a means of production is provided or fully financed by the Buyer, it must not be used for the manufacture of goods for parties other than the Buyer or its Affiliated Undertakings and authorised service partners without the prior express written consent of the Buyer. ◀

Example

Supplier's Obligations in respect of Buyer's Tooling. The Supplier shall: (a) properly keep, store, house and maintain Buyer's Tooling at a designated Supplier Premises as bailee for the Buyer or the Customer (as applicable); (b) not use Buyer Property for any purpose other than for performance of the Contract; (c) use Buyer Property only in compliance with Buyer's or the OEM's instructions and in compliance with all Applicable Laws and not modify or tamper with it, or attach it to anything, or anything to it;[. . .]. ◀

---

[196] Cf. e.g. Communication from the Commission—The Future Competition Law Framework applicable to the motor vehicle sector (Text with EEA relevance) {SEC(2009) 1052} {SEC (2009) 1053} /* COM/2009/0388 final, para. 37.

[197] Bechtold et al. (2023, Vertikal-GVO, Art. 4 para. 48); Siegert (2022, Vertikal-GVO, Art. 4 para. 220).

[198] Zöttl (2020, Vertikal-GVO, Art. 4 para. 150 (on Article 4(e) VBER 2010)).

References

Autohaus (2022) Agenturvertrieb: Was Hersteller und Importeure planen. https://www.autohaus.de/nachrichten/autohandel/was-hersteller-und-importeure-planen-3177844. Accessed 12 Feb 2023

Baron M (2020) 7. Teil.B. Vertikalvereinbarungen. Vert-GVO. In: Loewenheim U et al (eds) Kartellrecht, 4th edn. C.H. Beck, Munich

Bechtold R, Bosch W, Brinker I (2014) EU-Kartellrecht, 3rd edn. C.H. Beck, Munich

Bechtold R, Bosch W, Brinker I (2023) EU-Kartellrecht, 4th edn. C.H. Beck, Munich

Bernhard J (2019) Die Geoblocking-Verordnung in der Praxis. NJW 2019:472–476

Bortolotti F, Bortolotti S (2023) Antitrust rules of the European Union applicable to distribution, available through the International Distribution Institute (Turin)

Bundeskartellamt (2017) Hinweise zum Preisbindungsverbot im Bereich des stationären Lebensmitteleinzelhandels. https://www.bundeskartellamt.de/SharedDocs/Publikation/DE/Diskussions_Hintergrundpapier/Hinweispapier%20Preisbindung%20im%20Lebensmitteleinzelhandel.pdf. Accessed 10 February 2023

Distribution Law Center Countdown XX – Selective distribution (Reverse protection) (2022). https://distributionlawcenter.com/news-analysis/distribution-law-center-countdown-xx-selective-distribution-reverse-protection/. Accessed 10 February 2023

Dohrn D (2022) Vertikal-GVO Art. 4(c). In: Bacher K, Hempel R, Wagner-von Papp F, Beck OK (eds) Kartellrecht, 6th edn. C.H. Beck, Munich

Ellger R (2019) Verordnung (EU) Nr. 330/2010 der Kommission vom 20. April 2010 über die Anwendung von Artikel 101 Absatz 3 des Vertrages über die Arbeitsweise der Europäischen Union auf Gruppen von vertikalen Vereinbarungen und abgestimmten Verhaltensweisen-GVO. In: Immenga U, Mestmäcker E-J (eds) Wettbewerbsrecht, vol. 1, 6th edn. C.H. Beck, Munich

European Commission (2014) Commission Staff Working Document, Guidance on restrictions of competition 'by object' for the purpose of defining which agreements may benefit from the De Minimis Notice. SWD(2014) 1989 final, p. 4. https://ec.europa.eu/competition/antitrust/legislation/de_minimis_notice_annex.pdf. Accessed 10 February 2023

European Commission (2020) Online shopping: Commission and Consumer Protection authorities urge traders to bring information policy in line with EU law. Press release IP/20/156. https://ec.europa.eu/commission/presscorner/detail/en/IP_20_156. Accessed 10 February 2023

European Commission (2021) Summary of the replies of the national competition authorities of the European Competition Network provided during the targeted consultation for the impact assessment of the review of Regulation (EU) No 330/2010, para. II.a (https://ec.europa.eu/competition-policy/system/files/2021-06/VBER_IA_summary_contributions_from_NCAs.pdf). Accessed 10 February 2023

Haberer A, Fries H (2021) Entwurf der neuen Vertikal-GVO – Abschied vom "sicheren Hafen"? NZKart 2021:444–449

Höving M (2023) Das Vertriebsrecht und Social Media: (Wann) sind Influencer Handelsvertreter? ZVertriebsR 2023:Issue 3

Kerber W, Schwalbe U (2020) VII. Vertikale Vereinbarungen, vertikale und konglomerate Zusammenschlüsse. In: Säcker F-J, Karpenstein U, Ludwigs M (eds) Münchener Kommentar zum Wettbewerbsrecht, vol 1/2, 3rd edn. C.H. Beck, Munich. para. 480–572

Lettl T (2013) Informationsaustausch über die Preisgestaltung als vertikale Wettbewerbsbeschränkung. WRP 2013:1272–1279

Maritzen L (2022) Vertikal-GVO Art. 4(a), (b), (d). In: Bacher K, Hempel R, Wagner-von Papp F (eds) BeckOK, Kartellrecht, 6th edn. C.H.Beck, Munich

Martel A (2022) Rolex sagt dem Graumarkt den Kampf an. Neue Zürcher Zeitung 02.09.2022. https://www.nzz.ch/wirtschaft/rolex-lanciert-certified-pre-owned-programm-fuer-gebrauchte-uhren-ld.1714725. Accessed on 9 February 2023

Nolte S (2022) Nach Art. 101 AEUV. In: Langen E, Bunte H-J (eds) Kartellrecht, vol 2, 14th edn. Luchterhand, Munich

Ong B (2021) The Applicability of Art. 101 TFEU to Horizontal Algorithmic Pricing Practices: Two Conceptual Frontiers. IIC 2021:189–211

Plate D (2022a) Ford-Partner Verband: Kündigung und echte Agentur. Autohaus 10/2022 (23 May 2022):12–13

Plate D (2022b) Vertriebs-GVO. Es bleibt beim Trend zur unechten Agentur, Interview with Woltermann A. Autohaus 12/2022 (27 June 2022):12–13

Rahlmeyer D (2015) Welche Vorgaben eines Herstellers für den Onlinevertrieb seiner Produkte sind kartellrechtlich zulässig? ZVertriebsR 2015:144–150

Rohrßen (2016) Plattformverbote im Selektivvertrieb – der EuGH-Vorlagebeschluss des OLG Frankfurt vom 19.4.2016. ZVertriebsR 2016:278–284

Rohrßen B (2017) Internetvertrieb in der EU 2018 ff. – Online-Vertriebsvorgaben von Asics über BMW bis Coty. ZVertriebsR 2017:274–281

Rohrßen B (2018a) Vertriebsvorgaben im E-Commerce 2018: Praxisüberblick und Folgen des "Coty"-Urteils des EuGH. GRUR-Prax 2018:39–41

Rohrßen B (2018b, 2018) Internetvertrieb nach Coty – Von Markenware, Beauty und Luxus: Plattformverbote, Preisvergleichsmaschinen und Geoblocking. ZVertriebsR:277–285

Rohrßen B (2018c) Internetvertrieb von Markenartikeln: Zulässigkeit von Plattformverboten nach dem EuGH-Urteil Coty. DB, 300–306

Rohrßen B (2019) Internetvertrieb 2019/20 – Vertriebsvorgaben, (Best-)Preise & Platform-to-Business-Verordnung. ZVertriebsR 2019:341–347

Rohrßen B (2020) Online-Preisbrecher – Wie Markenhersteller damit umgehen. ZVertriebsR 2020: 406-408

Rohrßen B (2021) Online-Vertrieb in der EU – Vertriebskartellrecht: Die neue Vertikal-GVO 2022. ZVertriebsR 2021:293–298

Schultze J-M, Pautke S, Wagener DS (2019) Vertikal-GVO, Gruppenfreistellungsverordnung für vertikale Vereinbarungen, 4th edn. Deutscher Fachverlag, Frankfurt am Main

Siegert R (2022) Vertikal-GVO Art. 4(f). In: Bacher K, Hempel R, Wagner-von Papp F (eds) BeckOK, Kartellrecht, 6th edn. C.H. Beck, Munich

Siegert R, Schneider R (2022) Art. 6 Geoblocking-VO. In: Bacher K, Hempel R, Wagner-von Papp F (eds) BeckOK Kartellrecht, 6th edn. C.H. Beck, Munich

Spenner K 2nd (2021) Chapter. In: Martinek M, Semler FJ, Flohr E (eds) Formularsammlung Vertriebsrecht, 2nd edn. C.H. Beck, Munich

Stäuber R (2022) Preisbindung durch Preisempfehlung – Urteile des Schweizer Bundesgerichts zu Hors-Liste-Arzneimitteln. NZKart 2022:388–391

Wegner AC, Schwenker B, Altdorf S (2022) Die neue Vertikal-Gruppenfreistellungsverordnung (EU) 2022/720 nebst Vertikal-Leitlinien - Kontinuität und Umbruch in der Vertriebspraxis. ZWeR 2022:243–283

Wijckmans F, Tuytschaever F (2018) Vertical agreements in EU competition law, 3rd edn. Oxford University Press, Oxford

Zöttl J (2020) Vertikal-GVO. In: Säcker F-J, Karpenstein U, Ludwigs M (eds) Münchener Kommentar zum Wettbewerbsrecht, vol 1/2, 3rd edn. C.H. Beck, Munich

Article 5 VBER: Excluded Restrictions—Grey Clauses

5

Abstract Article 5 VBER lists four types of restrictions which are excluded from the benefit of the VBER—and thus called "excluded restrictions", or "grey clauses" as their impact on the agreement is less severe than that of the black clauses in Article 4: Only the grey clauses, as far as they can be severed from the remaining agreement, are excluded from the benefit of the VBER and require an individual assessment instead. There is, however, "no presumption that the obligations listed in Article 5 of the Regulation fall within the scope of Article 101(1) of the Treaty or fail to satisfy the conditions of Article 101(3) of the Treaty" .[1]

5.1 What's New for Grey Clauses?

The wording of the grey clauses has vastly remained the same as under the VBER 2010. Editorial clarifications apart,[2] two things have changed:

- **Evergreening non-competes can be exempt**: Non-competes may now be renewed and yet benefit the VBER. The respective sentence that non-compete obligations which are tacitly renewed beyond a period of 5 years shall be deemed concluded for an indefinite term[3] has been deleted. The Vertical Guidelines now explicitly allow for such renewal.[4]
- **Across-platform retail parity obligations** requested by online intermediation services, as e.g. on the hotel booking platforms, are now **excluded**, i.e. require an

[1] VGL, para. 246.

[2] Using numerals instead of spelling out numbers ("5" instead of "five), adding the word "point" to describe paragraphs initiated with letters, clarifying that the post-term compete requires "all" the conditions of Article 5(3) to be fulfilled.

[3] I.e. the former Article 5(1) Sentence 2 VBER 2010.

[4] VGL, para. 248.

B. Rohrßen, *VBER 2022: EU Competition Law for Vertical Agreements*, Law for Professionals, https://doi.org/10.1007/978-3-031-35024-5_5

individual assessment.[5] The other forms of parity obligations are, however, block exempt.

All in all, Article 5 VBER now lists **four types of grey clauses**: (i) Non-compete obligations, (ii) post-contractual non-competes, (iii) non-compete obligations in selective distribution and, new, (iv) MFN in agreements with online intermediation services.

5.2 Non-compete Obligations, Article 5(1)(a) and (2) VBER

Non-compete obligations are obligations addressed to the buyer. In contrast to the situation under the VBER 2010,[6] non-compete obligations may now also be tacitly extended over a period of 5 years—provided that there are adequate possibilities for termination or renegotiation so that the buyer can withdraw from the non-competition obligation at the end of the 5 years.

Non-compete obligations are defined by Article 1(1)(f) VBER as follows:

▶ **Definition** 'non-compete obligation' means any

- direct or indirect obligation causing the buyer not to manufacture, purchase, sell or resell goods or services which compete with the contract goods or services, or
- any direct or indirect obligation on the buyer to purchase from the supplier or from another undertaking designated by the supplier more than 80% of the buyer's total purchases of the contract goods or services and their substitutes on the relevant market, calculated on the basis of the value or, where such is standard industry practice, the volume of its purchases in the preceding calendar year.

Non-competes accordingly cover both direct obligations such as single purchase obligations (for the contract goods and competing goods) and indirect obligations such as minimum purchase obligations or category management. Moreover, the EU competition law concept of non-competes is broader than its name suggests, as it already kicks in where a buyer is obliged to buy 80% of its contract products and competing products from the supplier. Any scheme which makes the buyer actually buy more than 80% of its required goods or services from one specific supplier is a non-compete. This includes e.g. quantity forcing, in the form of incentives or obligations to concentrate the buyer's purchases in the supplier, minimum purchase requirements, stocking requirements and bonus or non-linear pricing schemes. As

[5] Article 5(d) VBER.

[6] Tacit contract extensions are currently treated as open-ended contracts, i.e. they are *not* exempted under Art. 5 of the Vertical Block Exemption Regulation, cf. ECJ, judgment of 8.6.1995, Rs. T-7/93 para. 137 f. ("*Langnese-Iglo*").

with vertical restraints in general, the indirect obligations are those where contract drafting requires utmost care.

Example

The Buyer is obliged to purchase Products per calendar year from the Supplier in a quantity[7] equal to at least 80% of Buyer's Total Annual Demand in the *previous* year (the "Minimum Purchase Obligation").[8] ◀

Exclusive sourcing is an alternative example. Exclusive sourcing requires the buyer (distributor) to buy the supplier's brand directly from the supplier[9]:

Example

The Buyer shall purchase all contract products from the Supplier. The Buyer must not purchase products which compete with the contract products. ◀

Example

The Buyer shall purchase all contract products from the Supplier. The Buyer may purchase and resell competing products. ◀

5.2.1 Maximum Term: Five Years

The VBER 2022 has granted suppliers **more leeway**. While non-competes previously required a maximum five-year term, many distribution agreements either stipulated renegotiating the non-compete every 5 years, or the entire contract (as many suppliers chose to simply agree to contracts with a five-year-term).

Example

For a period of 5 years from the Effective Date or, if the contract ends earlier, for the duration of the contract, the buyer must not purchase, distribute or manufacture products that compete with the contract products, unless the supplier consents. Without consent, the distributor must also not directly or indirectly participate in a competitor of the supplier or promote its business operations in any other way. The Parties undertake to renegotiate extending the term of this

[7] Please specify the relevant measuring unit.

[8] Ideally combined with an information right by the supplier/information obligation by the buyer to inform when coming close to/reaching/exceeding the threshold.

[9] VGL, para. 129 (definition); para. 393 (as example of non-compete).

non-competition clause 6 months before the expiry of the 5-year period, in the light of the then applicable competition law standards. ◀

Now, the distribution contracts can be drafted as evergreen contracts, i.e. with an automatic renewal of the non-compete obligation. This is what the Vertical Guidelines now stipulate[10]—and thereby reduce the scope of Article 5(1)(a) VBER as the latter excludes non-compete obligations whose duration is "indefinite or exceeds 5 years". What duration, however, does in effect have an evergreening non-compete if not an indefinite one? It would thus have been preferable (because clearer and binding also the courts and national competition authorities) to amend Article 5(1)(a) VBER.

5.2.2 New: Evergreening Non-compete Obligations

For a "tacitly renewable" non-compete to be **exempt** for a period beyond 5 years, Article 5(1)(a) VBER together with the Vertical Guidelines now sets up **two requirements**:

(1) The buyer must be able to effectively renegotiate or terminate the respective vertical agreement (for which, considering the objective of avoiding market foreclosure, renegotiating or terminating the non-compete obligation alone should suffice, even though the Vertical Guidelines refer to the "vertical agreement containing the obligation"). In practice, however, suppliers that have started with distributors that do not sell competing goods will often be willing to only agree to distribution contracts with non-competes—or prefer having no contract at all.
(2) The buyer must be able to renegotiate or terminate at a reasonable notice period and at a reasonable cost. This requirement is given if the buyer can effectively switch suppliers when the five-year period expires. This includes that there must be no indirect obstacles, such as loans having to be paid back, or ("not relationship-specific") equipment that the buyer requires.

5.2.3 Re-Exception: Outlets Owned or Leased by Supplier

If the buyer sells the contract goods or services from premises and land owned or leased by the supplier from third parties, the parties may also agree on longer non-compete obligations, up to, as maximum, the term of the period of occupancy of the premises and land by the buyer (Article 5(2) VBER). Attempts to avoid the five-year-limit by agreeing on a temporary transfer of ownership from the buyer to

[10] VGL, para. 248.

the supplier fail.[11] What works instead (if practical), are permanent sale-and-lease-back situations.

The same goes for mobile outlets. Though the wording literally only refers to "premises and land", it also applies—by analogy—to mobile outlets.[12]

5.2.4 Individual Assessment of Non-Competes

Non-compete obligations may occur in different ways, including by single branding obligations or quantity forcing. The same effects also usually result from English clauses, which require the buyer to report any better offer and allow the buyer to accept such an offer only if the supplier does not match it.[13]

Where not block exempt, their **individual assessment** requires reviewing the risk of foreclosure, focusing on the supplier's market position[14] and countervailing buyers' power,[15] asking especially whether the supplier's market coverage combined with the duration of the non-compete makes it hard for buyers to switch to other suppliers. Besides, the goods concerned—intermediate or final products—and the level within the distribution chain are relevant[16]: Foreclosure, making it more difficult for new suppliers to enter the market, is less likely with intermediate products at the wholesale level and more likely with final products at the retail level. In the light of the rationale behind Article 5(2) VBER, non-competes tied to premises and land (or, in analogue interpretation, mobile outlets) owned or leased by the supplier will usually have only limited foreclosure effects.

While non-competes will regularly not produce anti-competitive effects where numerous competitors with similar market strength exist; a foreclosure of new market entrants due to cumulative effects or collusion between the existing market players must be avoided, too.[17] As a **rule of thumb**, the Commission considers single and cumulative foreclosure effects **unlikely** where the largest **supplier's market share is below 30%** and the **overall market share of the five largest suppliers is below 50%**[18] (hence applying the same threshold as for declaring the VBER inapplicable according to Article 7 VBER). Finally, the duration of the non-compete works as an adjusting screw: the shorter, the higher the chances for buyers to switch suppliers, the lower the risk for producing anti-competitive

[11] VGL, para. 249.

[12] VGL, para. 249; see also VGL 2010, para. 67.

[13] VGL, para. 298.

[14] VGL, para. 301 et seq.

[15] VGL, para. 306.

[16] VGL, para. 307–310.

[17] For details on the individual assessment, including examples, cf. VGL, para. 298, 301–320.

[18] VGL, para. 304.

Table 5.1 Classification of non-competes by degree of restrictiveness

Explicit non-competes, including exclusive purchasing, exclusive sourcing[a] and single branding[b]		
	Quantity forcing, e.g. minimum purchase requirements, stocking requirements, equipment requirements, non-linear pricing	
		English clauses, i.e. requiring the buyer to report any better offer and allowing the buyer to accept such an offer only if the supplier does not match[c]

[a]Defined in VGL, para. 129
[b]Provided single branding is understood in its literal sense, i.e. focusing on the brand of a single supplier, i.e. including sourcing from another supplier that sells the same brand. Insofar, it may leave more freedom for the buyer
[c]VGL, para. 298

effects.[19] In descending order according to the degree of restrictiveness, suppliers especially apply the tools listed in Table 5.1.

Despite the greater freedom to act, shown here from left to right/to bottom, quantity forcing may have the same anti-competitive effect as explicit no-competes. Whereas English clauses may even be worse as they facilitate collusion where the buyer is obliged to provide market information of the supplier's competitor(s).

5.3 Post-Contractual Non-Competes, Article 5(1)(b) and (3) VBER

After termination of contract, the buyer (distributor) shall be free to manufacture, purchase, sell or resell goods in services. Therefore, Article 5(1)(b) VBER generally excludes a respective direct or indirect obligation from the benefit of the VBER. However, two exceptions exist from this prohibition of post-contractual—or post-term,[20] as the Vertical Guidelines say—non-compete obligations:

[19]VGL, para. 312, which refers to sectors where selling one brand only from a single site.
[20]Though this term is rather used to refer to "prolonged pregnancy".

5.3.1 Direct Non-Compete Obligations

Non-compete obligations after termination are **exempt** if they fulfil—as now explicitly stipulated "all of the following"[21] **four requirements** (not three, as the Vertical Guidelines stipulate, leaving out no. 2 below[22]): The non-compete

(1) relates to the contract goods or services.
(2) is limited to the distribution premises.
(3) is necessary to protect know-how transferred by the supplier to the buyer.
(4) is limited to a period of 1 year after termination of the agreement.

When drafting/agreeing on such post-contractual non-compete, the parties should bear in mind the applicable distribution laws, as they may provide for a right of the distributor to be compensated for not competing. It is hence worth weighing the payments for an intermediary simply for a negative action (refraining from working) against alternative payments for positive actions (such as for further marketing the brand in the territory). In case of a German distributor, such "adequate compensation" will regularly be calculated on the average annual margin the distributor made in the last 2, 3 to 5 years, reduced, as a rule of thumb, to 70–75% in order to reflect the costs saved.[23]

5.3.2 Indirect Non-Compete Obligations

If the non-compete is the result of **secret know-how**, restrictions on the use and disclosure of said know-how can be imposed without any time limit. This exception in Article 5(3) second sentence VBER is necessary because suppliers would be reluctant to disclose secret know how if they had to fear it would be made public on the day a distribution intermediary leaves.

5.4 Non-compete in Selective Distribution, Article 5(1)c) VBER

Suppliers may also agree on **general non-competes** with their selective distributors, e.g.:

Example

For a period of 5 years from the effective date of the contract, the distributor shall not purchase, distribute or manufacture products that compete with the contract products. ◀

[21] The previous version's language versions were not all clear about this, cf. Bechtold et al. (2023, Vertikal-GVO, Art. 5 para. 16 with further references).

[22] Cf. VGL, para. 250.

[23] Thume and Rohrßen (2023, § 90a HGB para. 19).

Suppliers shall, however, refrain from restricting their distributors with regard to one or more specific competitors because a non-compete "not to sell the brands of particular competing suppliers" is excluded from the exemption provided by the VBER.

This exclusion shall avoid that suppliers using the same distribution outlets block specific competitors from using the same distribution outlets for their competing goods or services.[24] In other words: Suppliers shall refrain from agreeing with their selective distributors to collectively boycott one or more specific competitor(s).

5.5 Parity Obligations, Article 5(1)(d) VBER

Parity obligations, also known as "most favoured customer" or "most favoured nation" clauses,[25] are now **partially explicitly regulated** by the VBER. **Across-platform retail parity obligations** are **excluded from the safe harbour** of the VBER. They require the supplier to sell the goods or services at least at the same favourable conditions as anywhere else and are thus also called "wide" retail parity obligations. In contrast, **"narrow" retail parity obligations** (i.e. requiring to sell the goods or services at least at the same favourable conditions as at one's direct sales channels) and **other parity obligations** (beyond retail) in principle **benefit** from the VBER. Nevertheless, national sector-specific regulations must also be observed, especially in the hotel room sector.

The key word for these obligations is "at least the same favourable" (or, negative: "no less favourable") as they require one party to sell its goods or services to "at least the same favourable conditions" to the other party (or: "at no less favourable conditions than to other parties). Such conditions may be the price itself, inventory, availability or any other terms of offer or sale. Again, as with all other Article 5-restrictions, the means may be direct or indirect, including by differential pricing incentivizing or disincentivizing the supplier's behaviour in providing the same favourable conditions.[26]

Parity obligations exist in **different shades**, i.e. with different degrees of restriction, from narrow parity obligations (which only restrict the buyer's direct sales), over across-platform retail parity obligations (which restrict sales on competing online intermediation services) to wide parity obligations (which restrict the sales on all sales channels).[27] Altogether, they are also called Most Favoured Nation clauses ("MFNs") and also sometimes Across-Platform Parity Agreements

[24] VGL, para. 252.

[25] VGL, para. 254(c) and para. 356. Though VGL, para. 356 states that parity obligations are also sometimes called most favoured nation clauses (MFNs) or Across-Platform Parity Agreements (APPAs), the latter term should be reserved for those parity obligations which oblige the supplier to provide the best terms over more than one sales channel ("across platforms").

[26] VGL, para. 357.

[27] VGL, para. 259 and para. 358; Rohrßen (2019, p. 343).

("APPAs"),[28] even where the obligation only refers to the direct sales and not to a third-party online platform,[29] which is why MFN or parity obligation are the best fitting terms. Among all types of parity obligations, only across-platform retail parity obligations are excluded from the VBER, while all other types can benefit from it.[30]

Across-platform retail parity obligations are defined by Article 1(1)(f) VBER as follows:

▶ **Definition** "any direct or indirect obligation causing a buyer of online intermediation services not to offer, sell or resell goods or services to end users under more favourable conditions via competing online intermediation services".

The conditions include every ascept of the sale, especially the price itself, but also the availability of the goods or services.[31]

5.5.1 What's New for Across-Platform Retail Parity Obligations?

New to the VBER is the **exclusion of across-platform retail parity obligations from the VBER's safe harbour**. So far, only some EU Member States (France,[32] Belgium,[33] Italy,[34] and Austria[35]) had regulated and restricted the use of best price clauses, while in others the national competition authorities and courts took decisions.

---

[28] VGL, para. 356.

[29] Cf. the definition of the Commission in VGL, para. 356 and the corresponding definition by the OECD (2016).

[30] VGL, para. 254.

[31] VGL, para. 253.

[32] Article L311-5-1 Code du tourisme (introduced by the Law 2015-990 of 6 August 2015): "... l'hôtelier conserve la liberté de consentir au client tout rabais ou avantage tarifaire, de quelque nature que ce soit, toute clause contraire étant réputée non écrite".

[33] "Loi relative à la liberté tarifaire des exploitants d'hébergements touristiques dans les contrats conclus avec les opérateurs de plateformes de réservation en ligne" vom 30.7.2018, "Art. 5: Le prix de la location d'un hébergement touristique est déterminé librement par l'exploitant. Il a également la liberté de consentir tout rabais ou avantage tarifaire, de quelque nature que ce soit. Art. 6: Toute clause d'un contrat conclu entre un exploitant et un opérateur de plateforme qui est contraire à l'article 5 est réputée non écrite et nulle de plein droit."

[34] Legge 4 agosto 2017, n. 124 ("Legge annuale per il mercato e la concorrenza"), Art. 1, para. 166 (sic): "È nullo ogni patto con il quale l'impresa turistico-ricettiva si obbliga a non praticare alla clientela finale, con qualsiasi modalità e qualsiasi strumento, prezzi, termini e ogni altra condizione che siano migliorativi rispetto a quelli praticati dalla stessa impresa per il tramite di soggetti terzi, indipendentemente dalla legge regolatrice del contratto".

[35] § 1 UWG i. V. m. Nr. 32 Anhang zum UWG: "Das Verlangen eines Betreibers einer Buchungsplattform gegenüber einem Beherbergungsunternehmen, dass dieses auf anderen Vertriebswegen inklusive seiner eigenen Website keinen günstigeren Preis oder keine anderen günstigeren Bedingungen als auf der Buchungsplattform anbieten darf."

Now, Article 5(1)(d) VBER has been added, together with further updated provisions,[36] to reflect the online platform economy. Parity obligations are quite usual, especially in the hotel room market. The VBER only excludes retail parity obligations, i.e. those which concern the conditions under which goods or services are sold to end users.[37]

Example

"Best price and availability guarantee: As a matter of principle, the hotel portal service provider "H" expects its hotel partners to offer the lowest possible room rates including all taxes and charges (so-called final rates) as well as the highest possible availability. The hotel thus undertakes that a) H always receives the at least equally favourable prices and price conditions (hereinafter jointly "price" or "rate") which the hotel offers or allows to be offered on other booking and travel platforms on the Internet and its own distribution channels (so-called parity rate)... ."[38] ◀

As with all other Article 5-restrictions, **both direct and indirect restraints are excluded**, no matter whether price parity is the result of pressure or of incentives, e.g. better visibility/ranking on the platform or differential pricing according to the readiness the buyer of the online intermediation services to offer or to refrain from offering the goods or services on competing platforms.

The above **example** contains a **broad retail parity obligation,** as it requires the hotel to give the online intermediation service the same favourable rates as the hotel offers or allows to be offered on other platforms and its own distribution channels. It has been neither block-exempt (because the platform's market share exceeded the 30% threshold of Article 3 VBER), nor individually exempt under Article

[36] Further provisions tackling the online platform economy are the definitions of online intermediation services (Article 1(1)(e) VBER) and active sales (Article 1(1)(l) VBER), the clarification that online intermediation services may also be suppliers (Article 1(1)(d) VBER), the re-exception of vertical agreements for online intermediation services (Article 2(6) VBER), the hardcore restriction safeguarding the effective use of the internet (Article 4(e) VBER) the mentioning of online intermediation services as example case for the withdrawal of the VBER in Article 6(1).

[37] VGL, para. 357 on the definition of retail parity obligations.

[38] Example from Hotel Reservation Service, translated from Higher Regional Court of Düsseldorf, Decision of 9 January 2015, Case No.VI-Kart 1/14(V), para. 4 et seq. The clause basically continued: "... In this context, the hotel also undertakes to oblige its other distribution partners (such as tour operators) accordingly and to ensure that H also receives this price in the event that the hotel can be booked at a lower price, (b) it settles a valid claim by a H customer for breach of the Best Price Guarantee with the guest in the course of invoicing. In addition, the hotel shall immediately amend the H-Price accordingly, (c) H is not treated less favourably than other distribution channels in terms of availability, so that rooms still available on other distribution channels are always made available on H as well, d) G is not treated worse than other distribution channels with regard to booking and cancellation conditions for the customer, so that more favourable conditions, which the hotel offers or has offered on other booking and travel platforms on the Internet as well as its own distribution channels online or offline, also apply at H."

101(3) TFEU (because both the Bundeskartellamt[39] and the Higher Regional Court of Düsseldorf[40] found it reduced competition between established platforms and hindered the market entry of new platforms. Whereas the broad retail parity obligation was thus not exempt in the cases of HRS.com[41] and Booking.com,[42] the Higher Regional Court of Düsseldorf found the broad retail parity obligation used by Expedia.de to be exempt according to Article 2 VBER as it did not contain any black or grey clauses.[43]

While across-platform retail parity obligations are not block-exempt, they may still be exempt under Article 101(3) TFEU based on an **individual assessment**, even though they raise competition concerns because they are likely to soften competition, facilitate collusion between online intermediation service providers or foreclosure.[44]

5.5.2 Other Parity Obligations

All other parity obligations may be exempt under the VBER. That goes especially for the three types listed by the Vertical Guidelines as they do either not restrict the sales via competing platforms, do not concern retail sales, or concern the purchase (not sale) of goods or services:

- Narrow retail parity obligations, i.e. retail parity obligations relating only to the direct sales channels of buyers of online intermediation services, not restricting sales via competing platforms (thus called 'narrow' retail parity obligations). They generally allow the buyer of the online intermediation services to offer the goods or services elsewhere at more favourable conditions, except on their direct sales channels. Where, however, there are few other online intermediation services, the narrow retail parity obligations may lead to higher prices as the competition exerted by the direct sales channels is missing.[45]
- Non-retail related parity obligations (also called "upstream parity obligations"[46]), i.e. parity obligations relating to the conditions under which goods or services are offered to undertakings that are not end users. They include, for example, parity

[39] BKartA, 20 December 2013, Case No. B9-66/10.

[40] Higher Regional Court of Düsseldorf, 9 January 2015, Case No. VI-Kart 1/14(V) para. 81.

[41] Higher Regional Court of Düsseldorf, 9 January 2015, Case No. VI-Kart 1/14 (V) para. 121.

[42] Higher Regional Court of Düsseldorf, 4 May 2016, Case No. VI-Kart 1/16 (V) para. 63.

[43] Higher Regional Court of Düsseldorf, 4 December 2017, ECLI:DE:OLGD:2017:1204.VI.U.KART5.17.00 para. 25, 34 et seq.

[44] VGL, para. 360; for details on the individual assessment cf. VGL, para. 361 et seq., including the relevant factors, such as market position, market shares, homing behaviour of buyers and end users, entry barriers, the significance of direct sales.

[45] For details on the individual assessment of narrow retail parity obligations cf. VGL, para. 372–375.

[46] VGL, para. 376.

obligations imposed by retailers on suppliers concerning the conditions (except the price, as this would constitute RPM) at under which the supplier sells the goods to other retailers.[47] Where not block exempt, their individual assessment requires reviewing the situation of competition downstream, i.e. between the undertakings that buy goods or services. The Commission will apply the same rules and principles to these non-retail related parity obligations as to the retail related ones.[48]

- Most favoured customer obligations, i.e. parity obligations relating to the conditions under which manufacturers, wholesalers or retailers purchase goods or services as inputs.[49] They do not directly affect competition downstream. Where not block exempt, their individual assessment requires reviewing the size and market power of the supplier and buyer that are party to the parity obligation, the market share covered and the supplier's cost of input in relation to the buyers' total cost,[50] hence the price paid. The Commission considers most favoured customer obligations in particular regularly being individually exempt under Article 101(3) TFEU where they relate to long-term supply relationships as they motivate the buyer to invest in new products (as they may take away the buyer's fear that subsequent buyers may free-ride on their investment for such input goods or services).[51]

References

Bechtold R, Bosch W, Brinker I (2023) EU-Kartellrecht, 4th edn. C.H. Beck, Munich

OECD (2016) Competition and across platform parity agreements. https://www.oecd.org/daf/ 1088competition/competition-cross-platform-parity.htm. Accessed 9 Feb 2023

Rohrßen B (2019) Internetvertrieb 2019/20 – Vertriebsvorgaben, (Best-)Preise & Platform-to-Business-Verordnung. ZVertriebsR 2019:341–347

Thume KH, Rohrßen B (2023) §§ 84 et seq. Handelsgesetzbuch. In: Röhricht V, Graf von Westphalen F, Haas U (eds) HGB, Kommentar zu Handelsstand, Handelsgesellschaften, Handelsgeschäften, besonderen Handelsverträgen und internationalem Vertragsrecht, 6th edn. Otto Schmidt, Cologne

[47] VGL, para. 368.

[48] VGL, para. 376, referring to para. 360–374 on narrow retail parity obligations.

[49] VGL, para. 254.

[50] VGL, para. 377.

[51] VGL, para. 378.

Article 6 and 7 VBER: Withdrawal/Non-application

6

Abstract Both tools, the withdrawal and the non-application of the VBER, recur on the Regulation on the implementation of the EU competition rules.[1] Reason for this right of individual withdrawal or right of abstract non-application as may be required as the VBER covers quite a vast number of categories and confers, in the Commission's words, a "presumption of legality",[2] which may be withdrawn.

Article 6 on the withdrawal of the benefit in individual cases is re-introduced into the material part of the VBER. The right (or risk, from the undertaking's perspective) of withdrawal has anyway existed earlier, based on Article 29 of the Regulation No 1/2003 of 16 December 2002 on the implementation of the rules on competition. A typical case could consist of parallel agreements/parallel networks of agreements with cumulative anti-competitive effects.[3]

Article 7 of the VBER allows for the competition authorities to take away the benefit of the VBER by regulation. It may be made use of especially in cases of parallel networks whose cumulative effect restricts competition, provided the agreements with their vertical restraints cover more than 50% of the relevant market.

6.1 What's New for Withdrawing the Benefit of the VBER?

Withdrawing the benefit of the VBER is not new: The pre-predecessor, the VBER 2790/1999 already provided for quite similar rules in its Articles 6 (for the Commission) and 7 (for the national competition authorities).

The predecessor, the VBER 330/2010 referenced the Commission's and national competition authorities' right to withdraw the benefit of the VBER in recitals no. 13 (for the Commission) and 14 (for the national competition authorities), with

[1] Regulation (EC) No 1/2003 of 16 December 2002.

[2] VGL of 19 May 2010 on the VBER 330/2010, para. 74.

[3] VGL, footnote 26.

B. Rohrßen, *VBER 2022: EU Competition Law for Vertical Agreements*, Law for Professionals, https://doi.org/10.1007/978-3-031-35024-5_6

general rules in no. 15 (anti-competitive effects deriving from parallel networks of vertical agreements with similar effects). The individual withdrawal of the benefit has existed all this time, as it has also been laid down in Article 29 of the Regulation No 1/2003 of 16 December 2002 on the implementation of the rules on competition. Therefore, Article 6 VBER refers also to Article 29 of said Regulation.

6.2 Withdrawal of the Benefit in Individual Cases

Article 6 VBER empowers the competition authorities to withdraw the benefit of the VBER where an agreement has effects which are incompatible with Article 101(3) TFEU. Such withdrawal takes only effect for the future.

Withdrawals may occur in **two scenarios**, namely where a vertical agreement has anti-competitive effects, i.e. fulfils at least one of the four conditions of Article 101(3) TFE,

- either in itself ("in isolation"[4]).
- or in conjunction with parallel networks (i.e. similar agreements entered into by competitors, such as retail parity obligations, selective distribution or non-compete obligations,[5] especially where they may lead to market foreclosure).

As example, Article 6 VBER lists the—highly concentrated—market for the supply of online intermediation services, where competition by providers is restricted by the cumulative effect of parallel networks of similar agreements. E.g. they may restrict the access to or lead to foreclosure of the market. Other examples are that of

- multiple exclusive dealerships at retailer level in an oligopolistic market, which bears the risk of collusion between the few market leaders,[6]
- qualitative[7] selective distribution of a rather simple product for which the criteria lead to reduced inter-brand competition between the leading brands,[8]
- of single branding of dominant undertakings,[9]

[4] VGL, para. 257.

[5] VGL, para. 258–260.

[6] VGL, para. 141.

[7] VGL, para. 164 last paragraph refers to "quantitative selective distribution", apparently a typo as the case refers to qualitative selection criteria such as having a brick and mortar shop, trained personnel, pre-sales services, minimum area dedicated, the product type must represent ≥30% of the shop's total turnover, etc.

[8] VGL, para. 164.

[9] VGL, para. 303 and 310.

- exclusive supply agreements[10] into which enter a number of major buyers,[11]
- narrow parity obligations where there is no or limited risk of freeriding and no other efficiencies in terms of Article 101(3) TFEU are generated.[12]

The withdrawal is limited to those undertakings and their agreements which **appreciably restrict competition**. Where, instead, the suppliers' or distributors' market share **amounts to a maximum 5%**, they will be outside such withdrawal as their agreements are presumed to have **no appreciable effect**.[13]

Competent competition authorities are either the **Commission** or,—where the agreement's effects are limited to the territory of a Member State, or a part thereof, which has all the characteristics of a distinct geographic market,—the **national competition authorities** of a respective Member State, cf. Article 6(2) VBER. The authorities may start such investigations on their **own initiative—or** upon a (especially competitor's or other market player's) **complaint**. If the agreement affects several separate national or regional markets, each competent national competition authority may take action. In that case, they have to provide any decision to the Commission.[14] Alternatively, the national competition authorities may also ask the Commission to apply withdrawal—or they may follow up through the European Competition Network, whose Advisory Committee is to be consulted prior to the Commission taking a withdrawal decision.[15] The burden of proof lies with the respective competition authorities. It is hence up to them to prove that the specific vertical agreement restricts competition within the meaning of Article 101(1) TFEU—and that its effects are incompatible with Article 101(3) TFEU, i.e. fails to fulfil one of the four requirements.

So far, there have been only two cases where the withdrawal has occurred in practice:[16]

Example

Langnese-Iglo GmH: The Commission withdraw the benefit of the then current VBER[17] to the exclusive agreements "whereby retailers undertook to buy, offer for sale or sell only the ice-cream of those producers, to the exclusion of the

[10] Defined as restrictions that oblige or induce the supplier to sell the contract products only or mainly to one buyer, VGL, para. 321. Covered by Article 4(f) VBER and by the Subcontracting Notice (see above).

[11] VGL, para. 325.

[12] VGL, para. 374 et seq.

[13] VGL, para. 261.

[14] Article 11(4) Regulation (EC) No. 1/2003 on the implementation of the competition rules.

[15] Commission Notice on cooperation within the Network of Competition Authorities (Official Journal C 101, 27/04/2004, p. 43), para. 59.

[16] VGL, para. 267 footnote 158.

[17] Regulation (EEC) No 1984/83 of 22 June 1983 on the application of Article 85(3) of the Treaty to categories of exclusive purchasing agreements (OJ 1983 L 173, p. 5).

ice-cream products "Mars", "Snickers", "Milky Way", and "Bounty" where the latter are offered to the final consumer as single-item products."[18] ◀

Example

Eco System/Peugeot:[19] The Commission has withdrawn the benefit of the then applicable MVBER[20] for the standard contract for the exclusive and selective distribution of Peugeot vehicles in Belgium and Luxembourg as it contained "clauses designed to prevent the parallel import or export of contract goods",[21] namely "it is implemented by all undertakings in the Peugeot network in the countries concerned, it is designed to prevent, and generally does prevent, the export to France of Peugeot vehicles purchased in Belgium or Luxembourg by French consumers using the services of Eco System. The sensitive nature of this restriction derives from the Peugeot make's important position on the Community market. Since the agreement, by definition, relates to cross-border trade, it is likely to affect trade between Member States; this has sensitive consequences, since, although the Peugeot vehicles reimported into France by Eco System account for only a small proportion of Peugeot sales, parallel imports are likely to make a significant contribution to reducing price differentials within the Community, while the circular sent out by Peugeot to the distributors in its network helps to perpetuate the partitioning of national markets."[22] ◀

6.3 What's New for Non-applying the VBER?

The answer is easy and short: **Nothing**. The provision stays exactly the same, but for changing its numbering, having been shifted from "Article 7" to "Article 8", simply making space for re-inserting the provision on the individual withdrawal (see above).

6.4 Non-application of the VBER

Article 7 VBER refers to the Commission's right to declare, by regulation, that the benefit of the VBER shall not apply to vertical agreements containing market-specific restraints where parallel networks of similar vertical restraints cover more

[18] ECLI:EU:T:1995:98 para. 4.

[19] Commission Decision 92/154/EEC of 4 December 1991.

[20] Commission Regulation No 123/85 of 12 December 1984.

[21] Commission Decision of 4 December 1991, 92/154/EEC, para. 25.

[22] Commission Decision of 4 December 1991, 92/154/EEC, para. 23.

than **50% of a market**—also called "**disapplication of the VBER**".[23] Whether the 50% threshold is exceeded will have to be measured—in lack of any statutory rule[24]—by summing up the market shares of every individual network which produces such similar effects,[25] whereas direct sales by the suppliers only count for calculating the overall market volume.[26]

Contrary to the individual exemption under Article 6 VBER, this tool generally excludes all agreements by all undertakings concerned. Due to its wider impact on the undertakings concerned and the entire relevant market, this tool is the last resort, compared to the individual withdrawal. The Commission will therefore—also in the light of the principle of proportionality laid down in Article 5(4) TFEU—consider first whether an individual withdrawal suffices to restore the anti-competitive effects.

What cases may that be? Such non-application or disapplication may especially occur with parallel selective distribution networks where they create cumulative anti-competitive effects,[27] especially foreclosure of other distributors. Such cumulative effects may especially occur if the agreements rely on selection criteria which are not required by the goods or services[28] or discriminate certain types of distribution, i.e. treat them differently for no reason. As a **rule of thumb**, the stronger the position of the distributors not applying selective distribution, the less likely is foreclosure.

As effect, the VBER does not apply to the restraints and markets concerned—which is why the Commission must specify the product(s) and market(s) plus the vertical restraint(s) concerned. The Commission may also, again in the light of the principle of proportionality, limit the disapplication under such regulation to certain vertical restraints which restrict competition the most. As an example, given by the Commission, the regulation may be limited to disapply the VBER to non-compete obligations that exceed a specific term or specific selection criteria as non-competes or quantity forcing,[29] i.e. obliging or incentivizing the buyer to concentrate its purchases to a large extent with the supplier.[30]

The undertakings concerned will at least have a **transitional period of six months** to fix the agreement(s) concerned as this minimum transition period is

[23]While the VBER uses the term "non-application" (Article 7), the VGL refer to "disapplication" (e.g. in para. 256, 269 et seq.), also the French ("non-application" vs. "exclusion"), Italian ("Non applicazione" vs. "disapplicazione"), Spanish (No aplicación vs. "Inaplicación"), while German ("Nichtanwendung") or Swedish ("Icke-tillämpning") use consistently the same term.

[24]Article 8 only applies to calculating the market share threshold in Article 3; at best, Article 8 (e) VBER may be applied by analogy here, thus adding up the market shares held by each undertaking within such networks.

[25]VGL, para. 270.

[26]Bechtold et al. (2023, Vertikal-GVO, Art. 7 para. 5); Schultze et al. (2019, para. 1055 (e Art. 6 VBER 2010).

[27]VGL, para. 155 and para. 270.

[28]Which also may suffice for the individual withdrawal according to Article 6 VBER, cf. VGL, para. 152.

[29]VGL, para. 272.

[30]For the definition of quantity forcing, see also VGL, para. 298.

stipulated by law.[31] Such fixing may not even require any action (but review), provided that the agreement by the respective supplier falls either outside Article 101(1) TFEU for being non-appreciable or is individually exempt under Article101 (3) TFEU.[32]

In practice, the **Commission has not made use of this tool**, does not feel obliged to use it[33]—and likely can go without it as the Commission could change the VBER itself instead.[34]

References

Bechtold R, Bosch W, Brinker I (2023) EU-Kartellrecht, 4th edn. C.H. Beck, Munich

Bretthauer S (2022) Vertikal-GVO Art. 5-11. In: Bacher K, Hempel R, Wagner-von Papp F (eds) BeckOK, Kartellrecht, 6th edn

Schultze J-M, Pautke S, Wagener DS (2019) Vertikal-GVO, Gruppenfreistellungsverordnung für vertikale Vereinbarungen, 4th edn. Deutscher Fachverlag, Frankfurt am Main

[31] Article 1(a) Regulation No. 19/65/EEC (the "Empowerment Regulation of 1965", as amended by Regulation No 1215/1999): "... fix a period at the expiry of which the Regulation pursuant to Article 1 would no longer be applicable in respect of the relevant agreements or concerted practices on that market; such period must not be shorter than six months".

[32] Bretthauer (2022, Vertikal-GVO, Art. 7 para. 6); apparently dissenting: Bechtold et al. (2023, Vertikal-GVO, Art. 7 para. 7: exemption ceases to apply, restraints void according to Article 101(2) TFEU).

[33] VGL, para. 270: "Article 7 ... does not require the Commission to adopt such regulation where the 50% market coverage ratio is exceeded."

[34] Bretthauer (2022, Art. 7 para. 2); Schultze et al. (2019, para. 1052 re VBER 2010).

Franchise Systems

7

Abstract Before diving into the VBER, the first question to answer is whether the vertical restraints in franchise agreements are already outside the scope of Article 101(1) TFEU because franchising requires uniform products and a uniform appearance on the market and those obligations necessary to safeguard the uniformity are outside of Article 101(1) TFEU.[1]

Franchise systems are not defined nor explicitly tackled by the VBER. However, there is clear case law and also the Vertical Guidelines explain the Commission's competition law perspective on franchise systems.[2] While EU law lacks any definition of "franchising", "franchise systems" or "franchise agreements",[3] there has been

[1] ECLI:EU:C:1986:41 ("Pronuptia") para. 17: "the franchisor must be able to take the measures appropriate to protect the identity and the name of the sales organisation symbolised by the business name. Consequently, the provisions regulating the control indispensable for this purpose are also not restrictions of competition". Cf. Wolf-Posch and Samek (2018, pp. 302 et seq.); Schultze et al. (2019, para. 775).

[2] Cf. especially VGL, para. 165–169; moreover, selectively in para. 16(f) and 318 [know-how as justification for non-competes/know-how protection as solution to the otherwise arising hold-up issue], 16(h) [franchise as distribution model, next to selective distribution, that preserves uniformity and standardization], 72, 77, 85, 86 [franchise as IP-related type of agreements where IP however is not the primary object and thus eligible for the VBER's safe harbour, cf. Article 2(3) VBER], 87 [list of seven obligations generally considered necessary to protect the franchisor's intellectual property rights and thus if in the scope of Article 101(1) TFEU at all, exempt under the VBER], 98 [potentially necessary information exchange in the light of Article 2(5) VBER], 174 [calculating the market share of a franchisor which franchises a business method (goods and services combined with intellectual property rights) on the basis of the franchisee's sales], 197 (b) [price fixation by exception exempt for coordinated low-price campaigns], 318 [non-competes].

[3] European Parliament resolution of 12 September 2017 on the functioning of franchising in the retail sector (2016/2244(INI)), Recital A; Directorate-General for Internal Policies of the European Union, Report issued in 2016 on Franchising, p. 185.

B. Rohrßen, *VBER 2022: EU Competition Law for Vertical Agreements*, Law for Professionals, https://doi.org/10.1007/978-3-031-35024-5_7

one, which still can be relied on, in the—outdated[4]—Franchise Block Exemption Regulation.[5] Franchise agreements are defined by Article 1(3)(b) Franchise Block Exemption Regulation as follows:

▶ **Definition** "An agreement whereby one undertaking, the franchisor, grants the other, the franchisee, in exchange for direct or indirect financial consideration, the right to exploit a franchise[6] for the purposes of marketing specified types of goods and/or services; it includes at least obligations relating to:

- the use of a common name or shop sign and a uniform presentation of contract premises and/or means of transport,
- the communication by the franchisor to the franchisee of know-how,
- the continuing provision by the franchisor to the franchisee of commercial or technical assistance during the life of the agreement".[7]

Franchise systems are perfect to expand a brand. They are a distribution type which allows establishing a uniform network for the distribution of goods or services

[4]The Franchise Block Exemption Regulation, originally expiring according to its Article 9 on 31 December 1999, had been prolonged until 31 May 2000. From 1 June 2000, franchise agreements have been covered by the VBER (first Regulation 2790/1999, then 330/2010, now 720/2022), same as exclusive purchasing agreements and exclusive distribution agreements, previously block exempt by the Commission Regulation (EEC) No 1984/83 of 22 June 1983 on the application of Article 85 (3) of the Treaty to categories of exclusive purchasing agreements, respectively No 1983/83 of 22 June 1983 on the application of Article 85 (3) of the Treaty to categories of exclusive distribution agreements.

[5]Commission Regulation (EEC) No 4087/88 of 30 November 1988 on the application of Article 85 (3) of the Treaty to categories of franchise agreements. Different from the VBER, the Franchise Block Exemption Regulation contained in Articles 2 and 3 also white clauses, i.e. clauses which the regulation positively listed as exempt.

[6]Defined by Article 1(3(a) of the Franchise Block Exemption Regulation as "a package of industrial or intellectual property rights relating to trade marks, trade names, shop signs, utility models, designs, copyrights, know-how or patents, to be exploited for the resale of goods or the provision of services to end users".

[7]Cf. also the explanation of franchise agreements in VGL, para. 165. Further enlightening definitions can be found e.g. by the German Franchise Association ("GFA", a non-government body), cf. Deutscher Franchiseverband e.V. (2013). The GFA defines franchising as (translated) "a sales and distribution system by means of which goods, services or technologies are marketed. It is based on a close and ongoing cooperation between legally and financially independent and self-employed companies, the Franchisor and the Franchisees. The Franchisor grants its Franchisees the right, at the same time as imposing the obligation on them, to run a business according to its concept. This right entitles and obliges the Franchisee, in return for direct or indirect remuneration, within the framework and for the term of a written Franchise Agreement concluded between the parties for this purpose, to utilise, under ongoing technical and economic support by the Franchisor, the system's name, the trademark, the service mark, copyright and/or other intellectual property rights, as well as know-how, economic and technical methods and the business system of the Franchisor".

with a marginal investment, as the franchisee bears the entrepreneurial risk.[8] The franchisor not only makes use of the franchisee's entrepreneurial energy, his willingness to invest his local know-how and his motivation to increase his own business, but also receives a remuneration, often calculated as a share of the franchisee's income or turnover. The franchisee usually pays up-front an initial fee to become part of the franchising business,[9] covers the costs of setting up the franchise, training the staff and launching the business and pays a percentage of its revenue throughout the duration of the franchise agreement.

From the perspective of pure commercial and distribution law, franchise agreements are only regulated in a few EU Member States.[10] Regardless of any regulation and definition, franchise agreements **usually merge the following elements of various types of contracts**, such as

- agency and supply contract,
- contracts providing the right of use against payment (e.g. lease of premises, trademarks, concept),
- purchase contracts,
- service contracts, and
- licence contracts.[11]

These elements' weight differs from franchise agreement to franchise agreement.

Different from commercial agents and similar to (independent) distributors, franchisors and franchisees act each in their own name and for their account, usually on different levels of the distribution chain. They thus stand in a vertical relationship to each other. Any restraints within this relationship are therefore basically subject to Article 101(1) TFEU. This is also why EU competition law may serve as drafting guideline and one of the building blocks of franchise law,[12] especially where Member States do not regulate franchising, such as German law.

The **organisation and monitoring in franchising** are much more distinctive than in distribution and an authorized distributor lacks the franchise-typical tight organisation oriented towards uniformity. Moreover, a franchise agreement typically contains licence agreements, contrary to distribution agreements. Also, the franchisee's company name generally disappears, due to the franchise-typical uniform appearance in the market, while a distributor (or authorized dealer) often places its company name next to the manufacturer's trademark.

---

[8] Cf. also ECLI:EU:C:1986:41 ("Pronuptia") para. 15; Bortolotti and Bortolotti (2023, p. 99 et seq.).

[9] For a comparison of current initial and ongoing franchise fees (aka "royalties") Rohrßen (2022, pp. 139–151).

[10] Cf. the overview by Rothermel (2021, Chapter H.III. para. 109 et seq.).

[11] Cf., from the perspective of German law, Higher Regional Court of Frankfurt, decision of 27 September 1994, Case No. 11 U (Kart) 30/94 ("Pronuptia III"); Higher Regional Court of Hamm, decision of 13 March 2000, Case No. 8 U 113/992000.

[12] Not just one, but "the" building block ("der Baustein") of franchising law according to Flohr (2022a, p. 73).

The characteristic duties of the franchisor vis-à-vis the franchisee include the transfer of its know-how, typically by means of training courses and franchise manuals, a duty to provide any useful information for a proper set up and management of the franchise, duties of system integration and consistent business assistance through consulting, support and other services, as well as a duty to create, maintain and optimize a marketing concept. Characteristic duties of the franchisee include the payment of all due fees (e.g. entrance fees, as a consideration for system integration services, franchise fees, as a consideration for business assistance by the franchisor, advertising or marketing fees and possible further fees), the establishment of a functional system operation, the duty to promote sales, the duty to maintain a coherent system, especially with regard to the application of the business concept, the duty to comply with the franchisor's interests and accept the latter's goods or services, as well as the duty to keep the franchisor informed about and to disclose any customers' requests.

7.1 What's New for Franchising?

For franchising, the **VBER** does not contain any specific news; it simply **continues to apply**.[13] However, the VBER contains **news** as far as franchising faces **digitalization** and **dual distribution**. Furthermore, all the news of the VBER apply to franchising agreements, too, as far as they fall within the grid of the VBER.[14] The compliance test for franchising continues to be threefold, with a special focus on Article 101(1) TFEU, as shown in Fig. 7.1.

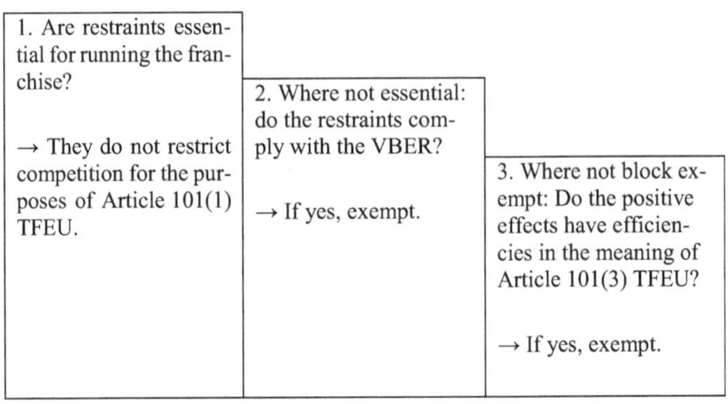

Fig. 7.1 Competition compliance test for franchising agreements

[13] Article 2(3) establishes that contracts that transfer intellectual property rights or their use (in case franchising especially trademarks and know-how) can in principle also be block-exempted.

[14] Flohr (2022b, p. 1164).

7.2 Which Competition Rules to Comply with in Franchising?

Franchise agreements do not only combine different traditional contract types, but also different vertical restraints, e.g. exclusive or selective distribution, internet sales restrictions, and non-compete obligations, sometimes also RPM.[15] As the VBER lacks franchise-specific rules, franchise agreements require compliance and review under those **rules** of the VBER **which fit to the specific case** (or, as the Vertical Guidelines put it, "most closely correspond to the particular franchise agreement"[16]).

Prior to diving into the VBER, however, vertical restraints in franchise agreements will **regularly** already fall **outside the scope of Article 101(1) TFEU**, as far as the restraints are necessary to protect the know-how and safeguard the uniformity of the franchise system. Restraints that are essential for running the franchise do not restrict competition for the purposes of Article 101(1) TFEU as they are only ancillary restraints.[17] As the European Court of Justice put it in its key decision "Pronuptia" concerning a fashion franchise:

> It follows that provisions which establish the means of control necessary for that purpose do not constitute restrictions on competition for the purposes of Article 85(1).
>
> The same is true of the franchisee's obligation to apply the business methods developed by the franchisor and to use the know-how provided.
>
> That is also the case with regard to the franchisee's obligation to sell the goods covered by the contract only in premises laid out and decorated according to the franchisor's instructions, which is intended to ensure uniform presentation in conformity with certain requirements. The same requirements apply to the location of the shop, the choice of which is also likely to affect the network's reputation. It is thus understandable that the franchisee cannot transfer his shop to another location without the franchisor's approval.
>
> The prohibition of the assignment by the franchisee of his rights and obligations under the contract without the franchisor's approval protects the latter's right freely to choose the franchisees on whose business qualifications the establishment and maintenance of the network's reputation depend.
>
> By means of the control exerted by the franchisor on the selection of goods offered by the franchisee, the public is able to obtain goods of the same quality from each franchisee. It may in certain cases – for instance, the distribution of fashion articles – be impractical to lay down objective quality specifications. Because of the large number of franchisees, it may also be too expensive to ensure that such specifications are observed. In such circumstances a provision requiring the franchisee to sell only products supplied by the franchisor or by suppliers selected by him may be considered necessary for the protection of the network's reputation. Such a provision may not, however, have the effect of preventing the franchisee from obtaining those products from other franchisees.
>
> Finally, since advertising helps to define the image of the network's name or symbol in the eyes of the public, a provision requiring the franchisee to obtain the franchisor's approval for all advertising is also essential for the maintenance of the network's identity, so long as that provision concerns only the nature of the advertising.[18]

---

[15] Bunte and Stancke (2022, § 4 para. 61).

[16] VGL, para. 167 and 169 (example of a franchising format selling sweets).

[17] ECLI:EU:C:1986:41 ("Pronuptia") para. 16 et seq.

[18] ECJ, ECLI:EU:C:1986:41 ("Pronuptia") para. 16–21.

In particular, the following restrictions are generally considered necessary to protect the franchisor's intellectual property rights and, where such obligations fall within the scope of Article 101(1) of the Treaty, they are also covered by the VBER:

- non-compete obligations (engaging neither directly nor indirectly in any similar business, including not to acquire shares in such competing undertaking which would allow influencing it);
- non-disclosure obligations on the franchisor's know-how;
- obligations of informing of and granting licences on foreground gained in exploiting the franchise;
- obligation to inform of and take legal action against infringements of the franchisor's intellectual property rights
- an obligation to use franchised know-how only for the franchise business;
- an obligation not to assign the franchise agreement without the franchisor's consent.[19]

In light of the Pronuptia case, franchise agreements require only **a reduced review** under the VBER:[20] **Only where restraints fall in the scope of Article 101(1) TFEU, the VBER comes into play.** Though these principles have been established for the traditional product distribution franchising, the European Commission considers that service franchising (aka: business format franchising) can in principle be treated the same way.[21]

Those vertical restraints which have fallen through the Article 101(1) TFEU grid are to be reviewed in line with (i) **the general principles of the VBER** such as RPM and (ii) **the principles concretely applying to the distribution system corresponding most closely to the particular franchise agreement**.

As regards the general principles, two issues are most relevant: **RPM** and **information exchange in dual distribution**:

RPM are in principle prohibited according to Article 4(1) VBER. Franchise agreements are, however, one of the few exceptions where RPM may, for short-term low-price campaigns, be exempt, provided the campaign's pro-competitive effects outweigh the negatives ones.[22] Insofar, nothing has changed as the Vertical Guidelines have foreseen this exception already under the previous VBER 2010.[23]

Dual distribution, i.e. the scenario where the supplier competes with its independent distributors, will occur in franchising where franchisors operate outlets themselves, hence in competition to the franchisees. In such case, the strict rules on information exchange as per Article 2(5) VBER will apply.

---

[19] VGL, para. 87.

[20] Pautke and Schultze (2022, p. 27).

[21] Commission Decision of 14 November 1988 (Service Master), OJ 1988 L 332, 38, 39 (para. 6).

[22] VGL, para. 197(b). For details, see above in Sect. 4.1.

[23] VGL 2010, para. 197(b).

A way out for the franchisor from these strict rules on information exchange is to run the outlets through other entities, provided the entities are not connected undertakings within the meaning of Article 1(2) VBER. Otherwise, the parties must take care that the information exchanged (i) relates to the implementation of the franchise agreement and (ii) is necessary to improve the production or distribution of the contract goods or services. Insofar, the non-exhaustive blacklist and whitelist of information provided by the Vertical Guidelines may be of help.[24]

Where franchise agreements fall in the scope of Article 101(1) TFEU and are not block exempt, the following **rule of thumb** applies: The more important the transfer of know-how, the more likely the vertical restraints will create efficiencies and are indispensable to achieve the benefits of Article 101(3) TFEU.[25]

References

Bortolotti F, Bortolotti S (2023) Antitrust rules of the European Union applicable to distribution, available through the International Distribution Institute (Turin)

Bunte HJ, Stancke F (2022) Kartellrecht mit Vergaberecht und Beihilfenrecht, 4th edn. C.H. Beck, Munich

Deutscher Franchise-Verband e.V. (2013) Existenzgründung mit System. Ein Leitfaden des Deutschen Franchise-Verbandes e.V. 2013. DFV, Berlin

Flohr E (2022a) Franchise-Recht – Ein Konglomerat-Rechtsgebiet? (Teil 2). ZVertriebsR 2022:71–80

Flohr E (2022b) Entwicklungen im Franchise-Recht (Teil 3): Die neue EU-Gruppenfreistellungsverordnung für vertikale Vertriebsbindungen. ZAP 2022:1163–1174

Pautke S, Schultze JM (2022) Expert Report on the review of the Vertical Block Exemption Regulation Information exchange in dual distribution. https://competition-policy.ec.europa.eu/system/files/2022-02/kd0122032enn_VBER_dual_distribution_2.pdf. Accessed 9 Feb 2023

Rohrßen B (2022) Franchiseverträge und Franchisegebühren – “Welcome to the Club!”. ZVertriebsR 2022:139–151

Rothermel M (2021) Internationales Kauf-, Liefer- und Vertriebsrecht, 2nd edn. Deutscher Fachverlag, Frankfurt am Main

Schultze J-M, Pautke S, Wagener DS (2019) Vertikal-GVO, Gruppenfreistellungsverordnung für vertikale Vereinbarungen, 4th edn. Deutscher Fachverlag, Frankfurt am Main

Wolf-Posch A, Samek P (2018) Aktuelle kartellrechtliche Fragen beim Internetvertrieb von Franchise-Produkten. ZVertriebsR 2018:302–308

[24] VGL, para. 99 and 100.

[25] VGL, para. 168.

Dual Distribution and Other Dualisms

8

Abstract Dualisms may appear on several levels in distribution: dual pricing as regards different pricing for products resold off- and online, dual role agents as regards agents acting for the same supplier both as independent distributor and agent and dual distribution as regards suppliers and their distributors competing. This chapter aims at briefly summarizing the relevant restrictions and guard rails in order to structure distribution correspondingly.

8.1 Dual Pricing

Dual pricing is defined by the Vertical Guidelines as follows:

▶ **Definition** "A requirement that the buyer pays a different wholesale price for products sold online than for products sold offline".[1]

Example

"Supplier will pay the distributor an additional [•]% discount on the purchase price for the goods sold offline."[2] ◀

Dual pricing does, as a term, not appear in the VBER. As dual pricing may lead to a different price for products resold off- versus online, an agreement on dual pricing **may fall under the new hardcore restriction** in Article 4(d) VBER. Under the previous VBER, dual pricing qualified as hardcore restriction.[3] This qualification was in line with the broader understanding of passive sales and the high value the

[1] VGL, para. 209, similar to the definition in VGL 2010, para. 52(d).
[2] Cf. for other examples of online sales restrictions Rohrßen (2018, p. 40).
[3] VGL 2010, para. 64 and 52.

B. Rohrßen, *VBER 2022: EU Competition Law for Vertical Agreements*, Law for Professionals, https://doi.org/10.1007/978-3-031-35024-5_8

Commission attached to online sales as a (if not: the) means to accomplish the internal market: "The internet is a powerful tool to reach a greater number and variety of customers than by more traditional sales methods . . .".[4] The underlying principle was clear: "Restrictions to limit the distributor's access to a greater number and variety of customers".[5]

Incentives where the distributor receives higher discounts or bonuses for goods sold stationary have been considered as a **hardcore restriction** of passive sales. According to the European Commission, dual pricing systems were only lawful where exempt under Article 101(3) TFEU, especially to prevent free-riding. The Bundeskartellamt also regarded such systems as a restriction of passive sales by object.[6] Accordingly, dual pricing systems were hardly common,[7] also because the often sophisticated discount systems required a differentiated effects analysis despite the clear requirement not to restrict online sales.[8]

Under the VBER 2022, dual pricing may already be exempt under the VBER (unlike in the past), as it may incentivise or reward investments in the different (online or offline) sales channels, as long as such dual pricing does not have the object of restricting the distributor's effective use of the internet.[9] The difference in the wholesale price offline versus online needs to be in a reasonable proportion to the differences in investments and costs incurred by the distributor in the respective distribution channel. Depending on the specific distribution scenario, considering such investments or costs may lead to both higher or lower wholesale prices for products sold online. For example, the supplier might intend to reward those distributors who give their customers an additional right to return, e.g. in the B2C sector beyond the cooling-off period required by EU law, as such right may lead to additional costs, e.g. for a higher return rate, more effort in incoming inspection, repackaging and other logistical issues.

Contract Drafting Advice

To contractually back up dual pricing, where practised, the parties may also expressly stipulate the objective of dual pricing, e.g. by stating if and which

(continued)

[4] VGL 2010, para. 52.

[5] VGL 2010, para. 52 sentence 8.

[6] Bundeskartellamt, Cases B7-11/13 (BSH), B5-144/13 (Gardena), B5-100/10 (Dornbracht).

[7] Kaiser (2017, p. 582).

[8] Pautke and Billinger (2016, pp. 40 et seq.). The Bundeskartellamt considered rebates to be lawful if the same for offline and online sales and based on discount-relevant, realisable services (quality requirements), even if "pure players" did not receive a full discount as a result (Bundeskartellamt, Case B7-11/13, Case Report of 23 December 2013, p. 5 [BSH]). Also fixed subsidies independent of turnover or volume, intended to cushion costs associated with stationary distribution, were seen as lawful (Bundeskartellamt 2013, p. 21).

[9] VGL, para. 209.

investments in the offline or online sales channels the dual pricing shall incentivise or reward. The invoicing may either occur later—or through an ex post balancing of accounts.

8.2 Dual Distribution

Dual Distribution is defined by the VBER as

▶ **Definition** "The scenario where a supplier sells goods or services not only at the upstream level but also at the downstream level, thereby competing with its independent distributors."[10]

Dual distribution scenarios are, according to Article 2(4) VBER, **exempt** if (i) the vertical agreement is non-reciprocal and (ii) the parties do not compete at the upstream level where the buyer buys the contract products. The VBER 2022 has given more legal certainty: While under the Verticals Block Exemption Regulation 2010 the requirements for information exchange were questionable,[11] the VBER 2022 gives more guidance.

Especially **three issues** require **specific consideration**: **First**, a dual distribution scenario is already given where the parties are **potential competitors**:

▶ **Definition** 'Potential competitor' means an undertaking that, in the absence of the vertical agreement, would, on realistic grounds and not just as a mere theoretical possibility, be likely, within a short period of time, to make the necessary additional investments or incur other necessary costs to enter the relevant market.[12]

This "short period of time" may be rather long: according to the official guidance, a year is "normally" still considered to be a "short period of time".[13] Such a broad concept of "short period of time" does not even exclude longer time periods beyond a year. With regard to active and well-performing companies, only the "realistic grounds" required by the definition above are those that separate the companies from being competitors. This threshold is rather low, as the Commission sees "no need to demonstrate with certainty that the undertaking will, in fact, enter the relevant market and that it will be capable of retaining its place there".[14] This interpretation

[10] VBER, Recital 12.

[11] Aberle (2022, p. 504).

[12] Article 1(1)(c) VBER.

[13] VGL, para. 90 and 106.

[14] VGL, para. 90.

is in line with the case of the European Court of Justice.[15] Ultimately, the decisive factors are the concrete market structure and the economic and legal context within which the undertaking concerned operates.[16]

Second, information exchange is **only exempt provided** it is **necessary** to improve production/distribution of goods/services. At least, though with caveats, the Vertical Guidelines contain **black and white lists** which help to find orientation. Information exchange is accordingly—in principle—exempt as regards technical information, supply-related information (production, stock, sales quantities, returns); aggregated customer information; current resale prices of buyer, RRP or maximum sale prices as long as not used for RPM or minimum price setting, marketing information, including on advertising campaigns; performance-related information, including aggregated information on marketing and sales activities of other customers; sales volumes and revenues with contract goods/services compared to competing ones. For further details and checklists, see Sects. 2.4.3 and 2.5.

Not exempt is especially the information on future resale prices (exception possible); customer-specific sales data (exception possible); information on competing private label products of the distributor. Possible competition concerns can be addressed by aggregation, delayed forwarding of information, or ring-fencing.

Third, agreements with **suppliers** of **Online Intermediation Service** are **not** exempt, Article 2(6) VBER. This is true, for example, for franchisors who allow franchisees to sell through the franchisor's sales through their website. For further details, see Sect. 2.6.

8.3 Dual Role Agents

What's new for dual agents? According to case law, commercial agents that also act as independent distributor for the same supplier do not benefit from the "agency privilege", i.e. their relationship to the supplier **falls entirely into the scope of Article 101(1) TFEU**, with the crucial consequence **that RPM (as other hardcore restrictions) is unlawful**. This has, however, been disputed.[17]

[15] EU:C:1991:91 (Delimitis), para. 21 ("whether there are real concrete possibilities for a new competitor . . ."); ECLI:EU:C:2020:52 (Generics [UK] and Others) para. 36 et seq. (". . . it must be determined whether there would have existed, in the absence of that agreement, real and concrete possibilities for that undertaking to enter that market and compete with the undertakings established in that market . . . there can be no finding of a potential competitive relationship as an inference merely from the purely hypothetical possibility of such entry or even from the mere wish or desire of the manufacturer of generic medicines to enter the market. Conversely, there is no requirement that it must be demonstrated with certainty that that manufacturer will in fact enter the market concerned and, a fortiori, that it will be capable, thereafter, of retaining its place there").

[16] Cf. only ECLI:EU:C:2020:52 (Generics [UK] and Others) para. 39; ECLI:EU:C:2021:243 (Lundbeck) para. 55.

[17] In favour of applying the agency-typical risk assessment under competition law also to dual role agents e.g. Metzlaff (2018, Artikel 101 para. 171).

The prohibition of anti-competitive agreements under Article 101(1) TFEU applies if the distributor acts in parallel as a commercial agent of the principal for the same product. The reason is that in such case he cannot be qualified as a commercial agent under competition law because there is a risk that the principal influences the pricing and conditions of the distribution intermediary as a dealer in the sale of the same product and does not bear all relevant financial and commercial risks in relation to the commercial agency relationship, i.e. that the principal abuses the commercial agency relationship in order to circumvent the applicability of the antitrust prohibition.[18]

Dual agents can, however, escape the application of Article 101(1) TFEU by delineating both roles and especially costs and investments. Thereby, the agent will be able to show that it bears no or only insignificant costs and risks.

References

Aberle L (2022) Informationsaustausch im dualen Vertrieb – Alle Unklarheiten beseitigt? NZKart 2022:504–509

Bundeskartellamt (2013) Vertical Restraints in the Internet Economy, 10 October 2013. https://www.bundeskartellamt.de/SharedDocs/Publikation/EN/Diskussions_Hintergrundpapiere/Vertical%20Restraints%20in%20the%20Internet%20Economy.pdf?__blob=publicationFile&v=2. Accessed 12 Feb 2023

Goßler J, Wentzel C (2021) Der Entwurf der neuen Vertikal-GVO im Lichte des Entwurfs der neuen Vertikal-Leitlinien. ZVertriebsR 2021:341–348

Kaiser F (2017) Die Sektoruntersuchung zum elektronischen Handel. WuW 2017:578–584

Metzlaff K (2018) Artikel 101 AEUV. In: Flohr E, Wauschkuhn U (eds) Vertriebsrecht, 2nd edn. C.H. Beck, Munich

Pautke S, Billinger J (2016) Doppelpreissysteme: Ausgewählte Rechts- und Anwendungsfragen zur Entscheidungspraxis des Bundeskartellamtes. ZWeR 2016:40–65

Rohrßen B (2018) Vertriebsvorgaben im E-Commerce 2018: Praxisüberblick und Folgen des "Coty"-Urteils des EuGH. GRUR-Prax 2018:39–41

[18] Cf. Goßler and Wentzel (2021, p. 344).

Digital Distribution: Online Sales and Online Platforms

9

Abstract Online sales are on the rise since the last decades. By 2040, 95% of all business will, according to NASDAQ Research, be facilitated via e-commerce.[1] Online sales include sales through the supplier's or distributor's own online stores and through the online intermediation service providers. Online sales, or in broader terms: digital distribution,[2] understood as sales where at least one part of the contracting or delivery process takes place in the digital world,[3] can be subject to vertical restraints. Which restraints are exempt has been at the heart of disputes under the VBER 2010, which did not even mention the term "online" once. A special focus lies on online intermediation services, as they break up the dualism between suppliers and buyers; they are something in between.

9.1 Online Sales Restriction, Practical Overview

With the e-commerce, online sales restrictions have increased over the recent years under the VBER 2010. They were in the focus of especially the German (but also of French, English and other Member States) courts and competition authorities, as the European Commission's sector inquiry into e-commerce[4] confirmed. In the **absence of specific legal rules**, the authorities and courts have developed the rules **case by case**, leading not directly to a uniform practice, but to **uncertainty** as to which requirements were lawful.[5] The spotlight has especially been on bans of sales through online platforms and the use of price comparison tools, e.g.:

---

[1] Nasdaq (2017).

[2] Digital distribution does not necessarily relate to digital products (which, in case of licensing as the primary object of the distribution agreement fall outside the scope of the VBER.

[3] Cf. Rohrßen (2021, p. 71).

[4] European Commission (2017, para. 10 et seq.).

[5] Cf. the earlier overview compiled on the occasion of the Coty ruling: Rohrßen (2018, pp. 39–41).

B. Rohrßen, *VBER 2022: EU Competition Law for Vertical Agreements*, Law for Professionals, https://doi.org/10.1007/978-3-031-35024-5_9

Example

It is prohibited to sell the goods on online platforms that offer used or damaged goods, allow sales by private end users, have multiple sellers for the same product or to not have a separate brand shop for each brand belonging to the manufacturer. ◀

Online platform bans, such as the example taken from Adidas' 2012 e-commerce terms and conditions, have been the most controversial quality requirements in e-commerce for several years.[6]

Example

The distributor may not support the functionality of price comparison engines, in particular provide application-specific interfaces ("APIs") for price comparison engines. ◀

This ban of price comparison platforms is taken from Asics' "Distribution System 1.0". Both the Bundeskartellamt and the courts in Germany have held it unlawful as it restricted passive sales to end consumers.[7]

The questions finally culminated in the **Coty case** in the preliminary ruling of the European Court of Justice.[8] The court took the opportunity to clarify issues that had arisen since the case ruling in the Pierre Fabre in 2009, but the decision also raised further questions. To sum up, said ruling allowed luxury labels to restrict their retailers' sales on online platforms.[9] In the aftermath, it was discussed whether only platform bans in selective distribution and/or only concerning luxury products were covered by the VBER.

According to the Vertical Guidelines 2022, the VBER 2022 reaffirms the case law that developed over the past decade, especially the Coty ruling. In any case, the Vertical Guidelines, together with the new hardcore restriction for online sales, provide more guidance and thereby **legal certainty**.

Since the Coty ruling, bans on online marketplaces ("platform bans") have been exempted at least for luxury products; for products below the luxury threshold, however, the question remains open.[10] The VBER 2022 does not provide a direct answer to this question either. However, **the Vertical Guidelines contain explanations, according to which platform bans are in principle exempt**.[11]

[6] Rohrßen (2016, p. 278); Rohrßen (2018, pp. 39 et seq.).

[7] Higher Regional Court of Düsseldorf, ECLI:DE:OLGD:2017:0405.VI.KART13.15V.00 para. 94, confirmed by the Federal Court, ECLI:DE:BGH:2017:121217BKVZ41.17.0.

[8] ECLI:EU:C:2017:941.

[9] ECLI:EU:C:2017:941.

[10] Cf. Rohrßen (2019, p. 342); Rohrßen (2018, p. 40 at para. II.).

[11] VGL, para. 335.

Why? Because platform bans concern, according to the Commission, the modalities of the buyer's online sales, platform bans do not limit sales into a specific territory or to a specific customer group.

For further details on the different lawful versus unlawful online sales restrictions, see Sect. 4.5,[12] for the changes between VBER 2010 and 2022 the overview in Sect. 10.2 and all relevant aspects of the VBER 2022 summarised in the appendix to Chap. 10.

9.2 Pure Digital Distribution

Pure digital distribution, referring to the digital sales and supply process, either is covered by the VBER—where such agreements actually encompass the selling of products. Where, however, agreements primarily consist of licensing one or more intellectual property rights, they fall outside the scope of the VBER, as Article 2(3) VBER stipulates. For more details, see Sects. 2.3 and 2.4.2.

9.3 Online Intermediation Services

While suppliers and buyers had clear roles in the "traditional" economy of the "brick and mortar age", the digital age has brought a new kid on the block, a new player that does not simply fit to the supplier-buyer dualism.[13] Or, as the Commission puts it:

> The undertakings active in the online platform economy enable new ways of doing business, some of which are not easy to categorise using the concepts traditionally associated with vertical ~~relationships between suppliers and distributors in the brick and mortar environment~~ agreements in the traditional economy.[14]

However, vertical agreements concluded with **hybrid online platforms** are not exempt under the VBER, i.e. **need** to be **assessed individually**.[15] Hybrid online platforms are online intermediation services which also compete in the sale of intermediaries with the undertakings for which they provide online intermediary services. For details, see Sect. 2.4.6.

The question is how online intermediation services (e.g. online marketplaces, app stores, price comparison tools, social media[16]) fit into this picture, i.e. whether they may qualify as agents and therefore any sales requirements are outside the scope of

[12] Cf. also VGL, para. 332–342 on use of online marketplaces and para. 343–355 on price comparison services.

[13] Mundt (2022).

[14] Draft VBER, recital no. 10, compared to VBER 2022, recital no. 10 (crossed out = deleted, underlined = amended in the VBER's final version).

[15] Article 2(6) VBER; cf. also VGL, para. 104–109.

[16] VGL, para. 64.

Article 101 TFEU. Undertakings active in the platform economy qualify as suppliers where they provide online intermediation services (Article 1(1)(d) VBER). Online intermediation services, again, are defined by Article 1(1)(e) VBER as follows:

▶ **Definition** 'Online intermediation services' means information society services within the meaning of Article 1(1), point (b), of Directive (EU) 2015/1535 of the European Parliament and of the Council which allow undertakings to offer goods or services: (i) to other undertakings, with a view to facilitating the initiating of direct transactions between those undertakings, or (ii) to final consumers, with a view to facilitating the initiating of direct transactions between those undertakings and final consumers".[17]

This definition differs slightly from the one of online intermediation services as used under the P2B-Regulation as the Vertical Guidelines indicate.[18] Thus: What do "online intermediation services" under the VBER have in common with those under the P2B-Regulation? The answer is given by Table 9.1 which shows both their similarities and their differences.

If an undertaking active in the online platform economy enters into a vertical agreement, the question is which requirements must be met in order to be exempt under the VBER. Figure 9.1 shows how to qualify such agreements and distinguishes, where necessary, the different types of undertakings:

While the rationale for this qualification is understandable and the consequence drawn consistent with the qualification of both the online intermediation services and the goods or services that are transacted being contract products.[19] However, such qualification is dispensable because Article 4(a) VBER generally covers restricting the sale price (not the "resale price"). It also seems hardly consistent with the stipulation that each function has to be assessed separately.[20]

[17] Article 1(1)(e) VBER.

[18] VBER, Recital 11. See the detailed comparison below.

[19] VGL, para. 60.

[20] VGL, para. 746.

Table 9.1 Online intermediation services: VBER vs P2B compliance

	VBER	P2B regulation
Definition	Article 1(1)(e) means **information society services** within the meaning of Article 1(1) (b) of Directive (EU) 2015/1535 which **allow undertakings to offer goods or services to** – other undertakings, with a view to facilitating the initiating of direct transactions between those undertakings **or** – final consumers, with a view to facilitating the initiating of direct transactions between those undertakings and final consumers irrespective of whether and where the transactions are ultimately concluded	Article 2(2) – constitute **information society services** within the meaning of Article 1(1) (b) of Directive (EU) 2015/1535 – **allow business users to offer goods or services** to **consumers**, with a view to facilitating the initiating of direct transactions between those business users and consumers, irrespective of where those transactions are ultimately concluded **and** – are provided to business users on the basis of contractual relationships between the provider of those services and business users which offer goods or services to consumers
Similarities	• **information society services** within the meaning of Article 1(1), point (b), of Directive (EU) 2015/1535 of the European Parliament and of the Council • Mediation activity independent of the actual conclusion of the transaction • Target: initiation of **direct transactions** for the mediation of **goods** and **services**	
Differences	• Mediation of direct transactions **to undertakings and final consumers** • **Undertakings**/as a contractual partner of the OIS	• Mediation of direct transactions **only to business users** • **business users** as a contractual partner of the OIS[a] • Provision of the services on the **basis of a contractual relationship**[b]

[a] The scope differs as the VBER refers to undertakings, the P2B to business users
[b] Explicitly required by P2B Regulation only. The VBER however, requires an agreement, too

Appendix: Digital Distribution—Selection Criteria

Table 9.2 provides a checklist of quality requirements for online sales which applies especially, but not only for selective distribution.[21]

[21] Cf. VGL 2010, para. 54 ("quality standards ... in particular [i.e. not only] for selective distribution").

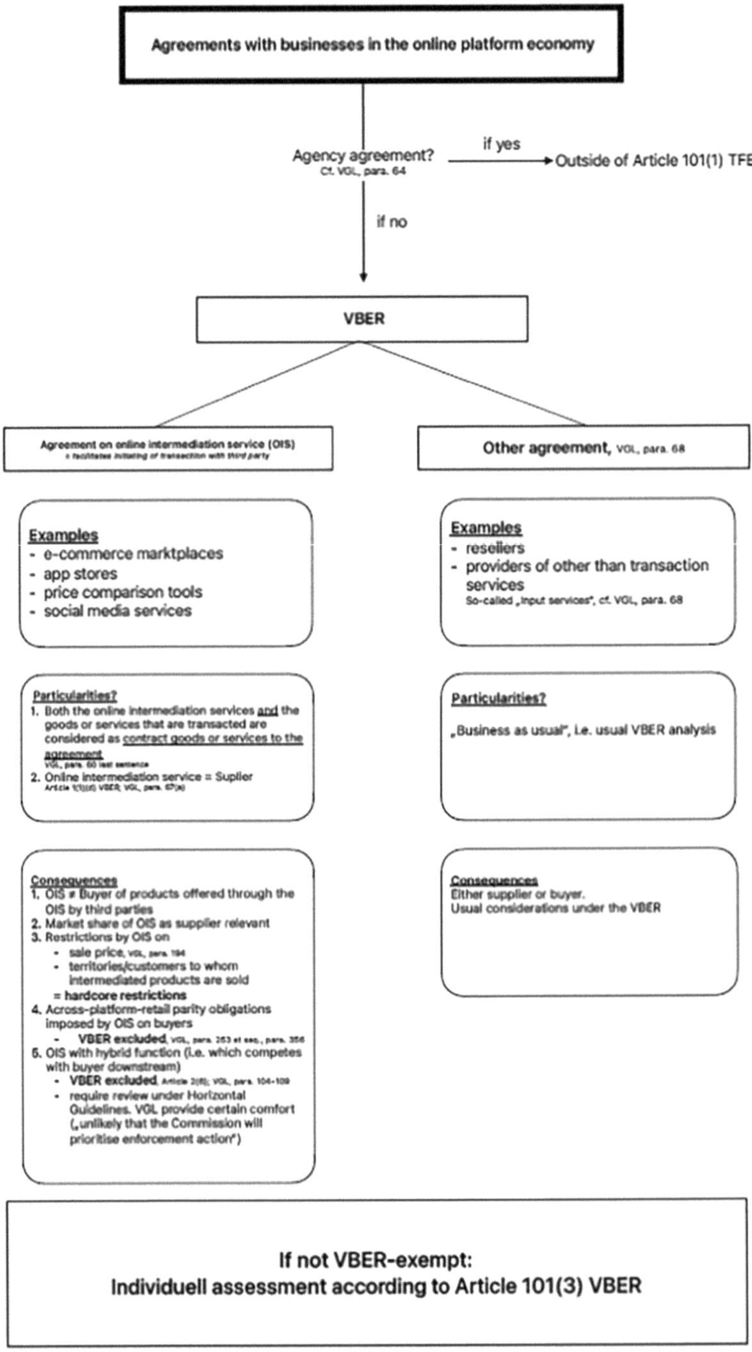

Fig. 9.1 Agreements with businesses in the online platform economy

Table 9.2 Checklist: quality requirements for online sales[a]

#	Quality scope	Quality requirements
1	Reason for selective distribution	• Branded or luxury goods or complex or technical products • Quality standard of the products, their environment and service, high customer expectations, positioning of the brand (s). • Sustainable protection
2	Requirements for admitting online sales	• Duty to effectively run at least one shop or showroom (brick and mortar clause[b]), i.e.: – Retail shop/Showroom – Minimum turnover/minimum purchase (fixed in absolute terms, not relative to online trading)
3	General requirements for online sales	• Internet address and domain: – Authorisation by supplier – No domains or terms that indicate inferior quality – Domain: Trademark is not a component – Reference to independence of the distributor from the supplier • Positioning website(s) as a specialist retailer in design, assortment, communication • Prohibition of sale via third party platforms – If applicable: limited only to open platforms or only with regard to certain platforms not approved by the supplier – General ban: All externally recognisable online platforms of third parties (logo clause[c])
4	Special requirements for the internet presence	
4.1	Website design	• Quality, e.g. functional and technical features: – Fast access and loading times – clear, uncomplicated navigation – High quality of the presentation – Various payment methods, secured through current encryption technology – Clearly understandable, clear ordering process • Look and Feel – High-quality design, presentation of goods – No ballyhooing, no puffery elements – No "sell-outs", "junk" sales, "flea market" atmosphere • Images, logos, trademarks – Visibility/Advertising on Homepage – Current material, either from supplier and/or professionally produced material – Control rights for supplier • Shop-in-shop presentation: exclusive presentation of the supplier's products on website • Sales: limited, customary, designation, maintaining quality of advice, brand environment
4.2	Website content	• Compliance with all legal, country-specific regulations (telemedia laws incl. provider identification, distance contract, e-commerce, consumer protection, unfair competition, data protection, data security). • Certification of the store as a "Trusted Shop" of Trusted Shops AG or comparable quality criteria:

(continued)

Table 9.2 (continued)

#	Quality scope	Quality requirements
		– Provider identification – Data protection and data security – Product description, distribution and marketing restrictions – Delivery information, availability and customer service – Payment – Right of withdrawal and purchase price refund – General terms and conditions • High rates of positive customer feedback • Product details (availability in real time, number of images per product from different perspectives, detailed, clear, correct product information, with official designation determined by the supplier). • Information about the supplier and links to the supplier • Information on the address of shops (if applicable, their availability of goods) • Stock availability, expected delivery time/delivery date, delivery status with minimum update requirements.
4.3	Product range on the website	• Website assortment • Assortment of contract goods • Promotion of new goods • Support for product range maintenance by suppliers • Stock
4.4	Processing online purchases	• Order processing (clear, up-to-date, high quality, professionally operated, secure, detailed overview before final purchase incl. legal price information, delivery costs, total amount, expected delivery date). • Order tracking (products, delivery date, right of withdrawal) • Delivery, delivery method • Data protection • Quantities customary for the end consumer
4.5	Customer service	• Customer advisory service • Customer service (information about supplier, distributors, website, products, comprehensive consulting, ordering, order processing) • Quality of advice (knowledge of contract products, features, fit, philosophy) • Counselling hours (hours/day, weekdays, response times) • Communication tools (e-mail, telephone, online chat, augmented reality; clearly indicated). • After-sales service (exchange, warranty, repairs, return costs in case of revocation)
4.6	Advertising	• Advertising by the specialist distributor (no terms with negative or disparaging content; to be send to supplier for inspection) • Advertising on authorised website (reference to products, no damage to image) • Restriction of marketing tools • External links: no image damaging links, no advertising or spyware, no pop-ups, forced-clicks, redirects, etc. • AdWord online marketing: subject to approval[d]

(continued)

Table 9.2 (continued)

#	Quality scope	Quality requirements
4.7	Sustainability	• Responsible sourcing and waste management • Online store: Emission goals/carbon footprint, especially concerning energy consumption (servers) • Eco-friendly delivery services

[a] The criteria for online and offline sales may be different. They do not need to be equivalent any more, as long as the criteria for online sales do not have the object of preventing the effective use of the internet as sales channel, cf. VGL, para. 235, thereby leaving the equivalence principle behind, set up in the previous VGL 2010, para. 56: "... the Commission considers any obligations which dissuade appointed dealers from using the internet to reach a greater number and variety of customers by imposing criteria for online sales which are not overall equivalent to the criteria imposed for the sales from the brick and mortar shop as a hardcore restriction"

[b] Cf. VGL, para. 208(d)

[c] Online marketplace bans may already fall out of the scope of Article 101 TFEU (if selective distribution complies with the "Metro criteria") or be block exempt, irrespective of the distribution system (if the ban does not have the object of preventing the effective use of the internet as sales channel, which "in principle" [VGL, para. 336, i.e. with exceptions is not the case where the buyer remains free to operate its own online store and advertise online]), cf. VGL, para. 150 and para. 208, 334 et seq

[d] Which must not be unreasonably withheld, especially not in regard to the supplier's trademarks or brand names, cf. VGL, para. 206(g)

References

European Commission (2017) Final Report on the e-commerce sector inquiry. 10 May 2017. https://competition-policy.ec.europa.eu/system/files/2021-10/2017_ecommerce_SI_final_report_en.pdf. Accessed 13 Feb 2023

Mundt A (2022) Die neue Vertikal-GVO – Bereit für die Zukunft ZVertriebsR 2022:205

Nasdaq (2017) UK Online Shopping and E-Commerce Statistics for 2017. https://www.nasdaq.com/articles/uk-online-shopping-and-e-commerce-statistics-2017-2017-03-14. Accessed 10 Feb 2023

Rohrßen B (2016) Plattformverbote im Selektivvertrieb – der EuGH-Vorlagebeschluss des OLG Frankfurt vom 19.4.2016. ZVertriebsR 2016:278–284

Rohrßen B (2019) Internetvertrieb 2019/20 – Vertriebsvorgaben, (Best-)Preise & Platform-to- 297 Business-Verordnung. ZVertriebsR 2019:341–347

Rohrßen B (2018) Vertriebsvorgaben im E-Commerce 2018: Praxisüberblick und Folgen des "Coty"-Urteils des EuGH. GRUR-Prax 2018:39–41

Rohrßen B (2021) Digitale Distribution in der EU – Digital Single Market: Neue Regeln im E-Commerce ab 2022. ZVertriebsR 2021:71–79

Practical Implementation of the VBER 2022 10

Abstract New agreements, new rules, existing agreements existing rules, but only until 31 May 2023. From 1 June 2023 all vertical agreements are subject to the latest Vertical Block Exemption Regulation. Fortunately, especially for suppliers, the new rules are generally more lenient and thus do not require to overhaul all agreements and templates. However, it is worth considering whether to use the new leeway granted, e.g. to opt for shared exclusivity, pass on territory and customer restrictions, or have non-compete clauses (or entire distribution and franchise agreements) evergreen. In the case of dual distribution, the business operations should be made aware of the more detailed rules on information exchange, while retail parity obligations have to be reviewed for compliance with the new, stricter rules. Also, OEM and other industrial buyers must allow their component suppliers to sell components as spare parts to wholesalers. In case of unlawful restrictions, thoughtful drafted severability clauses may be a way out of unwanted, unbalanced distribution and other supply agreements.

New agreements, new rules: The Vertical Block Exemption Regulation 2022 and the corresponding Vertical Guidelines 2022 **apply since June 2022** according to Article 10 VBER. All vertical agreements concluded since then require—to be block exempt—fulfilling the conditions of the new VBER.

Existing agreements still benefit from a transitional period**:** Vertical agreements that have been in force on 31 May 2022 must be adapted by 31 May 2023. Hence, as with its predecessor VBER 2010, also the new VBER 2022 provides for a **transition period of one year**.

The "reboot"[1] of the Vertical Block Exemption Regulation is accompanied by the review of other competition law regulations. In particular, the European Commission

[1] See above the introduction.

B. Rohrßen, *VBER 2022: EU Competition Law for Vertical Agreements*, Law for Professionals, https://doi.org/10.1007/978-3-031-35024-5_10

is putting the MVBER for the motor vehicles' aftermarket, the horizontal block exemption regulations and the market definition notice to the "test".[2]

10.1 Analysing the Business and the Supply Chain

Implementing the VBER first requires an **analysis of the status quo** of the supplier's operations, the market, the products and the objectives. Such analysis includes considering and **answering a set of questions** on the market, all parameters of competition, the supply chain and the planned strategy:

- **Where does the provider stand in relation to the market:** Is it brand new, long-established, or is market entry only in the planning stage? Does the supplier have or intend to establish an undertaking of its own on the market?
- **What is the market situation:** Does the supplier meet the market share thresholds set by the VBER? What is the market structure on the supply and purchase side[3]? What is the degree of market power of the parties to the agreement[4]? Who and how strong are the competitors? Who and how strong are existing or future/potential distribution intermediaries?
- **What are the supplier's objectives**, especially in the light of the products concerned: Is the supplier ready to invest and bear the risk of distribution? Does the supplier intend to establish a specific sale price/a uniform sale price in Europe? Does the product require specific quality of service in sales and/or aftersales, especially in the case of "technically advanced clocks and watches"[5] or other technically advanced products, e.g. "quality ceramic tableware"[6] or other "high-quality articles"[7]? Does the product require a uniform network?

Tailoring a distribution system to the business needs does not end with choosing a distribution structure that complies with the relevant competition law. It also requires considering product laws to ensure product compliant distribution set up. The structuring of distribution therefore is not only at the crossroads of distribution specific contract law and distribution specific competition law, but also at the crossroads with product law.[8] Insofar, the following questions are to be answered,

[2]Cf. European Commission (2020, pp. 14 et seq.).

[3]VBER, Recital 4.

[4]VBER, Recital 7.

[5]Commission Decision of 21 December 1976, Case No. IV/5715 (Junghans) Official Journal L 030, pp. 10 et seq. para. 22.

[6]Commission Decision of 16 December 1985, Case No. IV/30.665 (Villeroy & Boch) Official Journal L 376, pp. 15 et seq. para. 25.

[7]Commission Decision of 16 December 1991, Case No. IV/33.242 (Yves Saint Laurent Parfums) Official Journal L 012, pp. 24 et seq. para. 5.

[8]As if compliance with contract, distribution and product laws was not sufficient, the EU is continuously regulating the digital economy. Thus, market players have to look out for further laws, including data protection, consumer rights laws, digital services, product requirements.

too, in order to implement a **holistically structured distribution system** if the supplier is not manufacturing the products in the EU:

- **Has the supplier analysed its supply chain?** Is there an importer (e.g. company which sells the product to customers within the EU) or is the supplier delivering directly to the end-customer? Is the respective company prepared to serve as importer from product liability and safety side? Does the supplier agree with this company actually acting as its importer (e.g. is likely to gain insight to your IP relevant documents) or would the supplier prefer commissioning an authorized representative?
- If the supplier delivers the products directly to the customers within the EU: **Does the supplier already have a fulfilment service provider** (who takes care of warehousing, packaging, addressing and dispatching the products) or authorised representative (who has a written mandate to act on the supplier's behalf)[9]?
- **Do the products fulfil all labelling requirements** in terms of naming your importer and/or economic operator according to Article 4 European Market Surveillance Regulation? Is the EU declaration of conformity reflecting the distribution setup? Is the supplier/the importer/authorised representative registered with all relevant authorities/registers/platforms[10]? Does the importer/fulfilment service provider/authorised representative have sufficient expertise to control the incoming products for conformity with EU laws (in case of the importer), for ensuring the products are registered with a responsible, EU-based party (in case of the fulfilment service provider) or act as official EU point of contact and cooperate with national surveillance bodies/competent national authorities? Does the (non-EU established) supplier intend to sell the products via online marketplaces? Does the provider of the online market place have expertise to fulfil its obligations under the future General Product Safety Regulation[11]?

The best fit for distribution depends on the answers to the questions above. If the supplier seeks for the highest degree of control or influence, including the right to set the sale price, relying on own employees as inhouse sales force or on commercial agents is an option—because the relationship with employees and, in principle also with agents, is outside the scope of Article 101(1) TFEU (see above Sect. 1.1.5). For the same reason, employees and commercial agents are both also one option where the supplier is long established and has market shares beyond 30% and thus falls out of the scope of the VBER. Therefore, direct sales and verticalization (including shop-in-shop systems, consignment or commission models) have been on the rise in

[9]Cf. the Market Surveillance Regulation (EU) 2019/1020, with its general obligations for the economic operators in Article 4 and the specific rules for authorised representatives in Article 5.

[10]E.g. for waste electrical and electronic equipment ("WEEE"), where manufacturers are obliged to register with the authority stiftung ear https://www.ear-system.de/ear-verzeichnis/hersteller#no-back in Germany before placing electrical and electronic equipment or batteries on the market; distributors must submit annual statistical reports if they recycle the WEEE they take back.

[11]For details see Spiegel (2023).

the past decade, further boosted by the online sales.[12] Both employees and commercial agents require considering the constant (employees) or future (commercial agents) costs involved as employment and agency agreements are both subject to mandatory laws, including on termination notice (both), social security (employees) and indemnity at termination (agents). In both models, the sales risk remains with the supplier until the product is sold to the customer.

If, on the contrary, the supplier is new on the market and aims for a cost-effective means of distribution, the supplier may rather opt for the commercial agents as their remuneration is success-oriented. The contractual structure with commercial agents, at least where no multilevel structure exists and the distribution intermediary does not act as dual agent, is less sophisticated than for distributors or franchisees.

If suppliers already have an attractive, proven product and an elaborated sales strategy/know-how which they plan to roll out on a larger scale without investing in every single outlet and bearing a reduced sales risk, exclusive or selective distribution or franchise systems may be the way to go. Among the different distribution systems, however, franchise systems are at a "higher evolutionary stage"[13]—both in terms of the ramp up-work the supplier has to do to start the system and the know-how the supplier has to provide. Unlike employees or commercial agents, distributors and franchisees are not paid by the supplier—instead, they pay the supplier, for integrating the franchisees into the system, for providing the know-how and/or for selling the products. However, agreements with distributors and franchisees are subject to competition law—hence the supplier's control is limited. As a **rule of thumb**, the more integrated the distribution intermediary is with the supplier, the higher the general costs and the lower the competition law limits, i.e. the higher the degree of control (and vice versa).

10.2 Gap Analysis: Checklist of Change

As the VBER has been updated, the purchasing, sales and distribution operations must be reviewed. Existing agreements must be updated where competition law has become stricter, they can be updated where they provide more leeway. The synopsis of VBER 2010 versus 2022 in Appendix 1 shows the differences in the regulation's wording. The **checklist in** Table 10.1 supports the gap analysis of existing vertical agreements and templates for such agreements. The checklist provides **an overview of the most important points for drafting distribution agreements**. The first column lists the various vertical agreements (for which concerted practices are also sufficient,[14] so that an update of the operating staff is also due), the second

[12]Rohrßen (2022, p. 296).

[13]Emde (2018, p. 442).

[14]Cf. Article 101(1) TFEU: "The following shall be prohibited . . .: all agreements between undertakings . . . and concerted practices . . . which have as their object or effect the . . . restriction . . . of competition".

Table 10.1 Checklist of change from VBER 2010 to VBER 2022[a]

Vertical agreement	Need vs chance of change[b]	Change *(Unchanged rules in italics)*
Agency agreements	=	*Agent ≠ independent economic operator if no significant financial or commercial risk*[c] *→ Out of scope of Article 101(1) TFEU*
Dual role agents	>	**Agency privilege extends** to agents that act as agent + independent distributor for the same person for different products if four conditions are given[d]
Dual distribution	>	→ **Exemption explicitly extends to importers and wholesalers of goods**:[e] Exempt if (i) non-reciprocal vertical agreement and (ii) parties not competing upstream where buyer buys[f,g]
	~ **More clarity**	→ **Exempt: Information exchange if necessary** to improve production/ distribution
Dual distribution with hybrid online platforms	<	↓ **Excluded from VBER**:[h] Agreements with hybrid platforms require Article 101(1), (3) TFEU-test + Horizontal Guidelines
Pricing (Restricting the sale price)	= **In general** ~ **More clarity for fulfilment**	*→ Exempt: RRP* *→ Exempt: Maximum prices* *↓ Hardcore: RPM* *↓ Hardcore: MAP* → Clarification: Fulfilment scenario exempt
Dual pricing	>	→ **Exemption extended to dual pricing**, no longer hardcore restriction if to incentivize/reward investment. ↓ **Limit**: Must not prevent effective use of internet for online sales
Exclusive distribution	>	→ **Shared exclusivity**: Supplier may allocate exclusive sales territory/ customer group to up to five distributors. → **Passing on** the territory/customer restriction to distributors' direct customers
Selective distribution	>	→ **Intrusion protection extended**: Restricting active sales by selective or free distributors[i] and their direct customers (in)to exclusive territories/ customer groups[j] → **Passing on** the territory/customer restriction: to distributors' customers and their customers

(continued)

Table 10.1 (continued)

Vertical agreement	Need vs chance of change[b]	Change *(Unchanged rules in italics)*
		→ **Exemption extended to qualitative criteria that differ** between offline and online sales.[k] ↓ **Limit:** must not have object of preventing online sales
Free distribution	**= In general** **> Intrusion protection**	→ **Intrusion protection extended to selective distribution territories** (see selective distribution)
Franchising	**< Dual distribution with hybrid platforms** **> Exclusive/Selective distribution, Non-competes, Online sales restrictions**	(Non-)Exemptions follow the rules of the distribution system that most closely corresponds to concrete franchise agreement
Online sales and online advertising	**> Dual pricing, Quality criteria** **~ More clarity**	→ **Exemption extended to (i) dual pricing and (ii) different quality criteria** offline and online (see above) • **Clarification:** Online marketplace bans in principle exempt
Spare parts supply	<	↓ **Hardcore restriction extended** as regards buyers restricting component suppliers in selling spare parts **to unauthorized wholesalers**
Non-compete obligations	>	→ **Exemption extended to evergreening non-competes** if buyer can renegotiate or terminate with reasonable notice and cost[l]
Post-term non-compete obligations	=	→ *Exempt only under four conditions of Article 5(3) VBER*
Across-Platform Retail Parity Obligations[m]	<	**Excluded from VBER** due to competition concerns, require Article 101(3) TFEU-test[n]
Other Parity Obligations	=	→ *Exempt: All other types than across-platform retail parity obligations*
Exclusive supply (aka industrial supply)[o]	~	**Remains exempt**, even if Vertical Guidelines **seem to differ slightly**: Exclusive supply "is exempted" (VGL 2010, para. 193) versus "can benefit" from the VBER (VGL 2022, para. 322)
Upfront access payments[o]	~	**Remain exempt**, even if Vertical Guidelines **seem to differ slightly**: Upfront access payments "are exempted" (VGL 2010, para. 203), whereas VGL 2022 now are simply silent, only elaborate on the Article 101(3) TFEU-test (VGL 2022, para. 379)

(continued)

Table 10.1 (continued)

Vertical agreement	Need vs chance of change[b]	Change *(Unchanged rules in italics)*
Category management[o]	~	**Remains exempt**, even if Vertical Guidelines **seem to differ slightly**: Category management agreements "are exempted" (VGL 2010, para. 209) versus they "can benefit" from the VBER 2022 (VGL 2022, para. 385)
Tying[o]	~	**Remains exempt**, even if Vertical Guidelines **seem to differ slightly**: Tying "is exempted" (VGL, para. 218) versus it "can benefit" from the VBER (VGL 2022, para. 393)

[a] Cf. Rothermel and Rohrßen (2022, pp. 227 et seq.)
[b] ">" stands for new rules that expand the leeway ("opportunity to adjust"), "<" stands for new rules that reduce the leeway ("obligation to adjust"), "=" stands for rules that remain essentially identical, while "~" stands for rules which appear to be identical, but leave a backdoor for a less lenient assessment in the individual case
[c] VGL, para. 30
[d] VGL, para. 36
[e] Article 2(4)(a) VBER
[f] To be more precise: VBER if supplier is a manufacturer/wholesaler/importer and (downstream) importer/wholesaler/retailer, but the dealer is a (downstream) importer, wholesaler or retailer
[g] "Dual distribution exception", cf. VGL, para. 105
[h] Not exempt only means that the vertical agreement is not exempt under the VBER. It requires an individual assessment of whether it falls (i) inside the scope of Article 101(1) TEFU and, if so, (ii) it is exempt under Article 101(3) TFEU
[i] Article 4(b)(ii) and (d)(ii) VBER
[j] Article 4 VBER 2010 did not (explicitly) exempt suppliers who restricted sales into other distribution systems, it could nevertheless be interpreted to allow for such possibility, see Sect. 10.3.2
[k] VGL, para. 235
[l] VGL, para. 248
[m] Aka: "broad" versus "narrow retail parity obligation" which only apply to the buyer's direct sales channels
[n] VGL, para. 360; details on assessment: para. 360–368
[o] As exclusive supply, upfront access payment, category management and tying benefits from the exemption principle in Articles 2 and 3 VBER, there is no reason for reducing said exemption. Most likely, the different wording is, like others, due to the Commission's wish to keep all doors open

column shows the need or chance for changes, and the third column summarises the new issues. In other words, the second and third columns show where companies have the obligation or the opportunity to adapt (to stricter or to more lenient VBER rules).

10.3 Designing/Restructuring Distribution Systems

Suppliers are free to design and/or restructure the distribution of their products. When suppliers implement the VBER, their freedom is limited. In return for complying with the VBER, they receive legal certainty.

Furthermore, suppliers have many options even under the VBER. For example, they can set criteria for the sale of their products, irrespective of the distribution system: They may establish "... requirements imposed by the supplier on the buyer relating to the manner in which the contract goods or services are to be sold can benefit from the exemption provided by Article 2(1) of Regulation 2022/720 irrespective of the type of distribution system",[15] offline and online.[16]

Suppliers are free to combine different vertical restraints (see Sect. 10.3.1). Suppliers are also free to set up more than one distribution system in the EU/EEA. At least as long as the different systems refer to different products or different customers/territories (see Sect. 10.3.2); combining exclusive and selective distribution in the same territory for the same product, is, instead, in principle not exempt under the VBER (see Sect. 10.3.3). Finally, changes can benefit from statutory transition periods; alternatively, unlawful scenarios can be avoided by implementing a clear-cut roll-out of new agreements or by assessing and limiting the effects of transitional scenarios (Sect. 10.3.4).

10.3.1 Combining Vertical Restraints

Combinations of vertical restraints are lawful as long as they do **not** together **have an anti-competitive objective or effect**[17] (as the effect may indicate the objective; and the effect "suffices" for excluded restrictions and restrictions outside the VBER). Such combinations may lead to disapplication of the VBER—and such disapplication may be limited to specific restraints.[18] Insofar, combining vertical restraints is key—or risk, especially as the prohibition of anti-competitive agreements in Article 101(1) TFEU sanctions both direct and indirect restraints of competition: ".... which have as their object or effect ...", explicitly including agreements that "directly or indirectly fix purchase or selling prices".

---

[15] Cf. also VGL, para. 207.

[16] VGL, para. 208.

[17] Cf. the introductory sentence of Article 4 VBER: "... in isolation or in combination". Cf. also VGL, para. 202 and 203.

[18] VGL, para. 270, 272.

As a **rule of thumb**, restrictions can be combined—as long as none of them is hardcore and as long as their combination does not indirectly have the effect of appreciably affecting the competition. Table 10.2 summarizes the examples of many combinations covered by the Vertical Guidelines that are commonly taken into consideration in practice:

Table 10.3, instead, gives examples of combinations that are outside the vertical BER due to the parties' market share:

Table 10.2 Combinations of non-hardcore restrictions under the VBER

Exempt under the VBER	Not exempt under the VBER
→ **Non-hardcore restriction** combined with **other non-hardcore** restriction, unless their combination has the object of appreciably affecting competition	
→ **Exclusive distribution** combined with **other non-hardcore** vertical restraints[a]	↓ **Exclusive and selective** distribution for one product in the same territory = **hardcore** restriction[b]
→ **Exclusive distribution "in square"**: appoint exclusive distributor for particular customer group in specific territory[c]	
→ **Selective distribution** combined with **other non-hardcore** vertical restraints[d]	↓ **Selective distribution** must not be combined with **exclusive sourcing** as it would restrict cross-supplies[e]
→ **Selective distribution** combined with **non-competes** as long as they do not relate to one or more specific competing suppliers as it could lead to foreclosure[f] Article 5(1)(c) VBER	
→ **Agency and independent distribution** ("agents with dual role"). Exempt if agent bears only insignificant/no financial/economic risks. Therefore, investments and costs between both functions must be clearly delineated[g]	
→ **Franchising** itself is usually a combination of different restraints (e.g. selective distribution and non-competes, IPR related restrictions)[h]	
→ Restricting **two or more forms** of **online advertising** (e.g. the use of specific price comparison services plus others)[i]	

[a] VGL, para. 120
[b] VGL, para. 236
[c] VGL, para. 221
[d] VGL, para. 151
[e] VGL, para. 237
[f] VGL, para. 252
[g] VGL, para. 37
[h] VGL, para. 165
[i] VGL, para. 354 (whether such combination has a net anti-competitive effect)

Table 10.3 Combinations of non-hardcore restrictions outside the VBER

Combination outside VBER	How to handle/Article 101(3) TFEU
↓ **Exclusive distribution** and **single branding** outside VBER	**Assess and monitor** cumulative anti-competitive effects[a]
↓ **Exclusive distribution** and **exclusive sourcing** outside VBER	**Assess & monitor** competition concerns (intra-brand competition[b])
↓ **Selective distribution** combined with **single branding** (non-compete): competition concerns outside VBER	**Assess individually**, risk of foreclosure of other suppliers[c]
↓ **Selective distribution** combined with **location** clause outside VBER	**Exempt if indispensable** to e.g. protect investments by distributors, especially if service criteria alone insufficient[d]

[a] VGL, para. 128, 137
[b] VGL, para. 129
[c] VGL, para. 160
[d] VGL, para. 162

10.3.2 Combining Different Distribution Systems: Reciprocal Protection

Suppliers are free to set up different distribution systems in the EU/EEA.[19] The VBER also allows (or: obliges[20]) to reciprocally protect the different systems against each other, as laid down in Article 4(b)(ii), Article 4(c)(i)(1) and Article 4(d)(i) and (ii):[21,22]

Suppliers can prohibit distributors in exclusive and free distribution systems to sell (actively or passively) to unauthorized distributors in territories where the supplier operates a selective distribution system. Vice versa, suppliers may also prohibit distributors in selective and free distribution systems to actively sell into territories or to customer groups where the supplier operates an exclusive distribution system. Suppliers may also pass on such territory/customer restriction to their buyers (distributors) and request them to pass them on—in relation to exclusive

[19] Argumentum e contrario VGL, para. 236; see below Sect. 10.3.3.

[20] Operating a selective distribution system requires per definition that "the *supplier undertakes* to sell the contract goods or services, either *directly or indirectly*, *only* to distributors selected" (Article 1(1)(g) VBER), while operating an exclusive distribution system requires suppliers to "restrict(..) all its other buyers from actively selling into the exclusive territory or to the exclusive customer group", Article 1(1)(h) VBER. Moreover, the applicable national distribution laws may provide for a duty to protect the distributor against sales from the outside.

[21] These are carve-outs from the hardcore restrictions concerning exclusive, selective and free distribution.

[22] Article 4 VBER 2010 did not (explicitly) exempt suppliers who restricted sales into other distribution systems. Nevertheless, there has been one interpretation that allows for such possibility by establishing the principle that suppliers can require their distributors to comply with the distribution systems in other territories, cf. Bechtold et al. (2014, Artikel 1 VO 330/2010 para. 35); Bechtold et al. (2023, Vertikal-GVO Art. 1 para. 37).

territories/customer groups to the next level in the distribution chain, and in relation to selective territories/customer groups to all levels of the distribution chain.[23]

10.3.3 Combining Exclusive and Selective Distribution in a Territory?

The combination of different distribution systems for one and the same product in one territory is **not exempt** because of the diametric setup of both distribution types. This applies also, according to the Vertical Guidelines, at different levels of distribution, for example, exclusive distribution at the wholesale and selective distribution at the retail level.[24]

Does, however, this view hold true for every scenario? More specifically, the question is twofold: (i) Is such a combination exempt and (ii) if it is exempt, is it effective, i.e. does it allow to protect the respective other distribution type from intrusion?[25]

While operating selective distribution ("SD") and exclusive distribution ("ED") in different territories is exempt and a mutual protection may be set up,[26] different scenarios for combining both distribution types in the same territory have to be distinguished, as shown in Table 10.4.

All in all, the answer to the above two-fold question is: Yes and no: Although some scenarios can be designed to fall under the VBER, they generally lead to gaps in the distribution network which make the combination hardly effective.[27] In the end, two principles can be used: (i) Retailers' operations can always be restricted to their place of establishment,[28] and (ii) wholesalers' sales to end users can be prohibited.[29] These, however, do not suffice to close all the gaps of each distribution network.

Alternatively, other, less restrictive options exist, especially for who prefers following the explicit guidance provided by the European Commission:[30] Instead of combining selective and exclusive distribution, suppliers may simply implement location clauses (binding the distributors to sell the products only out of a specific

---

[23] Cf. e.g. VGL, para. 240 for free distribution systems: "The restriction [concerning territories with selective distribution] may cover active or passive sales [to unauthorized distributors] at any level of trade".

[24] VGL, para. 236.

[25] The latter question has been negated by the prevailing opinion in legal literature under the VBER 2010, cf. only Baron (2020, Vert-GVO Art. 4 para. 331).

[26] Cf. Sect. 10.3.2.

[27] The situation, thus, is as under the VBER 2010, cf. for the then prevailing opinion in legal literature Schultze et al. (2019), para. 911 et seq.; Baron (2020, Vert-GVO Art. 4 para. 331).

[28] Article 4(b)(iii) VBER; Article 4(c)(i)(3) VBER.

[29] Article 4(b)(iv), Article 4(c)(i)(4) and (d)(iv) VBER.

[30] Which the Commission suggests instead, VGL, para. 236.

Table 10.4 Combining selective and exclusive distribution

#	Scenario		VBER 2022
	Wholesale	Retail	
1	ED	ED	Wholesaler's sales to end users can be restricted.[a] Retailer must be free to sell to others.[b]
2	SD	SD	Wholesaler's sales to end users can be restricted.[c] Retailer must be free to sell to other authorised retailers.[d]
3	ED	SD	Wholesaler's sales to end users can be restricted.[e] Retailer must be free to sell to other authorised retailers.[f]
4	SD	ED	Wholesaler's sales to end users can be restricted.[g] Retailer must be free to sell to others (as #1), including other wholesalers. Structure **contradicts SD** as Supplier must only sell "directly or indirectly" to selected distributors, cf. Article 1(1)(g) VBER.
5	Supplier	ED + SD	SD must be free to sell to end customers and other authorised retailers, Supplier must only sell to authorised (selected) distributors.[h] Structure **contradicts SD** because ED must be free to sell also to unauthorised retailers. **Way out: ED (up to five distributors) combined with quality criteria.**
6	ED + SD	Others	**As #5.**

[a] Article 4(b)(iv) VBER
[b] Article 4(b) introductory sentence VBER
[c] Article 4(c)(i)(4) VBER
[d] Article 4(c)(ii) VBER
[e] As scenario #1
[f] Article 4(c)(ii) VBER
[g] Article 4(c)(iii) in conjunction with Article 4(c)(1) VBER. Thanks for the fruitful discussions with the *cher confrère* Jean-Philippe Arroyo/J.P. Karsenty & Associés, Paris and members from the European Commission, especially at the conferences of the International Distribution Institute and the AIJA T.R.A.D.E. and Antitrust Commissions in June 2022
[h] Article 1(1)(g) VBER

place of [physical, offline] establishment[31] or they may stipulate an exclusive supply (binding the supplier to sell contract products only or mainly to one buyer). Furthermore, the shared exclusivity, together with a reasonable allocation of territories/customer groups, opens up new options for suppliers, as exclusive distribution can be combined with quality requirements.

10.3.4 Transition Periods for Implementing Change

Implementing changes takes time, especially in complex distribution systems which cover multiple territories/customer groups and multiple levels of trade. Therefore, the VBER has foreseen a **transitional one-year period** in Article 10 VBER: While

[31] This restriction is exempt throughout all distribution systems, cf. Article 4(b)(iii), (c)(i)(3) and (d)(iii) VBER; restricting the online presence is, however, not covered hereby (see above Sects. 4.2.5 and 4.3.7).

the VBER came into force on 1 June 2022, **agreements that have already existed at that date have (had) time until 31 May 2023** to adapt—provided they satisfied the conditions for exemption under the VBER 2010.

Changes may be required by the VBER 2022—or optional. Or they may occur later, when suppliers consider restructuring their distribution systems, for whatever reason, e.g. future changes in (case) law, or technical, service- or market-related developments. For such temporary reorganization periods, unlawful restraints by effect may be disregarded. Or, as the European Commission puts it:

> Where, for practical reasons and not with the object of preventing parallel trade, the exclusive territory or customer group is not protected from active sales by certain buyers for a temporary period, for example where the supplier modifies the exclusive distribution system and requires time to re-negotiate active sales restrictions with certain buyers, the exclusive distribution system may still benefit from the exemption provided by Article 2(1) of Regulation (EU) X.)[32]

Better than relying on leniency in cases of transition, the transition ideally follows a clear schedule for roll-out where all the gears mesh properly. If need be, e.g. restructuring starts at the upstream level of distribution, the scenario should be assessed individually upfront[33] and document the overweighing pro-competitive effects: Distribution agreements which fall inside the scope of Article 101(1) TFEU but for whatever reason outside the VBER, may nevertheless comply with Article 101 TFEU—if the parties can show that the vertical agreement leads to economic benefits that outweigh the negative effects of the restriction of competition. For a more detailed overview on the **four requirements** of Article 101(3) VBER see Sect. 1.7.

10.4 Severability Clauses as a Loophole?

What happens to distribution or supply contracts if one or more clauses are void because they violate competition law? The answer usually follows directly from the agreement itself, as severability clauses are among the boilerplate clauses used and reused in many agreements. Some severability clauses only provide for upholding the agreement, others also specify which rules to apply instead.

Example

Severability clause: The invalidity of one or more provisions of this contract shall not affect the validity of the remainder of the contract. The Parties shall replace the invalid provision with a provision that comes as close as possible to the economic purpose of this contract by joint agreement. The same shall apply to any loopholes in the contract. ◀

[32] VGL, para. 122.

[33] VGL, para. 181.

Such severability clauses will regularly be valid, depending on the applicable law, provided that they do not aim at circumventing the laws requiring the invalidity of the respective contractual clause. For example, the parties may explicitly express their intention to comply with competition law, specifically with the VBER, in the preamble or close by to the vertical restrictions.[34] Such stipulation may help when interpreting the contract, especially in scenarios where the law is ambiguous.

Without (valid) severability clauses, the consequences of invalid contractual clauses are provided by the applicable civil or commercial law, which usually upholds freedom of contract. The law of the EU Member States usually stipulates rules in case that parts of contracts are void—as does the Draft Common Frame of Reference. The Draft Common Frame of Reference is a project by the Study Group on a European Civil Code and the Research Group on EC Private Law (Acquis Group). They have sought an answer to the scattered state of European contract law. The Draft Common Frame of Reference answers both questions which arise when contract clauses are void: Shall the remaining contract survive—and, in the affirmative, what shall apply in place of the unenforceable contract clause?

Example

Section 3: Infringement of fundamental principles or mandatory rules

II.–7:301: Contracts infringing fundamental principles

A contract is void to the extent that: (a) it infringes a principle recognised as fundamental in the laws of the Member States of the European Union; and (b) nullity is required to give effect to that principle.

II.–7:302: Contracts infringing mandatory rules

(1) Where a contract is not void under the preceding Article but infringes a mandatory rule of law, the effects of that infringement on the validity of the contract are the effects, if any, expressly prescribed by that mandatory rule.
(2) Where the mandatory rule does not expressly prescribe the effects of an infringement on the validity of a contract, a court may; (a) declare the contract to be valid; (b) avoid the contract, with retrospective effect, in whole or in part; or (c) modify the contract or its effects.
(3) A decision reached under paragraph (2) should be an appropriate and proportional response to the infringement, having regard to all relevant circumstances, including: (a) the purpose of the rule which has been infringed; (b) the category of persons for whose protection the rule exists; (c) any sanction that may be imposed under the rule infringed; (d) the seriousness of the infringement; (e) whether the infringement was intentional; and (f) the closeness of the relationship between the infringement and the contract.

[34] As suggested for a single supply obligation which according to its wording restricts the supplier of components, thereby exceeding Article 4(f) VBER, cf. Schultze (2019, para. 960); Nolte (2022, Nach Art. 101 AEUV para. 583).

II.–7:303: Effects of nullity or avoidance

(1) The question whether either party has a right to the return of whatever has been transferred or supplied under a contract, or part of a contract, which is void or has been avoided under this Section, or a monetary equivalent, is regulated by the rules on unjustified enrichment.
(2) The effect of nullity or avoidance under this Section on the ownership of property which has been transferred under the void or avoided contract, or part of a contract, is governed by the rules on the transfer of property.
(3) This Article is subject to the powers of the court to modify the contract or its effects.

II.–7:304: Damages for loss

(1) A party to a contract which is void or avoided, in whole or in part, under this Section is entitled to damages from the other party for any loss suffered as a result of the invalidity, provided that the first party did not know and could not reasonably be expected to have known, and the other party knew or could reasonably be expected to have known, of the infringement.
(2) The damages recoverable are such as to place the aggrieved party as nearly as possible in the position in which that party would have been if the contract had not been concluded or the infringing term had not been included.[35] ◀

Quick drafting of contracts may tempt to provide for some standard severability clauses as they at least express the parties' intention to uphold a contract even if one or more contract clauses are void. However, before relying on such standard too quickly, thought should be given to the consequences, especially if the invalidity, nullity or unenforceability (altogether here: unenforceability) of a provision **can change the entire business relationship**. This applies in particular to unenforceability due to non-compliance with competition law because such invalidity might turn the distribution contract's objective on its head.

Therefore, every contract, especially if it is of long duration, should be examined to see whether the business intended with it will be **substantially affected** by the severance of the valid part. If there is a risk, e.g. legal uncertainty due to a lack of case law, it is worth designing a contract-specific **severability clause** as well. Such a clause may contain

- specific fall-back provisions,
- a specific right and procedure to agree on changes to the contract,
- a right to terminate the contract, possibly combined with a right for the party adversely affected by the unenforceability to be indemnified, provided this does not unlawfully circumvent the law which has resulted in the unenforceability.

[35] von Bar et al. (2009, pp. 227 et seq.).

Ideally, however, such a clause is not needed, especially because of the **pragmatic shortcut offered by the Vertical Block Exemption Regulation**. This shortcut to legally certain distribution and franchise agreements is briefly summarized in Table 10.5, i.e. it offers a shortcut to the shortcut.

Appendix to Chapter 10

Table 10.5 Vertical restraints—the VBER 2022 in one table[a]

#	Vertical restraints—how they are treated under the VBER 2022	VBER	VGL
In force since/from	1 June 2022 until 31 May 2034	Article 11	(-)
Transition for existing agreements	Until 31 May 2023	Article 10	(-)
Material scope	• Vertical agreements (incl. concerted practices) = purchasing, selling or reselling goods or services ("products"[b]) at different production/ distribution chain levels • Including franchise, licence or technology transfer unless IP rights = main subject matter	Recital 1–3, Article 2(1) and Article 1(1)(a)	para. 48–70
Out of scope	• IP agreements where transfer/use of IP rights is primary object → TTBER • Automotive aftermarket → MVBER • Research and development → R&DBER	Article 2(3) Article 2(7)	para. 71–87 and 110–114
Market shares	≤30% held by supplier on sales market and by buyer on purchase market	Recital 8–9 Articles 3, 8, 9	para. 67(b), 68; 170–176
Agency agreements	= Entrusting person with power to negotiate and/or conclude contracts on behalf of another ('principal'), in agent's own or principal's name, for purchase from or supply by principal[c]	(-)	para. 29–46

(continued)

Table 10.5 (continued)

#	Vertical restraints—how they are treated under the VBER 2022	VBER	VGL
	↑ Agent **out of scope** of Article 101(1) TFEU ≠ independent economic operator **if** no significant financial or commercial risk[d]		
Dual role agents	= Undertaking[e] is independent distributor + agent for the same person for different products[f] → Dual role agents' agency agreement **out of scope** of Article 101(1) TFEU **if** 1. activities and risks effectively delineated (for products with additional features),[g] 2. agent/independent distributor free to enter distribution/agency relationship, and 3. all significant[h] financial and economic risk are borne by the principal 4. does not facilitate collusion, e.g. several principals use same agent[i] (online platforms)	(-)	para. 36–40
Dual distribution	= Supplier sells products upstream AND downstream, thereby competes with distributors[j] → **Exempt if (i)** non-reciprocal vertical agreement **and (ii)** parties not competing at upstream level where buyer buys[k,l]	Recital 12–14 Article 2(3)-(4)	para. 88–96
	→ **Exempt: Information exchange if necessary** to improve production/distribution of products, e.g.: • **Exempt:** Technical	Article 2(5)	para. 96–103

(continued)

Table 10.5 (continued)

#	Vertical restraints—how they are treated under the VBER 2022	VBER	VGL
	info, supply-related info (production, stock, sales quantities, returns); aggregated customer info; current resale prices of buyer, RRP or maximum sale prices as long as not used for RPM or minimum price setting, marketing info, including on advertising campaigns; performance-related info, including aggregated info on marketing and sales activities of other customers; sales volumes and revenues with contract goods/services compared to competing ones. • **Non-exempt:** Info on future resale prices (exception possible); customer-specific sales data (exception possible); information on competing private label products of the distributor. Concerns about horizontal info sharing can be addressed through aggregation, delayed forwarding of information, or ring-fencing		
Dual distribution with hybrid online platforms	= Dual distribution where supplier of online intermediation services competes with buyer on the market for sale of intermediated goods.[m] ↓ **Not exempt.**[n] Platform Services Agreement (on online marketplace or price comparison site), require assessment under	Recital 14 Article 2(6)	para. 67(e), 104–109

(continued)

Table 10.5 (continued)

#	Vertical restraints—how they are treated under the VBER 2022	VBER	VGL
	Article 101(1), (3) TFEU + Horizontal Guidelines.		
Pricing (Restricting the sale price)	→ Exempt: RRP → Exempt: Maximum prices ↓ Hardcore: RPM (including indirect measures, e.g. combining RRP o maximum prices with incentives or pressure to apply certain price levels[o] or with supplier's price monitoring and information systems or distributor's reporting obligations[p]), Article 4 (a) ↓ Hardcore: MAP (exception: to prevent loss leaders, via Article 101(3) TFEU) → Clarification: Fulfilment scenario exempt	Recital 15 Article 4(a)	para. 185–201
Dual pricing	→ **Exempt** (no longer hardcore restriction) **if** objective is incentivizing/rewarding investment in distribution channel through price difference. ↓ Limit: Must not prevent effective use of internet for online sales.	Article 4(b)-(d)	para. 209
Exclusive distribution	= Distribution system where supplier allocates territory/customer group to itself or maximum five buyers and restricts all other buyers from actively selling thereto.[q] **Exempt:** → Territory/customer restriction: Supplier may restrict active sales of its exclusive distributors,	Article 1(1)(h) Article 4(b)	para. 217–226

(continued)

Table 10.5 (continued)

#	Vertical restraints—how they are treated under the VBER 2022	VBER	VGL
	selective distributors, free distributors and other buyers (in)to exclusive territories/ customer groups → Intrusion protection: Restricting active sales by selective or free distributors and their direct customers (in)to exclusive territories/ customer groups[r] → Shared exclusivity: Supplier may allocate exclusive sales territory/ customer group exclusively to up to five distributors. → Passing on the territory/customer restriction: Supplier may require its exclusive distributors to pass on the restriction to distributors' direct customers → Restriction of place of establishment[s] → Restriction of sales of wholesalers to end users[t] → Restriction of component sales to supplier's competitors[u] **Combinations**: ↓ Exclusive and selective distribution for one product in the same territory = hardcore restriction[v] → Exclusive distribution may be combined with other non-hardcore vertical restraints[w] → Exclusive distribution "in square": appoint exclusive distributor for particular customer group in specific territory[x]		

(continued)

Table 10.5 (continued)

#	Vertical restraints—how they are treated under the VBER 2022	VBER	VGL
	Outside VBER: ↓ Exclusive distribution and single branding: ASSESS & MONITOR cumulative anti-competitive effects[y]] ↓ Exclusive distribution and exclusive sourcing: ASSESS & MONITOR competition concerns (intra-brand competition[z])		
Selective distribution	= Distribution system where supplier undertakes to sell contract products, either directly or indirectly, only to distributors selected on specified criteria, while distributors refrain from selling products to unauthorised distributors within selective distribution system's territory.[aa] Criteria may be qualitative or quantitative. **Exempt:** ↑ Qualitative selective distribution: Outside Article 101(1) TFEU if three "Metro criteria" are given[ab] → Qualitative distribution and Quantitative distribution[ac,ad] → Territory/customer restriction: Restricting the sales (active or passive) by members to unauthorised distributors in system's territory. → Intrusion protection: Restricting sales by exclusive or free distributors and their customers to	Article 1(1)(g) Article 4(c)	para. 227–237

(continued)

Table 10.5 (continued)

#	Vertical restraints—how they are treated under the VBER 2022	VBER	VGL
	unauthorised members in system's territory.[ae] → Passing on the territory/customer restriction: Supplier may require its selective distributors to pass on the restriction to distributors' customers and their customers. → Qualitative criteria: May differ between offline and online sales channels,[af] limit: must not have object of preventing online sales → Restriction of place of establishment[ag] → Restriction of sales of wholesalers to end users[ah] → Restriction of component sales to supplier's competitors[ai] **Combinations:** → Selective distribution may be combined with other non-hardcore vertical restraints[aj] → Selective distribution can be combined with non-competes as long as they do not relate to one or more specific competing suppliers as it could lead to foreclosure,[ak] Article 5(1)(c) VBER ↓ Selective distribution must not be combined with exclusive sourcing as it would restrict the freedom of cross-supplies[al] ↓ Selective distribution must not be combined with exclusive distribution in the same		

(continued)

Table 10.5 (continued)

#	Vertical restraints—how they are treated under the VBER 2022	VBER	VGL
	territory for the same product[am] **Outside VBER:** ↓ Selective distribution may be combined with minimum purchases: net negative effects rather unlikely[an] ↓ Selective distribution combined with single branding (non-compete): competition concerns (foreclosure of other suppliers)[ao] ↓ Selective distribution combined with location clause: Article 101(3) exempt if indispensable to e.g. protect investments by distributors, especially if service criteria alone do not suffice[ap]		
Free distribution	= Distribution System where supplier operates neither an exclusive distribution system nor a selective distribution system[aq] concerning the relevant territory. **Exempt:** → Intrusion protection for exclusive distribution territories: Restricting active sales by free distributors and their direct customers (in)to exclusive territories/ customer groups[ar] → Intrusion protection for selective distribution territories: Restricting sales by free distributors and their customers to unauthorised members in the selective distribution territory.[as] → Restriction of place of establishment[at]	Article 4(d)	para. 238–244

(continued)

Table 10.5 (continued)

#	Vertical restraints—how they are treated under the VBER 2022	VBER	VGL
	→ Restriction of sales of wholesalers to end users[au] → Restriction of component sales to supplier's competitors[av]		
Franchising	= Using a uniform network (uniform business name, uniform business methods) for distribution of the franchisor's products for which franchisor provides licence to business method, trademarks or signs and know-how.[aw] **Exempt:** ↑ Franchise agreements fall outside of Article 101(1) TFEU if strictly necessary for the functioning of the franchise system (as in the Pronuptia case), e.g. restrictions on using the know-how for competitors, non-competes for ensuring uniformity → Franchise agreements are VBER-exempt; vertical restraints are to be assessed according to applicable distribution system that most closely corresponds to the concrete agreement → Article 101(3) TFEU: The more important the know-how transfer, the more likely restrictions create efficiencies and are indispensable	(-)	para. 16(h), 72(d), 165–169, 174, 318
Online sales and online advertising	↓ Hardcore restriction: Agreements having the object of preventing effective use of internet for online sales and	Article 4(e)	para. 203, 206, 209, 335, 347

(continued)

Table 10.5 (continued)

#	Vertical restraints—how they are treated under the VBER 2022	VBER	VGL
	advertising → **Exempt:** • Restricting online sales, without prohibiting them entirely, i.e. keeping the online sales channel open for sales, e.g.: – Online marketplace bans – Webshop languages – Prohibition of pure online business: Brick-and-mortar clause – Quality criteria for online sales; not necessarily equivalent to those for offline sales – Dual pricing, i.e. Price incentivisation of offline sales – Other measures such as pre-launching new products online on supplier's (online) store. • Restricting online advertising, except having the object of preventing an entire online advertising channel, e.g. – Prohibition of specific price comparison tools (but no general ban of search engines or price comparison tools) – Prohibition of active advertising (in)to exclusive territories/ customer groups		
Spare parts supply	↓ **Hardcore restriction:** Restricting a component supplier in selling the components as spare parts to end users, repairers, wholesalers or other service providers not entrusted by the buyer	Article 4(f)	para. 245

(continued)

Table 10.5 (continued)

#	Vertical restraints—how they are treated under the VBER 2022	VBER	VGL
Non-compete obligations	= Any direct or indirect obligation causing the buyer not to manufacture, purchase, sell or resell products which compete with contract products, or any direct or indirect obligation on buyer to purchase from supplier or from other undertaking designated by supplier more than 80% of buyer's total purchases of contract products and substitutes on relevant market, calculated on basis of value or, where such is standard industry practice, volume of its purchases in preceding calendar year. **Not exempt, but excluded restriction.** Same effect: Single branding[ax] or English clauses[ay] or exclusive sourcing[az] **Exempt:** → Block exempt if ≤5 years → Block exempt if indefinite term where buyer can effectively renegotiate or terminate the vertical agreement with a reasonable period of notice and at a reasonable cost[ba] → Block exempt in selective distribution unless addressed against particular competitors	Article 1(1)(f) Article 5(1)(a)	para. 247–249
Post-term non-compete obligations	= Non-compete obligations (see above) for the time after termination	Article 5(1)(b) and Article 5(3)	para. 250–251

(continued)

Table 10.5 (continued)

#	Vertical restraints—how they are treated under the VBER 2022	VBER	VGL
	↓ **Not exempt, but excluded restriction.** → **Exempt only under four conditions:** 1. relates to the contract products; 2. is limited to the distribution premises, 3. is necessary to protect know-how transferred by the supplier to the buyer and 4. is limited to one year after termination.		
Across-Platform Retail Parity Obligations[bb]	= Obligation causing buyer of online intermediation services not to offer, sell or resell the products to end users under more favourable conditions (prices, inventory, availability, etc.[bc]) via competing online intermediation services ↓ **Not exempt, but excluded restriction.** Article 101(3) TFEU: Competition concerns as they soften competition.[bd]	Article 5(1)(d)	para. 253; 258, 259; 360–368
Other Parity Obligations	→ **VBER-exempt:** All other types than across-platform retail parity obligations, including • retail parity obligations (aka "narrow retail parity obligations"[be]); Article 101(3) TFEU: More likely to fulfil the efficiency than the across-platform parity obligations[bf] • non-retail ("upstream") parity obligations; Article 101(3) TFEU: Similar assessment as for retail parity obligations[bg]	Article 5(1)(d); Article 6(1)	para. 254; 356–359, 369–378

(continued)

Table 10.5 (continued)

#	Vertical restraints—how they are treated under the VBER 2022	VBER	VGL
	• most favoured customer obligations on products as input;[bh] Article 101(3) TFEU: May create efficiencies, especially minimize transaction costs, address hold-ups[bi] • Platform service agreements with parity obligations are listed as example subject to withdrawal of the VBER benefit where the market of platform service providers is highly concentrated.		
Combinations[bj] are possible as long as they do not collectively have an anti-competitive objective or effect[bk] (as the effect may indicate the objective; and the effect "suffices" for excluded restrictions and restrictions outside the VBER). Such combinations may only lead to disapplication—and such disapplication may again be limited to specific restraints[bl]	↓ Exclusive and selective distribution for one product in the same territory = hardcore restriction[bm] → Exclusive distribution combined with other non-hardcore vertical restraints[bn] → Exclusive distribution "in square": appoint exclusive distributor for particular customer group in specific territory[bo] ↓ Exclusive distribution and single branding outside VBER: ASSESS & MONITOR cumulative anti-competitive effects[bp] ↓ Exclusive distribution and exclusive sourcing outside VBER: ASSESS & MONITOR competition concerns (intra-brand competition[bq]) → Selective distribution combined with other non-hardcore vertical	Recital 15 Article 4	para. 236, 120, 221, 270, 272, 128, 137, 129, 151, 252, 237, 160, 162, 37, 165, 354

(continued)

Table 10.5 (continued)

#	Vertical restraints—how they are treated under the VBER 2022	VBER	VGL
	restraints[br] → Selective distribution combined with non-competes as long as they do not relate to one or more specific competing suppliers as it could lead to foreclosure[bs] Article 5(1)(c) VBER ↓ Selective distribution must not be combined with exclusive sourcing as it would restrict cross-supplies[bt] ↓ Outside VBER: Selective distribution combined with single branding (non-compete): competition concerns (foreclosure of other suppliers)[bu] ↓ Outside VBER: Selective distribution combined with location clause: Under Article 101(3) exempt if indispensable to e.g. protect investments by distributors, especially if service criteria alone do not suffice[bv] → Agency and independent distribution = agents with dual role = exempt if agent only bears insignificant or no financial or economic risks, i.e. investments and costs between both functions must be clearly delineated[bw] → Franchising itself is usually a combination of different restraints (e.g. selective distribution and non-competes, IPR		

(continued)

Table 10.5 (continued)

#	Vertical restraints—how they are treated under the VBER 2022	VBER	VGL
	related restrictions)[bx] → Restricting more than one form of online advertising (e.g. the use of price comparison services plus others)[by]		
Online intermediation services	= Information society services which allow undertakings to offer products: (i) to other undertakings, for facilitating the initiating of direct transactions between those undertakings, or (ii) to final consumers, for facilitating the initiating of direct transactions between those undertakings and final consumers, irrespective of whether and where transactions are ultimately concluded[bz] → Vertical agreements with online intermediation services **generally exempt by VBER**, key for VBER-interpretation in line with the Commission: (i) OIS ≠ Buyer of products offered by third parties;[ca] (ii) both the online intermediation services and the products intermediated are contract goods for the purpose of the VBER[cb] ↓ **Not VBER-exempt:** Platform service agreements with hybrid platforms[cc] (i.e. which compete with buyer downstream[cd,ce]) → VBER-excluded,[cf] require review under Article 101(1), (3) TFEU	Recital 10, 11, 14, 16 Article 1(1) (d) and (e), Article 2(6), Article 5(1)(d), Article 6	para. 60, 64–68; 104–109, 194; 253–254, 259, 332, 357, 358, 360–374, 376

(continued)

Table 10.5 (continued)

#	Vertical restraints—how they are treated under the VBER 2022	VBER	VGL
	and Horizontal Guidelines,[cg] certain comfort given: "it is unlikely that the Commission will prioritise enforcement action"[ch] ↓ Not VBER-exempt: across-platform retail parity obligations imposed by OIS on buyers → VBER-excluded.[ci]		
Exclusive supply (aka industrial supply)	= Restrictions that oblige/induce supplier to sell contract products only or mainly to one buyer.[cj] → **Exclusive supply** can be combined with other non-hardcore restraints[ck] Outside VBER: May be exempt, especially where suppliers are strong[cl]	(-)	para. 16(e), 321–331
Upfront access payments	= Fixed fees paid by suppliers to distributors at the beginning of a period, e.g. slotting allowances, pay-to-stay fees and payments for accessing distributor's promotion campaigns → **VBER: Exempt** Article 101(3) TFEU: Assessment as with exclusive supply as suppliers may tend to prefer the distributor paid for. Assessment as with single branding where distributor is strong. May, however, also contribute to efficient allocation of shelf space.	(-)	para. 379–384

(continued)

Table 10.5 (continued)

#	Vertical restraints—how they are treated under the VBER 2022	VBER	VGL
Category management	= Distributor entrusts the supplier (the 'category captain') with the marketing of a category of products[cm] → **Exempt.** Article 101(3) TFEU. May work as non-compete/single-branding. May cause upstream foreclosure[cn] or facilitate collusion.[co] Efficiencies: Distributors gain access to supplier's marketing expertise. Distributors may achieve economies of scale.[cp]	(-)	para. 385–388
Tying	= Supplier requires buyer of one product (tying product) also to purchase another distinct product (tied product) from the same supplier or a third party designated by the supplier[cq] → **Exempt**, also combined with non-hardcore restrictions,[cr] e.g. non-competes, quantity-forcing or exclusive sourcing. **Outside VBER:** Depending especially on supplier's market share: Where competitors are strong, there may not even be anti-competitive effects. Whereas combining tying with non-competes increases the supplier's market power and thus the risk of foreclosure.[cs]	(-)	para. 389–397

(continued)

Table 10.5 (continued)

#	Vertical restraints—how they are treated under the VBER 2022	VBER	VGL
	Potential efficiencies: Passing on cost reductions to consumers; ensuring uniformity/ quality standards.[ct]		

[a] In the table, = refers to definitions, ↑ means outside of Article 101(1) TFEU, → exempt under VBER, ↓ not exempt under VBER, requires Article 101(3) TFEU-test

[b] The term "products" is used as shorthand to cover both goods and services here

[c] VGL, para. 29

[d] VGL, para. 30

[e] Indirectly defined in VGL, para. 3, 56 as persons (natural and legal) who act for their trade, business, craft or professional purposes

[f] VGL, para. 36

[g] So that investments and costs for each function can be clearly delineated, VGL, para. 37

[h] VGL, para. 36 refers to "all relevant risks", which, read together with para. 31–32, must refer to significant financial or commercial risks

[i] VGL, para. 44. Collusion is a general negative requirement; agreements must not lead to foreclosure, cf. only VBER, Recital 10

[j] VBER, Recital 12

[k] More specifically: The VBER applies if the supplier is a manufacturer/wholesaler/importer and (downstream) importer/wholesaler/retailer, but the buyer is a (downstream) importer, wholesaler or retailer

[l] "Dual distribution exception", cf. VGL, para. 105

[m] VBER, Recital 14

[n] Not exempt only means that the vertical agreement is not exempt under the VBER. It requires an individual assessment of whether it falls (i) inside the scope of Article 101(1) TEFU and, if so, (ii) it is exempt under Article 101(3) TFEU

[o] VGL, para. 188

[p] VGL, para. 190

[q] Article 1(1)(h) VBER

[r] Article 4(c)(i)(2) and Article 4(d)(i) VBER

[s] Article 4(b)(ii) VBER

[t] Article 4(b)(iv) VBER

[u] Article 4(b)(v) VBER

[v] VGL, para. 236

[w] VGL, para. 120

[x] VGL, para. 221

[y] VGL, para. 128, 137

[z] VGL, para. 129

[aa] Article 1(1)(g) VBER

[ab] VGL, para. 148–150

[ac] May also be given where qualitative selection criteria are combined with minimum purchases

[ad] VGL, para. 151

[ae] Article 4(b)(ii) and Article 4(d)(ii) VBER

[af] VGL, para. 235

[ag] Article 4(c)(i)(3) VBER

[ah] Article 4(c)(i)(4) VBER

[ai] Article 4(c)(i)(5) VBER

(continued)

Table 10.5 (continued)

#	Vertical restraints—how they are treated under the VBER 2022	VBER	VGL

[aj] VGL, para. 151
[ak] VGL, para. 252
[al] Article 4(c)(ii) VBER; VGL, para. 237
[am] VGL, para. 236
[an] VGL, para. 156
[ao] VGL, para. 160
[ap] VGL, para. 162
[aq] Article 4(d) VBER
[ar] Article 4(d)(i) VBER
[as] Article 4(d)(ii) VBER
[at] Article 4(c)(i)(3) VBER
[au] Article 4(c)(i)(4) VBER
[av] Article 4(c)(i)(5) VBER
[aw] VGL, para. 165 et seq
[ax] = obliges or induces the distributor to concentrate its orders for a particular type of product with one supplier, VGL, para. 128, 298—though the difference to exclusive sourcing is not clear
[ay] VGL, para. 298–320
[az] Requires the distributor to buy the supplier's brand directly from the supplier, VGL, para. 129 (definition); para. 393 (as example of non-compete)
[ba] VGL, para. 248
[bb] Aka: "broad retail parity obligation", compared to narrow ones which only apply to the buyer's direct sales channels
[bc] VGL, para. 356
[bd] VGL, para. 360; details on assessment: para. 360–368
[be] VGL, para. 369
[bf] VGL, para. 374
[bg] VGL, para. 376
[bh] i.e. conditions under which manufacturers, wholesalers or retailers purchase products from their suppliers, cf. VGL, para. 377
[bi] VGL, para. 376
[bj] Combination is key—or risk, as the prohibition of anti-competitive agreements in Article 101(1) TFEU sanctions both restraints of competition by object and by effect and covers both direct and indirect measures (cf. only Article 101(1)(a) TFEU)
[bk] Cf. the introductory sentence of Article 4 VBER: "… in isolation or in combination". Cf. also VGL, para. 202 and 203
[bl] VGL, para. 270, 272
[bm] VGL, para. 236
[bn] VGL, para. 120
[bo] VGL, para. 221
[bp] VGL, para. 128, 137
[bq] VGL, para. 129
[br] VGL, para. 151
[bs] VGL, para. 252
[bt] VGL, para. 237
[bu] VGL, para. 160
[bv] VGL, para. 162
[bw] VGL, para. 37

(continued)

Table 10.5 (continued)

#	Vertical restraints—how they are treated under the VBER 2022	VBER	VGL

[bx] VGL, para. 165
[by] VGL, para. 354 (whether such combination has a net anti-competitive effect)
[bz] Definition used in Article 2(2) P2B-Regulation (EU) 2019/1150 adapted according to Recital 11 VBER as it here especially refers to "undertakings" due to the use in competition law context
[ca] VGL, para. 67(a)
[cb] VGL, para. 60 last sentence: "In the case of vertical agreements relating to the provision of online intermediation services, both the online intermediation services and the goods or services that are transacted via the online intermediation services are considered as contract goods or services for the purpose of applying Regulation (EU) 2022/720 to the agreement"
[cc] Article 2(6) VBER
[cd] VGL, para. 67(e). Hybrid function = online intermediation services which intermediate products and also compete with the buyer of the intermediation services on the market for sale of those very products
[ce] Care must be taken as the dual distribution exception does already not apply in case of potential competition, i.e. if the OIS can within less than a year make the necessary investments to enter the market for sale of the intermediated goods, cf. VGL, para. 106
[cf] Article 2(6) VBER; VGL, para. 104–109, excluded from VBER as they did not fulfil the rationale of dual distribution exceptions in Article 2(4) VBER, but would tend to favour their own sales
[cg] Cf. VGL, para. 107. The new, updated Horizontal Guidelines are to implemented in June 2023, see above, Sect. 1.6
[ch] VGL, para. 109
[ci] Article 5(1)(d) VBER
[cj] VGL, para. 321
[ck] VGL, para. 322
[cl] VGL, para. 327
[cm] VGL, para. 385
[cn] VGL, para. 386
[co] VGL, para. 387
[cp] VGL, para. 388
[cq] VGL, para. 389
[cr] VGL, para. 393
[cs] VGL, para. 395
[ct] VGL, para. 397

References

Baron M (2020) 7. Teil.B. Vertikalvereinbarungen. Vert-GVO. In: Loewenheim U et al (eds) Kartellrecht, 4th edn. C.H. Beck, Munich

Bechtold R, Bosch W, Brinker I (2014) EU-Kartellrecht, 3rd edn. C.H. Beck, Munich

Bechtold R, Bosch W, Brinker I (2023) EU-Kartellrecht, 4th edn. C.H. Beck, Munich

Emde R (2018) Weichenstellungen beim Entscheid über den Abschluss von Vertriebsverträgen. NJOZ 2018:441–445

European Commission (2020) Strategic Plan 2020-2024. comp_sp_2020_2024_en.pdf (europa.eu). Accessed 10 Feb 2023

Nolte S (2022) Nach Art. 101 AEUV. In: Langen E, Bunte H-J (eds) Kartellrecht, vol 2, 14th edn. Luchterhand, Cologne

Rohrßen B (2022) Online-Vertrieb in der EU – Vertriebskartellrecht: Die neue Vertikal-GVO 2022. ZVertriebsR 2021:293–298

Rothermel M, Rohrßen B (2022) Die neue Vertikal-GVO: Strukturelle Synopse und praktische Konsequenzen. IHR 2022:221–230

Schultze J-M, Pautke S, Wagener DS (2019) Vertikal-GVO, Gruppenfreistellungsverordnung für vertikale Vereinbarungen, 4th edn. Deutscher Fachverlag, Frankfurt am Main

Spiegel U (2023) Online-Marktplätze unter der Produktsicherheitsverordnung. ZVertriebsR 2023: 71–80

von Bar C, Clive E, Schulte-Nölke H (eds) (2009) Principles, definitions and model rules of European private law, Draft Common Frame of Reference (DCFR). Sellier Munich. https://doi.org/10.1515/9783866537279. Accessed 11 Feb 2023

Appendix 1: Synopsis VBER 2010 vs 2022

COMMISSION REGULATION (EU) *No 330/2010* 2022/720[1]

of 20 April 2010 **10 May 2022**

on the application of Article 101(3) of the Treaty on the Functioning of the European Union to categories of vertical agreements and concerted practices

(Text with EEA relevance)

THE EUROPEAN COMMISSION,

Having regard to the Treaty on the Functioning of the European Union,

Having regard to Regulation No 19/65/EEC of the Council of 2 March 1965 on the application of Article 85(3) of the Treaty to certain categories of agreements and concerted practices ([1]), and in particular Article 1 thereof,

Having published a draft of this Regulation (**[2]**),

After consulting the Advisory Committee on Restrictive Practices and Dominant Positions,

Whereas:

(1) Regulation No 19/65/EEC empowers the Commission to apply Article 101(3) of the Treaty *on the Functioning of the European Union ([2])* by regulation to certain categories of vertical agreements and corresponding concerted practices falling within Article 101(1) of the Treaty.

(2) Commission Regulation *(EC) No 2790/1999 of 22 December 1999 on the application of Article 81(3) of the Treaty to categories of vertical agreements and concerted practices* **(EU) No 330/2010** ([3]) defines a category of vertical agreements *which* **that** the Commission regarded as

[1] Wording in **bold** = added in VBER 2022, wording in *italics* = deleted in VBER 2022.

B. Rohrßen, *VBER 2022: EU Competition Law for Vertical Agreements*, Law for Professionals, https://doi.org/10.1007/978-3-031-35024-5

normally satisfying the conditions laid down in Article 101(3) of the Treaty. *In view of the overall positive experience* **Experience** with the application of *that* Regulation **(EU) No 330/2010**, which expires on 31 May *2010***2022**, *and taking* **has been positive overall, as shown by the evaluation of that Regulation. Taking** into account *further experience acquired since its adoption* **that experience as well as new market developments, such as the growth of e-commerce, and new or more prevalent types of vertical agreements**, it is appropriate to adopt a new block exemption regulation.

(3) The category of agreements which can be regarded as normally satisfying the conditions laid down in Article 101(3) of the Treaty includes vertical agreements for the purchase or sale of goods or services where those agreements are concluded between non-competing undertakings, between certain competitors or by certain associations of retailers of goods. It also includes vertical agreements containing ancillary provisions on the assignment or use of intellectual property rights. The term 'vertical agreements' should **be understood to** include the corresponding concerted practices.

(4) For the application of Article 101(3) of the Treaty by regulation, it is not necessary to define those vertical agreements which are capable of falling within Article 101(1) of the Treaty. In the individual assessment of agreements under Article 101(1) of the Treaty, account has to be taken of several factors, *and* in particular the market structure on the supply and purchase side.

(5) The benefit of the block exemption established by this Regulation should be limited to vertical agreements for which it can be assumed with sufficient certainty that they satisfy the conditions of Article 101(3) of the Treaty.

(6) Certain types of vertical agreements can improve economic efficiency within a chain of production or distribution by facilitating better coordination between the participating undertakings. In particular, they can lead to a reduction in the transaction and distribution costs of the parties and to an optimisation of their sales and investment levels.

(7) The likelihood that such efficiency-enhancing effects will outweigh any anti-competitive effects due to restrictions contained in vertical agreements depends on the degree of market power of the parties to the agreement and, *therefore* **in particular**, on the extent to which those undertakings face competition from other suppliers of goods or services regarded by their customers as interchangeable or substitutable for one another, by reason of the products' characteristics, their prices and their intended use.

(8) It can be presumed that, where the market share held by each of the undertakings party to the agreement on the relevant market does not exceed 30%, vertical agreements which do not contain certain types of

severe restrictions of competition generally lead to an improvement in production or distribution and allow consumers a fair share of the resulting benefits.

(9) Above the market share threshold of 30%, there can be no presumption that vertical agreements falling within the scope of Article 101(1) of the Treaty will usually give rise to objective advantages of such a character and size as to compensate for the disadvantages *which* **that** they create for competition. At the same time, there is no presumption that those vertical agreements are either caught by Article 101(1) of the Treaty or that they fail to satisfy the conditions of Article 101(3) of the Treaty.

(10) The online platform economy plays an increasingly important role in the distribution of goods and services. Undertakings active in the online platform economy make it possible to do business in new ways, some of which are not easy to categorise using concepts associated with vertical agreements in the traditional economy. In particular, online intermediation services allow undertakings to offer goods or services to other undertakings or to final consumers, with a view to facilitating the initiation of direct transactions between undertakings or between undertakings and final consumers. Agreements relating to the provision of online intermediation services are vertical agreements and should therefore be able to benefit from the block exemption established by this Regulation, subject to the conditions set out in this Regulation.

(11) The definition of online intermediation services used in Regulation (EU) 2019/1150 of the European Parliament and of the Council ([4]) should be adapted for the purpose of the present Regulation. In particular, to reflect the scope of Article 101 of the Treaty, the definition used in the present Regulation should refer to undertakings. It should also include online intermediation services that facilitate the initiation of direct transactions between undertakings, as well as those that facilitate the initiation of direct transactions between undertakings and final consumers.

(12) Dual distribution refers to the scenario where a supplier sells goods or services not only at the upstream level but also at the downstream level, thereby competing with its independent distributors. In that scenario, in the absence of hardcore restrictions, and provided that the buyer does not compete with the supplier at the upstream level, the potential negative impact of the vertical agreement on the competitive relationship between the supplier and buyer at the downstream level is less important than the potential positive impact of the vertical agreement on competition in general at the upstream or downstream level. This Regulation should therefore exempt vertical agreements entered into in such scenarios of dual distribution.

(13) **The exchange of information between a supplier and buyer can contribute to the pro-competitive effects of vertical agreements, in particular the optimisation of production and distribution processes. However, in dual distribution, the exchange of certain types of information may raise horizontal concerns. Therefore, this Regulation should only exempt information exchange between a supplier and a buyer in a dual distribution scenario where the information exchange is both directly related to the implementation of the vertical agreement and necessary to improve the production or distribution of the contract goods or services.**

(14) **The rationale for exempting vertical agreements in scenarios of dual distribution does not apply to vertical agreements relating to the provision of online intermediation services where the provider of the online intermediation services is also a competing undertaking on the relevant market for the sale of the intermediated goods or services. Providers of online intermediation services that have such a hybrid function may have the ability and the incentive to influence the outcome of competition on the relevant market for the sale of the intermediated goods or services. This Regulation should therefore not exempt such vertical agreements.**

(*10***15**) This Regulation should not exempt vertical agreements containing restrictions which are likely to restrict competition and harm consumers or which are not indispensable to the attainment of the efficiency-enhancing effects. In particular, **the benefit of the block exemption established by this Regulation should not apply to** vertical agreements containing certain types of severe restrictions of competition, such as minimum and fixed resale-*prices, as well as* **prices and** certain types of territorial protection, *should be excluded from the benefit of the block exemption established by this Regulation irrespective of the market share of the undertakings concerned.* **including the prevention of the effective use of the internet to sell or certain restrictions of online advertising. Accordingly, restrictions of online sales and online advertising should benefit from the block exemption established by this Regulation, provided that they do not, directly or indirectly, in isolation or in combination with other factors controlled by the parties, have the object of preventing the effective use of the internet by the buyer or its customers to sell the contract goods or services to particular territories or customers, or of preventing the use of an entire online advertising channel, such as price comparison services or search engine advertising. For instance, online sales restrictions should not benefit from the block exemption established by this Regulation where their objective is to significantly diminish the aggregate volume of online sales of the contract goods or services in the relevant market or the possibility for consumers to buy the contract goods or services**

online. The categorisation of a restriction as hardcore within the meaning of Article 4, point (e) may take into account the content and context of the restriction, but should not depend on market-specific circumstances or the individual characteristics of the parties.

(*11***16**) *In order* **This Regulation should not exempt restrictions for which it cannot be assumed with sufficient certainty that they satisfy the conditions of Article 101(3) of the Treaty. In particular,** to ensure access to *or* **and** to prevent collusion on the relevant market, certain conditions should be attached to the block exemption. To this end, the exemption of non-compete obligations should be limited to obligations which do not exceed a *defined* duration **of five years**. *For the same reasons, any direct or indirect obligation* **Obligations** causing the members of a selective distribution system not to sell the brands of particular competing suppliers should **likewise** be excluded from the benefit of this Regulation. **The benefit of this Regulation should not apply to retail parity obligations causing buyers of online intermediation services not to offer, sell or resell goods or services to end users under more favourable conditions via competing online intermediation services.**

(*12***17**) The market- share limitation, the non-exemption of certain vertical agreements and the conditions provided for in this Regulation *normally* **generally** ensure that the agreements to which the block exemption applies do not enable the participating undertakings to eliminate competition in respect of a substantial part of the *products* **goods or services** in question.

(*13***18**) The Commission may withdraw the benefit of this Regulation, pursuant to Article 29(1) of Council Regulation (EC) No 1/2003 *of 16 December 2002 on the implementation of the rules on competition laid down in Articles 81 and 82 of the Treaty (*[4]([5]), where it finds in a particular case that an agreement to which the **block** exemption *provided for in* **established by** this Regulation applies nevertheless has effects which are incompatible with Article 101(3) of the Treaty. **The competition authority of a Member State may withdraw the benefit of this Regulation where the conditions of Article 29(2) of Regulation (EC) No 1/2003 are fulfilled.**

(14) *The competition authority of a Member State may withdraw the benefit of this Regulation pursuant to Article 29(2) of Regulation (EC) No 1/ 2003 in respect of the territory of that Member State, or a part thereof where, in a particular case, an agreement to which the exemption provided for in this Regulation applies nevertheless has effects which are incompatible with Article 101(3) of the Treaty in the territory of that Member State, or in a part thereof, and where such territory has all the characteristics of a distinct geographic market.*

(19) **Where the Commission or the competition authority of a Member State withdraws the benefit of this Regulation, it has the burden of proving that the vertical agreement in question falls within the scope of Article 101(1) of the Treaty, and that the agreement fails to fulfil at least one of the four conditions of Article 101(3) of the Treaty.**

(*15***20**) In determining whether the benefit of this Regulation should be withdrawn pursuant to Article 29 of Regulation (EC) No 1/2003, the anti-competitive effects that may derive from the existence of parallel networks of vertical agreements that have similar effects, which significantly restrict access to a relevant market or competition therein, are of particular importance. Such cumulative effects may *for example* **in particular** arise in the case of **exclusive distribution, exclusive supply,** selective distribution, **parity obligations** or non -compete obligations.

(*16***21**) In order to strengthen **the** supervision of parallel networks of vertical agreements which have similar anti-competitive effects and which cover more than 50% of a given market, the Commission may by regulation declare this Regulation inapplicable to vertical agreements containing specific restraints relating to the market concerned, thereby restoring the full application of Article 101 of the Treaty to such agreements,

HAS ADOPTED THIS REGULATION:

Article 1

Definitions

1. For the purposes of this Regulation, the following definitions shall apply:

(a) 'vertical agreement' means an agreement or concerted practice *entered into* between two or more undertakings, each of which operates, for the purposes of the agreement or the concerted practice, at a different level of the production or distribution chain, and relating to the conditions under which the parties may purchase, sell or resell certain goods or services;

(b) 'vertical restraint' means a restriction of competition in a vertical agreement falling within the scope of Article 101(1) of the Treaty;

(c) 'competing undertaking' means an actual or potential competitor; 'actual competitor' means an undertaking that is active on the same relevant market; 'potential competitor' means an undertaking that, in the absence of the vertical agreement, would, on realistic grounds and not just as a mere theoretical possibility, *in case of a small but permanent increase in relative prices* be likely *to undertake*, within a short period of time, **to make** the necessary additional investments or **incur** other necessary *switching* costs to enter the relevant market;

(d) 'supplier' includes an undertaking that provides online intermediation services;

(e) 'online intermediation services' means information society services within the meaning of Article 1(1), point (b), of Directive (EU) 2015/1535 of the European Parliament and of the Council ([6]) which allow undertakings to offer goods or services:

(i) **to other undertakings, with a view to facilitating the initiating of direct transactions between those undertakings, or**

(ii) **to final consumers, with a view to facilitating the initiating of direct transactions between those undertakings and final consumers, irrespective of whether and where the transactions are ultimately concluded;**

(*d***f**) 'non-compete obligation' means any direct or indirect obligation causing the buyer not to manufacture, purchase, sell or resell goods or services which compete with the contract goods or services, or any direct or indirect obligation on the buyer to purchase from the supplier or from another undertaking designated by the supplier more than 80% of the buyer's total purchases of the contract goods or services and their substitutes on the relevant market, calculated on the basis of the value or, where such is standard industry practice, the volume of its purchases in the preceding calendar year;

(*e***g**) 'selective distribution system' means a distribution system where the supplier undertakes to sell the contract goods or services, either directly or indirectly, only to distributors selected on the basis of specified criteria and where these distributors undertake not to sell such goods or services to unauthorised distributors within the territory reserved by the supplier to operate that system;

(h) 'exclusive distribution system' means a distribution system where the supplier allocates a territory or group of customers exclusively to itself or to a maximum of five buyers and restricts all its other buyers from actively selling into the exclusive territory or to the exclusive customer group;

(*f***i**) 'intellectual property rights' includes industrial property rights, know **-** how, copyright and neighbouring rights;

(*g***j**) 'know-how' means a package of non-patented practical information, resulting from experience and testing by the supplier, which is secret, substantial and identified*: in this context,***;** 'secret' means that the know-how is not generally known or easily accessible; 'substantial' means that the know-how is significant and useful to the buyer for the use, sale or resale of the contract goods or services; 'identified' means that the know-how is described in a sufficiently comprehensive manner so as to make it possible to verify that it fulfils the criteria of secrecy and substantiality;

(*h*(**k**) 'buyer' includes an undertaking which, under an agreement falling within Article 101(1) of the Treaty, sells goods or services on behalf of another undertaking;

(i) 'customer of the buyer' means an undertaking not party to the agreement which purchases the contract goods or services from a buyer which is party to the agreement.

(l) 'active sales' means actively targeting customers by visits, letters, emails, calls or other means of direct communication or through targeted advertising and promotion, offline or online, for instance by means of print or digital media, including online media, price comparison services or advertising on search engines targeting customers in particular territories or customer groups, operating a website with a top-level domain corresponding to particular territories, or offering on a website languages that are commonly used in particular territories, where such languages are different from the ones commonly used in the territory in which the buyer is established;

(m) 'passive sales' means sales made in response to unsolicited requests from individual customers, including delivery of goods or services to the customer, without the sale having been initiated by actively targeting the particular customer, customer group or territory, and including sales resulting from participating in public procurement or responding to private invitations to tender.

2. For the purposes of this Regulation, the terms 'undertaking', 'supplier' and 'buyer' shall include their respective connected undertakings.

'Connected undertakings' means:

(a) undertakings in which a party to the agreement, directly or indirectly:
    (i) has the power to exercise more than half the voting rights, or
    (ii) has the power to appoint more than half the members of the supervisory board, board of management or bodies legally representing the undertaking, or
    (iii) has the right to manage the undertaking's affairs; **or**
(b) undertakings which directly or indirectly have, over a party to the agreement, the rights or powers listed in point (a); **or**
(c) undertakings in which an undertaking referred to in point (b) has, directly or indirectly, the rights or powers listed in point (a); **or**

(d) undertakings in which a party to the agreement together with one or more of the undertakings referred to in points (a), (b) or (c), or in which two or more of the latter undertakings, jointly have the rights or powers listed in point (a); **or**

(e) undertakings in which the rights or the powers listed in point (a) are jointly held by:
  (i) parties to the agreement or their respective connected undertakings referred to in points (a) to (d), or
  (ii) one or more of the parties to the agreement or one or more of their connected undertakings referred to in points (a) to (d) and one or more third parties.

Article 2

Exemption

1. Pursuant to Article 101(3) of the Treaty and subject to the provisions of this Regulation, it is hereby declared that Article 101(1) of the Treaty shall not apply to vertical agreements. This exemption shall apply to the extent that such agreements contain vertical restraints.

2. The exemption provided for in paragraph 1 shall apply to vertical agreements entered into between an association of undertakings and *its members* **an individual member**, or between such an association and *its suppliers* **an individual supplier**, only if all *its* **the** members **of the association** are retailers of goods and if no individual member of the association, together with its connected undertakings, has a total annual turnover exceeding EUR 50 million. Vertical agreements entered into by such associations shall be covered by this Regulation without prejudice to the application of Article 101 of the Treaty to horizontal agreements concluded between the members of the association or decisions adopted by the association.

3. The exemption provided for in paragraph 1 shall apply to vertical agreements containing provisions which relate to the assignment to the buyer or use by the buyer of intellectual property rights, provided that those provisions do not constitute the primary object of such agreements and are directly related to the use, sale or resale of goods or services by the buyer or its customers. The exemption applies on **the** condition that, in relation to the contract goods or services, those provisions do not contain restrictions of competition having the same object as vertical restraints which are not exempted under this Regulation.

4. The exemption provided for in paragraph 1 shall not apply to vertical agreements entered into between competing undertakings. However, *it* **that exemption** shall apply where competing undertakings enter into a non-reciprocal vertical agreement and **one of the following applies**:

(a) the supplier is **active at an upstream level as** a manufacturer *and a distributor*, **importer, or wholesaler and at a downstream level as an importer, wholesaler, or retailer** of goods, while the buyer is *a distributor* **an importer, wholesaler, or retailer at the downstream level** and not a competing undertaking at the *manufacturing* **upstream** level **where it buys the contract goods**; or
(b) the supplier is a provider of services at several levels of trade, while the buyer provides its *goods or* services at the retail level and is not a competing undertaking at the level of trade where it purchases the contract services.

5. The exceptions set out in paragraph 4, points (a) and (b) shall not apply to the exchange of information between the supplier and the buyer that is either not directly related to the implementation of the vertical agreement or is not necessary to improve the production or distribution of the contract goods or services, or which fulfils neither of those two conditions.
6. The exceptions set out in paragraph 4, points (a) and (b) shall not apply to vertical agreements relating to the provision of online intermediation services where the provider of the online intermediation services is a competing undertaking on the relevant market for the sale of the intermediated goods or services.
*5*7. This Regulation shall not apply to vertical agreements the subject matter of which falls within the scope of any other block exemption regulation, unless otherwise provided for in such a regulation.

Article 3

Market share threshold
1. The exemption provided for in Article 2 shall apply on condition that the market share held by the supplier does not exceed 30% of the relevant market on which it sells the contract goods or services and the market share held by the buyer does not exceed 30% of the relevant market on which it purchases the contract goods or services.
2. For the purposes of paragraph 1, where in a multi -party agreement an undertaking buys the contract goods or services from one undertaking **that is a** party to the agreement and sells the contract goods or services to another undertaking **that is also a** party to the agreement, the market share of the first undertaking must respect the market share threshold provided for in that paragraph both as a buyer and a supplier in order for the exemption provided for in Article 2 to apply.

Article 4

Restrictions that remove the benefit of the block exemption—hardcore restrictions
The exemption provided for in Article 2 shall not apply to vertical agreements which, directly or indirectly, in isolation or in combination with other factors under the control of the parties, have as their object:

(a) the restriction of the buyer's ability to determine its sale price, without prejudice to the possibility of the supplier to impose a maximum sale price or recommend a sale price, provided that they do not amount to a fixed or minimum sale price as a result of pressure from, or incentives offered by, any of the parties;

(c) the restriction of active or passive sales to end users by members of a selective distribution system operating at the retail level of trade, without prejudice to the possibility of prohibiting a member of the system from operating out of an unauthorised place of establishment;

(b) **where the supplier operates an exclusive distribution system,** the restriction of the territory into which, or of the customers to whom, *a buyer party to the agreement, without prejudice to a restriction on its place of establishment, may* **the exclusive distributor may actively or passively** sell the contract goods or services, except:

(i) the restriction of active sales *into* **by** the exclusive **distributor and its direct customers, into a** territory or to *an exclusive* **a** customer group reserved to the supplier or allocated by the supplier *to another buyer, where such a restriction does not limit sales by the customers of the buyer,* **exclusively to a maximum of five other exclusive distributors;**

(ii) the restriction of active or passive sales by the exclusive distributor and its customers to unauthorised distributors located in a territory where the supplier operates a selective distribution system for the contract goods or services;

(iii) the restriction of the exclusive distributor's place of establishment;

(*ii***iv**) **the restriction of active or passive** sales to end users by *a buyer* **an exclusive distributor** operating at the wholesale level of trade**;**

(*iii*(**v**) the restriction of the exclusive distributor's ability to actively or passively sell components, supplied for the purposes of incorporation, to customers who would use them to manufacture the same type of goods as those produced by the supplier;

(iv) the restriction of the buyer's ability to sell components, supplied for the purposes of incorporation, to customers who would use them to manufacture the same type of goods as those produced by the supplier;

(c) where the supplier operates a selective distribution system,

(i) **the restriction of the territory into which, or of the customers to whom, the members of the selective distribution system may actively or passively sell the contract goods or services, except:**

(1) **the restriction of active sales by the members of the selective distribution system and their direct customers, into a territory or to a customer group reserved to the supplier or allocated by the supplier exclusively to a maximum of five exclusive distributors;**

(2) **the restriction of active or passive sales by the members of the selective distribution system and their customers to unauthorised distributors located within the territory where the selective distribution system is operated;**
(3) **the restriction of the place of establishment of the members of the selective distribution system;**
(4) **the restriction of active or passive sales to end users by members of the selective distribution system operating at the wholesale level of trade;**
(5) **the restriction of the ability to actively or passively sell components, supplied for the purposes of incorporation, to customers who would use them to manufacture the same type of goods as those produced by the supplier;**

(ii) **the restriction of cross-supplies between the members of the selective distribution system operating at the same or different levels of trade;**
(iii) **the restriction of active or passive sales to end users by members of the selective distribution system operating at the retail level of trade, without prejudice to points (c)(i)(1) and (3);**

(d) *the restriction of cross-supplies between distributors within* **where the supplier operates neither an exclusive distribution system nor** a selective distribution system, **the restriction of the territory into which, or of the customers to whom, the buyer may actively or passively sell the contract goods or services, except:**

(i) **the restriction of active sales by the buyer and its direct customers into a territory or to a customer group reserved to the supplier or allocated by the supplier exclusively to a maximum of five exclusive distributors;**
(ii) **the restriction of active or passive sales by the buyer and its customers to unauthorised distributors located in a territory where the supplier operates a selective distribution system for the contract goods or services;**
(iii) **the restriction of the buyer's place of establishment;**
(iv) **the restriction of active or passive sales to end users by a buyer operating at the wholesale level of trade;**
(v) **the restriction of the buyer's ability to actively or passively sell components, supplied for the purposes of incorporation, to customers who would use them to manufacture the same type of goods as those produced by the supplier;**

(e) **the prevention of the effective use of the internet by the buyer or its customers to sell the contract goods or services, as it restricts the territory into which or the customers to whom the contract goods or**

services may be sold within the meaning of points (b), (c) or (d), without prejudice to the possibility of imposing on the buyer:

(i) **other restrictions of online sales; or**
(ii) **restrictions of online advertising that do not have the object of preventing the use of an entire online advertising channel;**

(*e***f**) the restriction, agreed between a supplier of components and a buyer who incorporates those components, of the supplier's ability to sell the components as spare parts to end- users or to repairers, **wholesalers** or other service providers not entrusted by the buyer with the repair or servicing of its goods.

Article 5

Excluded restrictions

1. The exemption provided for in Article 2 shall not apply to the following obligations contained in vertical agreements:

(a) any direct or indirect non-compete obligation, the duration of which is indefinite or exceeds *five* **5** years;
(b) any direct or indirect obligation causing the buyer, after termination of the agreement, not to manufacture, purchase, sell or resell goods or services;
(c) any direct or indirect obligation causing the members of a selective distribution system not to sell the brands of particular competing suppliers.**;**

For the purposes of point (a) of the first subparagraph, a non-compete obligation which is tacitly renewable beyond a period of five years shall be deemed to have been concluded for an indefinite duration.

(d) **any direct or indirect obligation causing a buyer of online intermediation services not to offer, sell or resell goods or services to end users under more favourable conditions via competing online intermediation services;**

2. By way of derogation from paragraph 1**, point** (a), the time limitation of five years shall not apply where the contract goods or services are sold by the buyer from premises and land owned by the supplier or leased by the supplier from third parties not connected with the buyer, provided that the duration of the non-compete obligation does not exceed the period of occupancy of the premises and land by the buyer.

3. By way of derogation from paragraph 1**, point** (b), the exemption provided for in Article 2 shall apply to any direct or indirect obligation causing the buyer, after termination of the agreement, not to manufacture, purchase, sell or resell goods or services where **all of** the following conditions are fulfilled:

(a) the obligation relates to goods or services which compete with the contract goods or services;
(b) the obligation is limited to the premises and land from which the buyer has operated during the contract period;
(c) the obligation is indispensable to protect know-how transferred by the supplier to the buyer;
(d) the duration of the obligation is limited to a period of one year after termination of the agreement.

Paragraph 1**, point** (b) *is* **shall be** without prejudice to the possibility of imposing a restriction which is unlimited in time on the use and disclosure of know-how which has not entered the public domain.

Article 6

Withdrawal in individual cases
1. The Commission may withdraw the benefit of this Regulation, pursuant to Article 29(1) of Regulation (EC) No 1/2003, where it finds in any particular case that a vertical agreement to which the exemption provided for in Article 2 of this Regulation applies nevertheless has effects which are incompatible with Article 101(3) of the Treaty. Such effects may occur, for example, where the relevant market for the supply of online intermediation services is highly concentrated and competition between the providers of such services is restricted by the cumulative effect of parallel networks of similar agreements that restrict buyers of the online intermediation services from offering, selling or reselling goods or services to end users under more favourable conditions on their direct sales channels.
2. The competition authority of a Member State may withdraw the benefit of this Regulation where the conditions of Article 29(2) of Regulation (EC) No 1/2003 are fulfilled.

Article 7

Non-application of this Regulation
Pursuant to Article 1a of Regulation No 19/65/EEC, the Commission may by regulation declare that, where parallel networks of similar vertical restraints cover more than 50% of a relevant market, this Regulation shall not apply to vertical agreements containing specific restraints relating to that market.

Article *78*

Application of the market share threshold
For the purposes of applying the market share thresholds provided for in Article 3 the following rules shall apply:

(a) the market share of the supplier shall be calculated on the basis of market sales value data and the market share of the buyer shall be calculated on the basis of market purchase value data. If market sales value or market purchase value data are not available, estimates based on other reliable market information, including market sales and purchase volumes, may be used to establish the market share of the undertaking concerned;
(b) the market shares shall be calculated on the basis of data relating to the preceding calendar year;
(c) the market share of the supplier shall include any goods or services supplied to vertically integrated distributors for the purposes of sale;
(d) if a market share is initially not more than 30%, but subsequently rises above that level *without exceeding 35%*, the exemption provided for in Article 2 shall continue to apply for a period of two consecutive calendar years following the year in which the 30% *market share* threshold was first exceeded;
(e) if a market share is initially not more than 30% but subsequently rises above 35%, the exemption provided for in Article 2 shall continue to apply for one calendar year following the year in which the level of 35% was first exceeded;
(f) the benefit of points (d) and (e) may not be combined so as to exceed a period of two calendar years;
(g**e**) the market share held by the undertakings referred to in *point (e) of the* **Article 1(2),** second subparagraph *of Article 1(2***, point** (**e**) shall be apportioned equally to each undertaking having the rights or the powers listed in point (a) of *the second* **that** subparagraph *of Article 1(2).*

Article 9

Article 8
Application of the turnover threshold
1. For the purpose of calculating total annual turnover within the meaning of Article 2(2), the turnover achieved during the previous financial year by the relevant party to the vertical agreement and the turnover achieved by its connected undertakings in respect of all goods and services, excluding all taxes and other duties, shall be added together. For this purpose, no account shall be taken of dealings between the party to the vertical agreement and its connected undertakings or between its connected undertakings.

2. The exemption provided for in Article 2 shall remain applicable where, for any period of two consecutive financial years, the total annual turnover threshold is exceeded by no more than 10%.

Article 910

Transitional period
The prohibition laid down in Article 101(1) of the Treaty shall not apply during the period from 1 June *2010* **2022** to 31 May *2011* **2023** in respect of agreements already in force on 31 May *2010* **2022** which do not satisfy the conditions for exemption provided for in this Regulation but which, on 31 May *2010***2022**, satisfied the conditions for exemption provided for in Regulation (*EC***EU**) No *2790/1999***330/2010**.

Article 1011

Period of validity
This Regulation shall enter into force on 1 June *2010* **2022**.
It shall expire on 31 May *2022* **2034**.
This Regulation shall be binding in its entirety and directly applicable in all Member States.
Done at Brussels, *20 April 2010* **10 May 2022**.

For the Commission

The President
José Manuel BARROSO
Ursula VON DER LEYEN

Appendix 2: List of Laws

Article 81(3) Guidelines	Guidelines on the application of Article 81(3) of the Treaty (2004/C 101/08)
Christmas notice	Notice on exclusive dealing contracts with commercial agents, dated 24 December 1962
Commission Recommendation of 6 May 2003 concerning the definition of micro, small and medium-sized enterprises	notified under document number C (2003) 1422 (Text with EEA relevance) (2003/361/EC)
Commission Regulation (EEC) No 1984/83	Commission Regulation (EEC) No 1984/84 of 22 June 1983 on the application of Article 85 (3) of the Treaty to categories of exclusive purchasing agreements
Commission Regulation No 1983/83	Commission Regulation No 1983/83 of 22 June 1983 on the application of Article 85 (3) of the Treaty to categories of exclusive distribution agreements
Council Regulation (EC) No 1/2003 of 16 December 2002	Council Regulation (EC) No 1/2003 of 16 December 2002 on the implementation of the rules on competition laid down in Articles 81 and 82 of the Treaty
De Minimis Notice 1997	Commission Notice on agreements of minor importance which do not appreciably restrict competition under Article 81(1) of the Treaty establishing the European Community (de minimis)

B. Rohrßen, *VBER 2022: EU Competition Law for Vertical Agreements*, Law for Professionals, https://doi.org/10.1007/978-3-031-35024-5

De Minimis Notice	Communication from the Commission—Notice on agreements of minor importance which do not appreciably restrict competition under Article 101(1) of the Treaty on the Functioning of the European Union 2014/C 291/01
Draft VBER	Commission Regulation (EU) . . ./. . .of XXX on the application of Article 101 (3) of the Treaty on the Functioning of the European Union to categories of vertical agreements and concerted practices DRAFT of 9 July 2021
Draft Horizontal Guidelines	Approval of the content of a draft for a Communication from the Commission – Guidelines on the applicability of Article 101 of the Treaty on the Functioning of the European Union to horizontal co-operation agreements, 2022/C 164/01.
Effect on Trade Guidelines	Commission Notice—Guidelines on the effect on trade concept contained in Articles 81 and 82 of the Treaty (2004/C 101/07)
EFTA De Minimis Notice	Notice of the EFTA Surveillance Authority Notice on agreements of minor importance which do not appreciably restrict competition under Article 53(1) of the EEA Agreement (de minimis)
EFTA Subcontracting Notice	Decision of the EFTA Surveillance Authority No 3/94/COL of 12 January 1994 on the issuing of 10 notices and guidelines in the field of competition, Official Journal L 153, 18/06/1994 P. 0001 - 0053
Franchise Block Exemption Regulation	Commission Regulation (EEC) No 4087/88 of 30 November 1988 on the application of Article 85 (3) of the Treaty to categories of franchise agreements

Geo-blocking Regulation	Regulation (EU) 2018/302 of the European Parliament and of the Council of 28 February 2018 on addressing unjustified geo-blocking and other forms of discrimination based on customers' nationality, place of residence or place of establishment within the internal market and amending Regulations (EC) No 2006/2004 and (EU) 2017/2394 and Directive 2009/22/EC
Horizontal Guidelines	Guidelines on the applicability of Article 101 of the Treaty on the Functioning of the European Union to horizontal co-operation agreements, 2011/C 11/01
Market Definition Notice	Commission Notice on the definition of relevant market for the purposes of Community competition law (97/C 372/03)
Market Surveillance Regulation	Regulation (EU) 2019/1020 on market surveillance and compliance of products and amending Directive 2004/42/EC and Regulations (EC) No 765/2008 and (EU) No 305/2011
Regulation (EU) No 1308/2013	Regulation (EU) No 1308/2013 of the European Parliament and of the Council of 17 December 2013 establishing a common organisation of the markets in agricultural products
SME Notice	Commission Recommendation of 6 May 2003 concerning the definition of micro, small and medium-sized enterprises (notified under document number 2003/L 124/36
Subcontracting Notice	Subcontracting Notice 1979/C 1/2 - Commission notice of 18 December 1978 concerning its assessment of certain subcontracting agreements in relation to Article 85(1) of the EEC Treaty
Treaty on European Union	Treaty on European Union 2012/C 326/13

Treaty on the Functioning of the European Union	Treaty on the Functioning of the European Union 2012/C 326/47
VABEO	Competition Act 1998 (Vertical Agreements Block Exemption) Order 2022
VABEO Guidance	Vertical Agreements Block Exemption Order guidance dance, first published on 12 July 2022
VBER	Commission Regulation (EU) 2022/720 of 10 May 2022 on the application of Article 101(3) of the Treaty on the Functioning of the European Union to categories of vertical agreements and concerted practices 2022/L 134/4
VBER 2022	See VBER
VBER 1999	Council Regulation (EC) No 1215/1999 of 10 June 1999 amending Regulation No 19/65/EEC on the application of Article 81(3) of the Treaty to certain categories of agreements and concerted practices 1999/L 336/21
VBER 2010	Commission Regulation (EU) No 330/2010 of 20 April 2010 on the application of Article 101(3) of the Treaty on the Functioning of the European Union to categories of vertical agreements and concerted practices 2010/L 102/1
VertBek	Swiss Vertical Notice (Vertikalbekanntmachung) of 12 December 2022
VertBek-Erläuterungen	Explanatory Notes on the Swiss Vertical Notice (Erläuterungen zur Vertikalbekanntmachung) of 12 December 2022
Vertical Guidelines	Guidelines on vertical restraints, 2022/C 248/01
VGL	See "Vertical Guidelines"

Index

B. Rohrßen, *VBER 2022: EU Competition Law for Vertical Agreements*, Law for Professionals, https://doi.org/10.1007/978-3-031-35024-5

MIX
Papier aus verantwortungsvollen Quellen
Paper from responsible sources
FSC® C105338
FSC
www.fsc.org

If you have any concerns about our products,
you can contact us on
ProductSafety@springernature.com

In case Publisher is established outside the EU,
the EU authorized representative is:
Springer Nature Customer Service Center GmbH
Europaplatz 3, 69115 Heidelberg, Germany

Printed by Libri Plureos GmbH
in Hamburg, Germany